Handel on the Stage

Of all the great composers of the eighteenth century, Handel was the supreme cosmopolitan, an early and extraordinarily successful example of a freelance composer. For thirty years the opera house was the principal focus of his creative work and he composed more than forty operas over this period. In this book David Kimbell sets Handel's operas in their biographical and cultural contexts. He explores the circumstances in which they were composed and performed, the librettos that were prepared for Handel and what they tell us about his and his audience's values, and the music he composed for them. Remarkably no Handel operas were staged for a period of 170 years between 1754 and the 1920s. The final chapter in this book reveals the differences and similarities between how Handel's operas were performed in his time and ours.

DAVID KIMBELL is Emeritus Professor of Music at the University of Edinburgh. His publications include *Verdi in the Age of Italian Romanticism* (Cambridge, 1981), *Italian Opera* (Cambridge, 1991) and *Vincenzo Bellini: Norma* (Cambridge, 1998). He has also contributed to *The Cambridge Handel Encyclopedia*, *The Cambridge History of Italian Literature* and *The Oxford Companion to Italian Literature*, and has edited volumes for the *Hallische Händel-Ausgabe* and for the *Works of Giuseppe Verdi*.

Handel on the Stage

DAVID KIMBELL

CAMBRIDGE
UNIVERSITY PRESS

CAMBRIDGE
UNIVERSITY PRESS

University Printing House, Cambridge CB2 8BS, United Kingdom

One Liberty Plaza, 20th Floor, New York, NY 10006, USA

477 Williamstown Road, Port Melbourne, VIC 3207, Australia

314-321, 3rd Floor, Plot 3, Splendor Forum, Jasola District Centre, New Delhi - 110025, India

79 Anson Road, #06-04/06, Singapore 079906

Cambridge University Press is part of the University of Cambridge.

It furthers the University's mission by disseminating knowledge in the pursuit of education, learning and research at the highest international levels of excellence.

www.cambridge.org
Information on this title: www.cambridge.org/9780521521604

First published 2016
First paperback edition 2018

A catalogue record for this publication is available from the British Library

Library of Congress Cataloging in Publication data
Names: Kimbell, David R. B., author.
Title: Handel on the stage / David Kimbell.
Description: New York : Cambridge University Press, 2016. |
Includes bibliographical references and index.
Identifiers: LCCN 2015042943 | ISBN 9780521818414 (hardback : alk. paper)
Subjects: LCSH: Handel, George Frideric, 1685–1759. Operas. | Opera–18th century.
Classification: LCC ML410.H13 K56 2016 | DDC 782.1092–dc23
LC record available at http://lccn.loc.gov/2015042943

ISBN 978-0-521-81841-4 Hardback
ISBN 978-0-521-52160-4 Paperback

For Ingrid, fifty years on.

Contents

Preface [*page* ix]
List of Abbreviations [xii]

1 Handel and opera: a biographical survey of the circumstances [1]

2 The libretto (1): argument – *dramatis personae* [48]

3 The libretto (2): words for music [73]

4 The music (1): mastering the medium [92]

5 The music (2): its role in the drama [127]

6 Aspects of the performance of Handelian opera in his time and ours [162]

Appendix: An overview of the repertory of the Royal Academy of Music [198]
Select bibliography [204]
Index [207]

Preface

This book is addressed to those who wish to know a little more about Handel's operas and to understand them a little better; and I hope it will be intelligible and helpful not just to professional musicians and musical scholars. Anyone writing on this topic in English does so in the shadow of two works (really the two parts of one single work) that have already covered the field with awe-inspiring comprehensiveness and mastery: *Handel's Operas 1704–1726* by Winton Dean and John Merrill Knapp, originally published by Oxford University Press in 1987, revised edition 1995, after Merrill Knapp's death; and *Handel's Operas 1726–1741* by Winton Dean, published by the Boydell Press in 2006. While deeply indebted to both these, my book is a quite different kind of undertaking. I have not attempted a systematic examination of all the operas; I have simply set out and reflected on some more general material about them – material of a kind I believe I should have found helpful and interesting when I first encountered the Handel operas myself: about the circumstances in which they were composed and performed; about the librettos that were prepared for Handel and what they tell us about his and his audience's values; about the music he composed for them, and the way it was (and is) performed. It is, in other words, in many ways a straightforward, traditional account of history, literary and musical achievement, and performance practice.

The ponderous title of the first chapter will alert the reader to the fact that it is something less than a balanced biography of Handel's opera-composing years – that it concerns itself only with those matters that have some real bearing on his work for the opera house. Even so, it is a long chapter, for fairly obvious reasons. Opera is a complex art form. To provide a useful context within which to understand it, political and social circumstances, evolving literary and musical tastes, the changing conditions in theatres and theatre companies all need to be considered – in Handel's case in three different countries. Some readers may be surprised, in this chapter and in the chapters about the music, that I have paid so much attention to his German years and to the one opera, *Almira* – very rarely performed – that survives from them. My response would be that, if we are to think sensibly about how Handel became a composer of Italian opera, we need to understand all we can about his years in Italy. As soon as we try to do that, we come face to face with a record of quite prodigious achievement, particularly during the first six months he spent there, and particularly in the circumstances under which he was then working: a new land, a new language, a new religion, a new social hierarchy. I sometimes find myself wondering whether there has ever been anything quite to match it in the whole history of musical precocity. And (to return to *Almira*) with that Italian period in our sights, it is scarcely possible to know enough about the young German musician who had left his homeland only a few months before.

The logic of dividing the material on the librettos into two chapters should be clear. But some readers may like to know that they are, very generally, organised according to the hierarchy classically defined, half a century before Handel's time, by Pierre Corneille. (For Handelians Reinhard Strohm's article on 'Dramaturgy' in *The Cambridge Handel Encyclopedia* is a helpful guide.) In the musical chapters my main aim has been to shed some light on what seems to me the clear truth that Handel's operatic music was composed with a dramatic purpose, which performers should understand even if they choose to override it. Chapter 4 describes the evolution of this musical language in his early years, up to the point when it was mature and wide-ranging enough to give voice to well-nigh anything in human experience that was likely to find a place in eighteenth-century drama. Chapter 5 shows what he then did with it, using for illustration some of the operas that are relatively frequently performed.

The chapter on Handelian opera in performance may seem ill-balanced – as elegantly proportioned as a pantomime horse, one kind reader has suggested. My excuse must be the strange history of the topic. The operas had disappeared from the theatre well before Handel died, and they did not return to it for some 170 years; indeed more than two centuries had elapsed before they became anything like standard items in the operatic repertory. When they did come back, the world's understanding of what the function of an opera house was, and what the balance of responsibility was in deciding how a 'work' should be performed there, had been utterly transformed. To try to shed some light on how things were done in Handel's time, and juxtapose it with what is done in our time, is necessarily a curious exercise, but I hope it can be a worthwhile one too.

An earlier and more extended version of the section 'Resources for characterisation' in Chapter 5 was published in *Händel-Jahrbuch* 54 (2008) as 'Heldinnen aus Ariost: Einige Gedanken über Händels Kunst der Charakterdarstellung'.

Acknowledgements

During my work on the book I have been assisted by staff in the erstwhile Reid Music Library at Edinburgh University, and The University Library itself; The National Library of Scotland; The British Library; The University Library, Cambridge – I thank them all. For kindnesses and assistance of various kinds I am grateful to Graham Diss, Barry Nisbet, Jürgen Stenzel, Colin Timms. And I am particularly grateful to Steuart Bedford, Andrew Jones, Roger Savage and Ruth Smith, who have read some of the chapters and made helpful suggestions about them. They are not, it need hardly be said, responsible for such *sottises* as may remain. And I thank Dr Victoria Cooper at Cambridge University Press for her patience during the inordinate length of time it has taken me to finish.

The music typesetting is by Derek Williams.

During the Easter Vacation in 1964 I went to Hamburg for the first time, to study some Handel opera manuscripts in the Staats- und Universitätsbibliothek. The Music Librarian who opened the door to me on that occasion and I are (D.V.) about to celebrate our Golden Wedding: to whom, then, but Ingrid could this little book be dedicated?

David Kimbell
Ely, Cambridgeshire

Abbreviations

CCH	*The Cambridge Companion to Handel*, D. Burrows (ed.) (Cambridge University Press, 1997)
CHE	*The Cambridge Handel Encyclopedia*, A. Landgraf and D. Vickers (eds.) (Cambridge University Press, 2009)
CHIL	*The Cambridge History of Italian Literature*, P. Brand and L. Pertile (eds.) (Cambridge University Press, 1996)
COJ	*The Cambridge Opera Journal*
EM	*Early Music*
GHB	*Göttinger Händel Beiträge*
HHA	*Hallische Händel-Ausgabe*
HHB 1	*Händel-Handbuch Band 1, Thematisch-systematisches Verzeichnis: Bühnenwerke*, B. Baselt, (Leipzig: VEB Deutscher Verlag für Musik, 1978)
HHB 4	*Händel-Handbuch Band 4, Dokumente zu Leben und Schaffen* (Leipzig: VEB Deutscher Verlag für Musik, 1985)
HIN	*The Handel Institute Newsletter*
HJb	*Händel-Jahrbuch*
JM	*Journal of Musicology*
JRMA	*Journal of the Royal Musical Association*
ML	*Music and Letters*
MQ	*The Musical Quarterly*
MT	*The Musical Times*
OIHO	*The Oxford Illustrated History of Opera*, R. Parker (ed.) (Oxford University Press, 1994)
SIMG	*Sammelbände der Internationalen Musik-Gesellschaft*
VIHAK	*Veröffentlichungen der internationalen Händel-Akademie, Karlsruhe*

1 Handel and opera: a biographical survey of the circumstances

Of all the great composers of the eighteenth century, Handel was the supreme cosmopolitan. Born in Halle,[1] he served his musical apprenticeship there and in Hamburg; during three years in Italy he became one of the most accomplished exponents of the internationally admired Italian style; he died an honoured and much loved British subject, and he lies now in Westminster Abbey among the greatest creative artists of his adopted home.

He was able to achieve these things because he was an early and extraordinarily successful example of a freelance composer; a man confident that his prodigious gifts would rise to any challenge, a man sufficiently urbane, cultivated and broadminded in his sympathies to feel at home in Lutheran Germany, in Catholic Italy and in Anglican England alike.

For thirty years, counting not quite continuously, the opera house was the principal focus of his creative work. He composed more than forty operas (considerably more than Mozart, more even than Verdi or Rossini), the first for Hamburg in 1704 when he was nineteen years old, the last (unless we count one or two of the oratorios as English operas) for the King's Theatre, London, in 1741 when he was fifty-six. And since this book concerns itself not with opera in any general or theoretical sense but quite specifically with Handel's operas, it will be worth starting with a biographical survey of those years he spent primarily in the theatre.

The German apprenticeship

Halle

Handel's breadth of sympathy and the capaciousness of his cultural and intellectual appetite he owed, in no small part, to the happy fact that he was born and brought up in Halle. With the transfer of the city to Brandenburg-Prussia in 1680, Halle had lost its princely court to nearby

[1] Halle is usually glossed 'in Saxony', and Handel was frequently described as a Saxon. However, at the time of his birth the city had recently been transferred from Saxony to Brandenburg-Prussia – a belated consequence of the Peace of Westphalia (1648).

Weissenfels; nevertheless, at the turn of the seventeenth to the eighteenth century it remained culturally a remarkable place, exemplary in many aspects of its civic and social amenities, its educational institutions and its musical life. After the last great plague had devastated the city in 1681–83 and catastrophically reduced the population, civic life had been rebuilt by the encouragement of immigration: French Protestants; Protestants from south Germany; Jews. These influxes in turn transformed commercial and cultural life and Halle became one of the most cosmopolitan and tolerant cities of the age.

One striking manifestation of that tolerance was the founding of a new university in 1694, a university where the great jurist Christian Thomasius, recently dismissed from Leipzig University for his liberal views, found a new home. Law, as taught by Thomasius, was no mere theory and practice of jurisprudence: it entailed ethical, philosophical and cultural reflections on human affairs – and the fact is worth mentioning because it was law that Handel himself is presumed to have studied when, in accordance with the hopes of his father, he enrolled at the university for a year in 1702–03. Thomasius, lecturing in German rather than the Latin traditional for jurists, helped turn Halle into the leading academic centre for Enlightenment thought in the German-speaking world, and by Handel's time young men were coming from all over Germany to study there. Among his contemporaries in Halle were two who later became colleagues in Hamburg: Barthold Hinrich Brockes, poet of the *Deutsche Arien* and of the Passion oratorio *Der für die Sünden der Welt gemarterte und sterbende Jesus*, who in his student years regularly arranged 'a little concert in my room';[2] and his cousin Barthold Feind, who is not known ever to have collaborated with Handel, but who will have known him well since he was a poet and librettist, and the leading polemicist of the Hamburg opera during the years Handel worked there.

Before enrolling at the university Handel must have studied at the Stadt-Gymnasium, where music played a central part in the curriculum. A principal duty of the school's choirs was to provide music for services in the city churches. And in being trained for his part in this role, Handel will have acquired not only a close practical experience of the obviously important items of the modern Lutheran repertory, but also a good working acquaintance with polyphonic masterpieces of the sixteenth-century

[2] Quoted, via the *Zeitschrift des Vereins für hamburgische Geschichte* (1847), in B. Baselt, 'Handel and His Central German Background', in Stanley Sadie and Anthony Hicks (eds.), *Handel Tercentenary Collection* (Basingstoke: Macmillan Music Division, 1987), p. 50.

Catholic tradition from Josquin to Lassus. One would dearly like to know more of these school days: for instance, what dealings he might have had with the Con-Rector of the school, August Christian Rotth (by marriage one of Handel's great-uncles), and in particular whether at this impressionable age Handel had absorbed anything of Rotth's 'poetics'. For this schoolmaster, who died in 1701 while Handel was a pupil at the school, was the author of a *Vollständige Deutsche Poesie*, which in its copious pages includes what has been deemed 'probably the most comprehensive and profound study of German Baroque dramaturgy'.[3]

What is certain, if Mainwaring's account is to be trusted,[4] is that, well before entering the Gymnasium, Handel had found the perfect music teacher in Friedrich Wilhelm Zachow (1663–1712), organist at the Marktkirche, the memory of whom he evidently cherished for the rest of his life. Zachow was the ideal man for Handel because, while on the one hand he insisted on the need to acquire an absolute mastery of the composer's metier – especially through the rigorous study of counterpoint and figured bass – he at the same time stimulated his imagination by the variety and freedom of his own compositions, vocal and instrumental, and by introducing Handel to a great deal of new music that he certainly would not have met with in the Halle churches as a matter of course: the best there was to be discovered from the Catholic south of Germany, and new instrumental music from Italy and France. And surely at some stage, however loyal to his employers Zachow may have been, he will also have discussed with his ambitious pupil the recurrent frustrations of a cantor-organist's work, the Pietist wing of the Lutheran church always being on the alert for opportunities to complain about 'the excessively long, unedifying and unintelligible performance of elaborate music'.[5]

So the foundations for Handel's exceptional range as a composer were already in place before he left Halle. He knew an extensive repertory of music, old and new and gathered from all the musical nations of Europe; he had acquired, while still a boy, a mastery of contrapuntal skills, which Mattheson was to compare with those of the redoubtable Kuhnau at the Thomaskirche in Leipzig; he had been encouraged to make fine music

3 G. Bimberg, 'Hallesche Anregungen zu einer Dramaturgie der frühdeutschen Oper', *HJb* 36 (1990), 35.

4 Mainwaring reports that, at the age of seven, Handel was already deputising for Zachow. See *George Frideric Handel Collected Documents, Volume 1 1609–1725*, Donald Burrows, Helen Coffey, John Greenacombe and Anthony Hicks (eds.), Cambridge University Press, 2013 (hereafter *Documents I*), pp. 18–19.

5 B. Baselt, citing W. Serauky, in 'Handel and His Central German Background', p. 51.

himself by opening up his imagination, giving his fancy free rein. And it is not difficult to imagine the relish with which he threw himself into all that: as he was to recall in later years, 'I used to compose like the devil in those days.'

But what of opera? Since the removal of the court to Weissenfels, Halle itself had had none; but there were several centres of operatic activity within easy reach of the city. Two of these are certainly germane to our purpose.

In 1701, when Handel was still a schoolboy, he became a good friend of the four-years-older Telemann, who ran a Collegium Musicum at Leipzig University. Ostensibly Telemann was a law student, as Handel was soon to become, but in addition to running the Collegium Musicum he also found time to compose fortnightly cantatas for the Thomaskirche and to direct the music at the Leipzig opera house. By his own account – the autobiographical sketch he wrote for Mattheson's *Ehrenpforte* in 1740 – he and Handel used to meet frequently, either in Halle or in Leipzig, encouraging one another particularly in acquiring the kind of 'modern' and 'melodious' style indispensable for success in opera.[6] So we can take it as certain that Handel will have gone over to Leipzig (roughly 25 miles distant) for at least some of the short seasons of opera that Telemann used to present each year around New Year, Easter and late September (St Michael's Day).

The other operatic establishment with which Handel will have been familiar was that at Weissenfels, where his father had been court surgeon, and whose Kapellmeister Johann Philipp Krieger was distantly related to Handel's mother. Being a court opera, Weissenfels might have been expected to provide a strikingly different model from that on offer in Leipzig, more Frenchified or Italianate. In fact it didn't, since, remarkably among court operas of that period, it always performed its operas in German: indeed, the ducal house believed that it owed a responsibility to play a exemplary role in the development and purification of the German language, and that opera could be an important medium in pursuit of that aim.[7] Little survives of the music Krieger composed for the opera at this time; such of it as there is suggests that courtly audiences still found simple continuo-accompanied songs adequate for most expressive purposes, whether mythology or allegory or history was the matter in hand.

The operas mounted at Weissenfels included guest performances by ensembles from the public theatres of Leipzig and Hamburg, the latter under the direction of Reinhard Keiser. Almost certainly it was Keiser who

[6] *Documents I*, pp. 31–2.

[7] W. Felix, 'Johann Philipp Krieger und die Hofoper in Weissenfels', *HJb* 36 (1990), 43.

was in some sense responsible for bringing Handel to Hamburg, whether he went out of his way to encourage him to try his luck there, or whether Handel himself made the leap, feeling that a man of Keiser's talents and musical personality was just the kind he wanted to work with.

Hamburg

At the beginning of the eighteenth century the free city of Hamburg, with something between 70,000 and 75,000 inhabitants, was, after Vienna, the most populous city in the ('Holy Roman') Empire; and since it was also its greatest international port, it was of all German cities the one most open to foreign, especially British, influence. Handel's residence fell within a period of religious controversy and political and social unrest which sometimes, and particularly in 1705–06, verged on anarchy; and the artistic community with which he was involved was not indifferent to these excitements of party. Nevertheless, Hamburg's commercial vitality was little impaired, its artistic life, if fractious, remained vigorous, and an established tradition of journalism ensured a well-informed and critical populace. Miniature havens of courtly seemliness were to be found at the residences of the diplomatic corps; music continued to flourish in at least some of the main churches and, most importantly for Handel, the city was the home of the senior and most illustrious of all German opera houses, the Theater am Gänsemarkt.

Handel spent two or three seasons at the Hamburg opera, the years during which he might have been continuing his studies at Halle university. He arrived in Hamburg in the summer of 1703,[8] and since he began his career as a second violinist in the opera orchestra, one assumes that that was for the start of the 1703–04 season. Mattheson gives a pleasant account of his graduation from so humble a position, but tells us neither when it happened, nor which opera it involved: 'at first he played second violin in the opera orchestra, and behaved as if he couldn't count up to five – for he was by nature much inclined to dry humour. But on one occasion, when the harpsichordist was missing, he let himself be persuaded to take his place; and he proved himself a Man'.[9]

8 The earliest report, 9 July (or possibly 9 June) 1703, is of his meeting with Johann Mattheson at the organ in the chapel of the former Maria-Magdalene cloister. Johann Mattheson, *Grundlage einer Ehren-Pforte*: Hamburg, 1740 (hereafter Mattheson, *Ehrenpforte*), p. 191; in *Documents I*, p. 39.

9 Mattheson, *Ehrenpforte*, pp. 93–4; in *Documents I*, pp. 37–8.

Early in the second season, indeed presumably before the season had even started, Handel was commissioned to compose two operas to librettos by Friedrich Christian Feustking. *Almira*, the first of these, had been intended for Keiser; but he had mysteriously abandoned it, and gone off to compose a revised adaptation of the same libretto for Weissenfels. Whose idea it was that Handel should take it over we do not know. Even less is known about the circumstances surrounding *Nero*, the second Feustking opera. But *Almira* was premiered with great success in January 1705; so in the space of some eighteen months preceding his twentieth birthday Handel had progressed from being a rank-and- file violinist, who 'behaved as if he couldn't count up to five', to become a feted composer of opera. Indeed, he might by this stage be said to have rounded off his education as a composer of German opera completely – except that there was one small crack in the comprehensiveness of his musicianship, which Mattheson, one feels, rather enjoyed pointing out; Handel couldn't, or didn't, really sing – at least not with any expressive finesse.[10]

What happened after this second, 1704–05, season in the opera house we do not know. Mattheson's account in the *Ehrenpforte*, in many particulars so exact, is here disappointingly vague, no doubt because he had himself retreated from the scene. Handel could certainly have stayed on for the 1705–06 season, but with teaching commitments too, which only allowed him to play a relatively modest role at the theatre; Mattheson remembered him having 'very many pupils' at this time.[11] Whatever he was up to, he needed to earn a substantial sum of money to finance the Italian journey which he was now determined to undertake, and on which he will have set out in the late summer or early autumn of 1706.

Excursus 1.1 – the mystery of *Florindo* and *Daphne*

So far I have accounted for only two of Handel's four Hamburg operas. The other two, *Der beglückte Florindo* and *Die verwandelte Daphne*, provide one of the most inscrutable enigmas of his operatic career. We have no sure information whatsoever about how and when they came to be composed, or when exactly, under what circumstances and with what measure of oversight on Handel's part they were performed. Such facts

[10] Mattheson noted this on a number of occasions, for example in *Ehrenpforte*, pp. 206–7; in *Documents I*, p. 517.

[11] Mattheson, *Ehrenpforte*, p. 95; in *Documents I*, pp. 49–50.

as we do have – really only two of them – are poor things. The first and more certain is that the librettos were both printed in Hamburg with the date 1708 on their title pages; and this date was endorsed in the catalogue of Hamburg opera premieres in Mattheson's *Patriot*. The circumstance in itself does not absolutely exclude the possibility of a 1709 premiere: the libretto of *Almira* had been printed in 1704, and was listed under 1704 in Mattheson's catalogue; however, it was premiered only in January 1705. But the likelihood of a similar circumstance having arisen with *Florindo* and *Daphne* is very small indeed. In 1704 *Almira* was the last opera listed, in 1708 *Florindo* and *Daphne* were the first, and the assumption must be that they were performed early in the (calendar) year. The other Hamburg fact is simply a rather vague testimony. In his translation of Mainwaring's biography of Handel, Mattheson asserts that in 1709, that is to say even after the two operas had been performed, 'Handel was still in Hamburg'.[12] The assertion flatly contradicts the usual understanding of these years, but as John Roberts has pointed out in this context, Mattheson did insist that everything he reported about Handel's Hamburg years was based on letters, diaries and his own first-hand knowledge.[13]

What happens when these Hamburg 'facts' are set alongside Handel's activities in Italy? Because the years surrounding the *Florindo* and *Daphne* premieres, 1706–09/10, were of course the years of Handel's Italian sojourn. Much of this Italian period is documented with gratifying fullness and specificity. But there are two lacunae: nothing is recorded about Handel's activities in Italy between early/mid November 1707 and late February 1708, nor between the autumn of 1708 (it is impossible to be more specific) and November 1709. While we do not know what Handel was doing in January 1708, we may agree with Ursula Kirkendale that it is difficult to imagine him popping back to Hamburg in midwinter to stage two operas there and being back in Rome before the end of February.[14] But there is no reason at all why he should not have spent much of 1709 there, as Mattheson reports. And that raises the question, whether *Florindo* and *Daphne* might

12 John Mainwaring, *G. F. Händel, nach Johann Matthesons deutscher Ausgabe von 1761 mit anderen Dokumenten herausgegeben* Bernhard Paumgartner (ed.), Zurich: Atlantis-Verlag, 1947 (hereafter Mainwaring–Mattheson), p. 51.

13 J. H. Roberts, 'A New Handel Aria, or Hamburg Revisited', in Klaus Hortschansky, and Konstanze Musketa (eds.), *Georg Friedrich Händel – ein Lebensinhalt. Gedenkschrift für Bernd Baselt (1934–1993)* (Halle, 1995) (herafter *Baselt Gedenkschrift*), p. 125. This essay is the most interesting contribution to the *Florindo/Daphne* puzzle.

14 A hypothesis offered in Roberts' 1995 essay – see U. Kirkendale, 'Händel bei Ruspoli: neue Dokumente aus dem Archivio segreto vaticano, Dezember 1706 bis Dezember 1708', *HJb* 50 (2004), 344.

not in fact have been composed and performed under Handel's direction during those months of 1708–09 when there is no account of any activity in Italy. At present the conundrum cannot be solved.

The presiding genius at the Hamburg opera was Reinhard Keiser (1674–1739), and he was surely the model for Handel's early achievements in the theatre. Mattheson declared him simply 'the greatest opera-composer in the world';[15] he was certainly one of the most productive, even if the 'well over 100' works attributed to him in Scheibe's 'Obituary' seems an exaggeration.[16] Given Handel's close personal links with Weissenfels, it is virtually certain that it will have been there that he first came across Keiser's music; for Keiser was a native of those parts and – as I mentioned earlier – reappeared there from time to time with visiting performers from Hamburg.

The relationship between Keiser and Handel developed and changed rapidly. It must surely have been Keiser who, directly or indirectly, sowed in Handel's mind the idea of giving up his university studies and his organist's post and trying his luck in Hamburg. During that first, impressionable season playing in the orchestra, it was Keiser's music almost exclusively from which Handel will have observed at close hand how opera worked.[17] The decision to give Handel the opportunity to set Feustking's *Almira* libretto, presumably in the summer of 1704, if not Keiser's alone, could hardly have been made without at least his agreement. *Almira*'s success may, however, have made the older composer a little nervous; and it is difficult not to agree with Roberts that *Octavia*, the exceptionally carefully composed and richly scored opera which Keiser produced in 1705, with its list of dramatis personae closely matching that of Handel's second opera, *Nero*, was designed 'to put his young competitor in his place'.[18] Feind and Hunold – neither of them, one must note, was an impartial witness – both asserted that *Octavia* drove *Nero* from the stage, 'a fierce flash of lightning [striking] Nero's bays of laurel', as Feind put it.[19]

15 The tribute comes in a poem Mattheson wrote in Mattheson, *Ehrenpforte*, p. 133; it was inspired by Keiser's death in September 1739.

16 *Der critische Musicus*, Part 56, (22 September 1739).

17 During Handel's first season and a half at the Hamburg opera (up to the premiere of *Almira*) the entire repertory, with the single exception of Mattheson's *Cleopatra*, was composed by Keiser.

18 J. H. Roberts, 'Keiser and Handel at the Hamburg Opera', *HJb* 36 (1990), 65.

19 In his panegyric on Keiser included in Keiser's *Componimenti musicali* of 1706: in *Documents I*, pp. 65–6.

Despite their best efforts, modern critics have not found it easy to give Keiser his due. He was not a master craftsman in the manner of Handel, or even Telemann; architectural design and tonal strategy are evidently not high priorities; Dean and Knapp find 'breathlessness', and a lack of poise even in his lyricism; 'cramped' and 'awkward' are other epithets bestowed. Keiser's contemporaries would have found these surprising perceptions. Mattheson, for instance, declared that 'everything he composed, especially in love-scenes, sang in the most charming way, falling on the ear so melodiously, spontaneously, richly and easily, that one had to love it almost more than admire it'.[20] And he did not doubt that Keiser's ability to sing his own music 'quite beautifully' helped him develop this gift. It was the relationship between poetry and melody in his operas that prompted Quantz to identify Keiser as one of those to whom the advance of 'good taste' in German music owed most. Be that as it may, whatever we think of Keiser's music, the important thing is that the memory of it haunted Handel for the rest of his life. Much of it he carried with him (whether literally in the form of early printed editions or copies of scores, or simply in his capacious memory, we do not know), and he returned to it, dipped into it, 'borrowed' or cribbed from it, reworked and adapted it throughout his career. This question will be discussed further in Chapter 4.

For young Handel the inspirational example of Keiser was complemented by a close friendship with Johann Mattheson (1681–1764). The fact that, compared with Handel, Mattheson was a very minor composer should not blind us to his exceptional accomplishments as a musician: at the very least a thoroughly capable composer, a superb harpsichordist, solo tenor in the Hamburg opera house between 1697 and 1705, and in due course the most encyclopedic musical theorist and journalist of the age. The range of his intellectual curiosity away from music was boundless too, and his work as a translator, principally of English novels, essays and pamphlets, and his responsibilities as tutor and secretary at the English 'Court' in Hamburg, entitle him to be regarded as the leading Anglophile in Germany's most Anglophile city – a fact of some interest in the light of Handel's later career – and therefore a figure of some importance in the German Enlightenment.

It is true that the friendship between the two men became a little edgy, and in due course faded, leaving Handel with we know not what feelings, and Mattheson with a residue of sadness and sometimes indignation. But the first year of their acquaintance, from the summer of 1703

[20] Mattheson, *Ehrenpforte*, cited in K. Zelm, *Die Opern Reinhard Keisers* (Munich and Salzburg: Katzbichler, 1975), p. 9.

to the autumn of 1704, was probably, I would suggest, the happiest of both their lives, its flavour nicely caught in the youthful 'affection and urgency' Mattheson felt so touched by in the letter Handel wrote him in March 1704.[21] It is amusing to find, both in *Ehrenpforte* and *Critica musica*, Mattheson making the same claim as Telemann: that Handel was already a past master at counterpoint, but that he knew nothing of the modern melodious operatic style until Mattheson took him in hand. But it is certain that Handel learned a huge amount from him: three years older, a worthy sparring partner in practical musical accomplishments,[22] vastly more experienced in opera, and surely someone who would already have been encouraging his younger friend to reflect more carefully on the relationship between dramatic action and poetry and music. Handel's admiration for Mattheson's authority in operatic matters comes out in that same March 1704 letter: 'without your presence it will be impossible to undertake anything at the opera.' Something of a cloud came over their relationship in November, when Mattheson was appointed to replace Handel as music tutor to the Wyche family; and the tension between the two men came to a melodramatic climax a few weeks later when they fought a duel after one of the performances of Mattheson's opera *Cleopatra*.[23] Mattheson rounds off his account of this episode: 'we were soon reconciled; because, on the same day, that is to say 30th December, I had the honour of giving Handel dinner at my home. Immediately afterwards, in the evening, we both attended the rehearsal of his *Almira*, and became better friends than before.' That last phrase doesn't ring quite true: for once *Almira* and *Nero* had been staged, the detailed, first-hand accounts of what the pair of them did together disappear from Mattheson's writings. Even so, I see no reason to doubt his claim to have exercised a kind of mentoring role at the time *Almira* was being composed – of how, as he put it, 'I well remember how [Handel] brought me his very first opera, scene by scene, and every evening wanted to hear what I thought about it; such was the labour it cost him to conceal the pedant.'[24]

[21] He quotes part of the letter in *Ehrenpforte*, p. 94; in *Documents I*, p. 42.

[22] See Mattheson's account of their journey together to Lübeck in August 1703: *Ehrenpforte*, p. 94; in *Documents I*, p. 40.

[23] Mattheson's version of the incident is in *Ehrenpforte*, pp. 94–5; in *Documents I*, pp. 44–5. A slightly different account, which must have come indirectly from Handel himself, is in John Mainwaring, *Memoirs of the Life of the Late George Frederic Handel*, London, 1760 (hereafter Mainwaring, *Memoirs*), pp. 30–5; in *Documents I*, pp. 45–6.

[24] J. Mattheson, *Critica musica*, 9 (January 1723); in *Documents I*, pp. 621–3. The music of *Almira* will be discussed in Chapter 4.

The Italian journey – patrons and colleagues

As the young rising star of the Hamburg opera, lapping up all there was to learn from Keiser, stimulated and perhaps from time to time infuriated by the opinionated Mattheson, mixing in the best society at the English 'Court', Handel must often have found his thoughts turning towards Italy; for Italy was the fount and origin of the art form with which he had become so fascinated, and which provided so ideal a focus for the encyclopaedic range of his musical gifts.

A vivid evocation of the spirit in which, many years later, Handel recalled (via John Christopher Smith the younger) his decision to undertake the journey to Italy is found in Mainwaring's *Memoirs*. A Medici prince temporarily resident in Hamburg has been 'discoursing' with Handel on matters musical. (Not all the details can be correct, but Mattheson in his translation offers no amendment.)

> The Prince would often lament that HANDEL was not acquainted with [the musicians] of Italy; shewed him a large collection of Italian Music; and was very desirous he should return with him to Florence. HANDEL plainly confessed that he could see nothing in the Music which answered the high character his Highness had given it. On the contrary, he thought it so very indifferent, that the Singers, he said, must be angels to recommend it. The Prince smiled at the severity of his censure, and added, that there needed nothing but a journey to Italy to reconcile him to the style and taste which prevailed there. [And so the conversation continued, until] the Prince then intimated, that if he chose to return with him, no conveniences should be wanting. HANDEL, without intending to accept the favour designed him, expressed his sense of the honour done him. For he resolved to go to Italy on his own bottom, as soon as he could make a purse for that occasion. This noble spirit of independency, which possessed him almost from his childhood, was never known to forsake him, not even in the most distressful seasons of his life.[25]

One notes the easy self-confidence with which, in a class-conscious age, the twenty-year-old Handel discoursed and disputed – presumably in French – with a prince from one of the most august houses in Europe.[26] And how urgently he needed that self-confidence, that sheer genius for finding patrons, for going directly to the men with power, influence and a taste for conspicuous consumption, when, steering a way past the scenes of havoc and desolation occasioned by the War of Spanish Succession, he arrived in Italy probably in the autumn of 1706! For the Battle of Turin in September

25 Mainwaring, *Memoirs*, pp. 39–42; in *Documents I*, pp. 66–7.
26 A cool appraisal of the Medici story is given in *CHE*, 'Medici, Ferdinando de' '.

had led to a new phase in the war, which continued for the greater part of Handel's sojourn in the peninsula. Austrian armies gradually wrested great swathes of the land from the control of the Bourbons. Many of the institutions on which the livelihood of musicians had depended were closed or had been destroyed, artistic patronage was in decline, a diaspora of Italian artists was in full train; poverty and famine were to reach terrible levels in the winter of 1708–09.

It may have been a Medici who provided the well-timed stimulus to send Handel off on his way to Italy, but Rome, not Florence, was his base for the greater part of his time there. By midwinter 1706–07 he was comfortably established in Rome, and already consorting with such princes of church and state as Ottoboni, Pamphili, Ruspoli, Colonna – men of enormous political influence, wealth and social standing; and because they were also great art lovers, they knew how to value Handel.

Cardinal Pietro Ottoboni was second in the papal hierarchy after the Pope himself: in that sense he was, as Mainwaring reported, Handel's most important patron in Rome. He was happiest in the company of artistic and learned men, and spent huge sums of money supporting musicians. He had a first-rate group of musicians in his employment, including Corelli, and his Wednesday evening salon was famous for the excellence of the music. Before a papal ban was imposed, he had even staged operas – for some of which he wrote the librettos himself – in the small theatre in his Palazzo della Cancelleria. While there appears to be no certain link between Ottoboni and any specific Handel piece, they must have seen much of one another. According to Mainwaring, it was Ottoboni who presided over that legendary 'trial of skill' between Handel and Domenico Scarlatti,[27] and he is reported to have welcomed Handel back with great cordiality when he returned briefly to Rome in 1729.

On that occasion Cardinal Carlo Colonna had to be avoided, for he was then harbouring the Old Pretender. But he too was a stimulating presence in Handel's Roman years, and as patron of the Carmelite order was clearly the man responsible for commissioning the Carmelite vesper music that Handel produced with such Counter-Reformation opulence in the early summer of 1707.

Of Cardinal Benedetto Pamphili Handel seems to have had less rosy memories, describing him to Charles Jennens as 'an old fool … who flattered me'.[28] But such an old fool he is unlikely to have been, embarrassing

[27] Mainwaring, *Memoirs*, pp. 60–2; in *Documents I*, pp. 70–1.

[28] *Documents I*, pp. 76–7.

as his footling cantata on Handel ('Hendel, non può la mia Musa', HWV 117) perhaps was. He held the senior librarian and archivist posts at the Vatican, was a discriminating connoisseur of music, and a respectable versifier who provided the poetry for several other Handel cantatas; he seems to have been Handel's 'first Maecenas' in Rome.[29] Moreover, in writing the text for *Il Trionfo del Tempo e del Disinganno* he provided the most theologically engaged libretto Handel set before *Messiah*.

Chief of Handel's patrons and hosts, however, was the Marquis Francesco Maria Ruspoli (Prince of Cerveteri only from 1709, by which time Handel had, in maybe more than one sense, parted from him). Since the autumn of 1706, when he inherited immense wealth, Ruspoli had been a most generous patron of the arts, outvying perhaps even his close friend Ottoboni. Handel was his guest for approximately two years. Besides the oratorio *La Resurrezione*, something like seventy of Handel's cantatas can be linked with Ruspoli, and most of them are likely to have been first performed at his celebrated Sunday *conversazioni*. During the summer months, at a 'Parrhasian grove' in his gardens at San Matteo in Merulana, Ruspoli hosted the gatherings of the Arcadian academy. Curiously, this most generous of Handel's Roman patrons does not feature at all in the recollections imparted to Mainwaring;[30] Ursula Kirkendale wonders whether Handel was offended by the appointment of Caldara as Ruspoli's resident maestro.[31]

None of these men was able to support Handel's progress as an opera composer directly, because opera was not staged in Rome in those years. Indirectly and collectively, however, what they contributed to his mastery of dramatic music was incalculable. Under their protection he became a respected colleague of Corelli, the Scarlattis, and the finest singers and string players of the age: week after week he was making music with them. He could immerse himself in the most subtle and masterly Italian music, and practise his hand at it; and he became a cultured gentleman: the letters written on his behalf at this time made much of his social and linguistic graces.[32] The commissions with which he was showered required regular practice from him in folding the finest qualities of modern Italian music into the native robustness he brought with him from Germany. And since his patrons were leading figures among the Arcadians, and Handel's music must often have been performed at their gatherings – their *adunanze* – he

[29] See particularly H. J. Marx, 'Händel in Rom: seine Beziehungen zu Benedetto Cardinal Pamphilj', *HJb* 29 (1983).

[30] *Documents I*, pp. 73–4.

[31] Kirkendale, 'Händel bei Ruspoli', 358.

[32] See C. Vitali, 'Italy – Political and Musical Contexts', in *CCH*, p. 43.

had the chance, if he cared to take it, to keep abreast of all their debates about taste, style and substance in poetry and drama.

Handel's time in Rome was being fruitfully spent, but if he wanted to continue with opera he needed to get out of the city. The two operas he composed during these years, *Vincer se stesso è la maggior vittoria* (which I shall henceforth call *Rodrigo*) and *Agrippina*, are the fruit of two such sallies, in the Autumn of 1707 to Florence and in the Autumn of 1709 to Venice. Both operas are still surrounded by more hopeful conjecture and blind surmise than one could wish.

Given Handel's association with the Medici family in Hamburg, it seems likely that he would have travelled to Rome via Florence. There perhaps he may have received the commission for *Rodrigo* sometime in 1706, and there perhaps he may have begun to plan the music before going on to Rome at the end of the year. In any event the likelihood is that he had composed all or most of it (on Roman paper) well before returning to Florence to rehearse and stage it, for there seems no other simple explanation for the many discrepancies between the autograph score (written before Handel knew the cast) and the libretto (recording what actually was done when *Rodrigo* was performed). This experience of adapting his work for the cast he found himself faced with will have been a valuable induction into one of the ever-recurring exigencies in the real life of the theatre.

Handel must also have learnt much from composing his first full-scale Italian opera libretto, a quite modern specimen of the new 'reform' opera,[33] especially if, as seems very likely, it had been arranged for the Florence production by Antonio Salvi. For Salvi, as well as being a physician, was theatre poet to the Medici, and Handel will have had ample opportunity to discuss the work with him. He liked Salvi's work well enough, he decided, to collect several of his librettos before he left Italy, and he acquired more in later years.

Agrippina has fair claim to be regarded as Handel's first operatic masterpiece. It is therefore the more frustrating that the story of its composition is so incomplete. Nothing is certain beyond the fact that it was premiered in Venice (the only city to have maintained its operatic life more or less unbroken through the years of the War of Spanish Succession) in the Teatro San Giovanni Grisostomo during the Carnival season 1709–10, when it enjoyed a successful run of twenty-seven performances. A key figure in the story as traditionally told is Cardinal Vincenzo Grimani. Scion of one of the wealthiest and most distinguished families in Venice, Grimani had

[33] The 'reform' of Italian opera in the early years of the century is discussed in Chapter 3.

as a young man (with his elder brother, Giovanni Carlo Grimani) rebuilt the family theatre, the aforementioned Teatro San Giovanni Grisostomo. He had become a zealous supporter of the Austrian cause in the war and, exiled from Venice since 1690, was, at the time of Handel's arrival in Rome, Viennese ambassador in that city; in July 1708 he moved to Naples as Austrian viceroy. It is just possible that his ways and Handel's will have crossed briefly in Naples as well as in Rome. The libretto of *Agrippina* has been ascribed to Grimani. The attribution is, however, late (1745) and unsupported by any firm contemporary documentation.[34] But there is no alternative attribution either, and pending the appearance of some better authenticated rival author, the hypothesis may be accepted. The story would then go as follows.

On his way to Florence and Rome Handel passed through Venice; he was there long enough to get a commission to compose an opera and buy a stock of Venetian music paper to write it on. Having arrived in Rome, he would have had the opportunity to plan the work with Grimani and make a start on it, sometime between early 1707 and early 1708, writing it in his 'early' Italian handwriting style on his stock of Venetian paper.[35] As with *Rodrigo*, therefore, much of the opera was written well before the rehearsals began, which would explain the many alterations that proved necessary.[36] The libretto, though modern in terms of its masterly unfolding of the plot, is, in terms of its ironic, witty tone, and the flexibility with which it accommodates a very large number of often small-scale arias, distinctly old-fashioned, as-it-were seventeenth-century Venetian. Such a style might come more naturally to Grimani than to a younger professional librettist.

Agrippina, this last major work of the Italian years, shows Handel applying on a grand scale all he had learned as a friend and colleague of Corelli and the Scarlattis; its triumph in a public theatre in Venice established him as one of the great Italian masters of the day. And since this was an age when Italian music was in great request all over Western Europe, the world was now his oyster – whether he chose to go back to seek a court position in Germany or to go and have a look at England, about which he had heard much in his Hamburg years, and where (as he would have heard from English

34 *Documents I*, pp. 173–4.

35 The analysis of the handwriting is that of K. Watanabe, cited in Kirkendale, 'Händel bei Ruspoli', p. 355.

36 Mainwaring's account of *Agrippina* (Mainwaring, *Memoirs*, p. 52), claiming that it was 'finished' in three weeks, has sometimes been held to go against this interpretation. But his choice of the word 'finished' surely does not exclude the probability that all the detailed work on the libretto and a great deal of the draft composition (at least) could have been done months if not years earlier.

noblemen he met in Italy) attempts were now being made to establish Italian opera on a regular footing. According to Mainwaring, the erstwhile British Ambassador in Venice, Charles Montagu, Earl of Manchester, had given Handel 'strong invitations to England'.[37] This is quite credible – in January 1709 Montagu was instrumental in persuading the greatest Italian castrato of the age, Nicolini, to go to England – but it can only have happened in 1708 or 1709, because by the time *Agrippina* was produced, the Earl was back in London.[38] Meanwhile some efforts seem to have been in train to get London ready for Handel. In January 1710 an unprecedented item of foreign news had appeared in the press, reporting from Venice that 'Mr. Hendle's Opera [*Agrippina*] is the best that was ever heard for the *Musick*'; and at the Queen's Theatre, revivals of Ben Jonson's *Alchemist* were being staged with music 'by an Italian master', who turned out to be Handel.[39]

The first years in England

After the successful staging of *Agrippina* Handel left Italy early in the spring of 1710.[40] Whether or not he had any formal invitations to carry away with him, he will have known from what had been said to him by some of the distinguished men he met in Italy that he would be a welcome visitor, and might reasonably hope to become more than a visitor, not only in London, but also at the Electoral courts in Düsseldorf and Hanover too. Hanover was the obvious place to investigate first: it was, with Hamburg, artistically the most important city in the Protestant north-west of Germany, and, because of its court, important in an interestingly different way. And it was the home base of Agostino Steffani, one of the composers of the previous generation whom Handel particularly admired. Presumably Handel also knew that Georg, Elector of Hanover, had in 1701 been adopted as heir to the British throne. Perhaps he knew too of Queen Anne's less than robust health. At any event he accepted the position of Court Kapellmeister at Hanover in June 1710, and retained it for three years.

This German interlude is not, strictly speaking, part of Handel's operatic career. The opera house in Hanover had closed down in 1697, and Steffani,

37 Mainwaring, *Memoirs*, p. 72; in *Documents I*, p. 180.

38 On Manchester's exertions on behalf of Italian music in England see *Documents I*, pp. 164 (*The Post-Boy*), and 180 (Mainwaring, *Memoirs*).

39 See Excursus 5.1, 'The overture to *Rodrigo*'.

40 Early in March he was reported as having just passed through Innsbruck (*Documents I*, pp. 177–8).

the composer of a distinguished line of operas in Hanover in the 1680s and 1690s, no longer held an official position at the court; he was now primarily occupied in deeds of ecclesiastical diplomacy. But he was still there in Hanover, as was his experienced librettist, the court poet Ortensio Mauro, and at some stage Handel established, or more likely re-established, a cordial relationship with him. Some forty years later he recalled their meeting for Sir John Hawkins: '[Steffani] received me with great kindness, and took an early opportunity to introduce me to the princess Sophia and the elector's son, giving them to understand that I was what he was pleased to call a virtuoso in music; he obliged me with instructions for my conduct and behaviour during my residence at Hanover.'[41] Since Handel was certainly intending within a year or two to make his way to London, he would also have reflected that a period spent in Hanover would help him establish useful relations with some princely figures who, in the near future, could be expected to be the most important patrons in England. The calculation – if that is what it was – worked beautifully, for Handel's harpsichord playing particularly delighted the youthful pair who, in due course, were to become King George II and Queen Caroline.[42]

The diplomatic facets of Handel's biography in these years are fascinating, and they have some bearing on his operas. In going to England he was going to a politically fraught land, a land where loyalties were divided, and where the divisions affected, perhaps more even than in Hamburg or in Italy, the attitude of patrons to what they heard in church or watched in the theatre; that in turn might be expected to influence the choice of plot and character and viewpoint in the operas staged. Between 1710 and 1715 Handel composed five new operas, all but the last of them, *Amadigi*, while he was officially Kapellmeister in Hanover – indeed proclaiming that fact in the printed librettos. His absences in London are unlikely to have been tolerated quite so readily had they not been very much in the interests of Hanover too.

[41] John Hawkins *A General History of the Science and Practice of Music* (London: Payne, 1776), p. 267. Colin Timms' suggestion that this visit was made when Handel was en route from Halle to Hamburg in 1703 rather than after the Italian years seems very plausible; not only did Handel claim to be 'under twenty' at the time, but after three years in the company of the grandest dignitaries in Rome and Florence it seems unlikely that he would have needed coaching in etiquette, even from the subtle Steffani. See C. Timms, *Polymath of the Baroque: Agostino Steffani and His Music* (New York: Oxford University Press, 2003), pp. 81–2.

[42] We learn this from two letters from the Dowager Electress of Hanover to her granddaughter Sophia Dorothea, Princess Royal of Prussia; *Documents I*, pp. 180–3.

These were the years in which the British monarchy was passing from the House of Stuart to the House of Hanover. It was a transfer made in the interests of ensuring the Protestant succession, though by no means all of Anne's subjects were happy to put their religious freedom before their loyalty to their legitimate sovereign. In these wavering times, Anne in London and Georg in Hanover needed to be kept informed, and discreetly informed, about one another; and someone spotted the fact that a brilliant and mannerly musician who was fluent in French and Italian, as well as his native German, could be a useful medium. It proved a signal piece of good fortune that Queen Anne's chief physician, John Arbuthnot, was a passionate and knowledgeable music-lover who immediately became Handel's 'great patron and friend'. As the Hanover resident in London, Christoph Friedrich Kreienberg, reported, Arbuthnot and Handel between them proved a very useful source of information both to him and, in the other direction, to the queen too.[43]

But as well as being the years preparing for the transfer of the British monarchy to the House of Hanover, these were also the years of 'The Peace'; and this was another delicate matter. The Tory election victory late in 1710 led to a series of diplomatic negotiations with France that culminated in the Peace of Utrecht in 1713. It was a Peace regarded by Britain's European allies as little better than a betrayal; those allies included Hanover. So Elector Georg cannot have been well pleased when he learned that his Kapellmeister had been composing a Te Deum and Jubilate to celebrate the Peace, not to mention a Birthday Ode for Anne, whose role in '[fixing] a lasting peace on earth' served as its triumphant refrain. If it was unlikely to have been Handel's long absences from Hanover that led to his dismissal from the Kapellmeistership, perhaps, as Donald Burrows suggested,[44] it was rather these enthusiastic hymnings of the Peace. And perhaps in any case Georg's discharge of his Kapellmeister was little more than a gesture of lordly pique. At any rate Kreienberg was able to reconcile the parties without difficulty or delay (though, remarkably, he dropped into code for part of the correspondence with Hanover dealing with the matter),[45] and when Georg, now King George I, arrived at his first Anglican Morning Prayer in September 1714, Handel was on hand with a new Te Deum to mark the occasion.

43 Report to the Electoral Court, Hanover; in *Documents I*, pp. 275–7.

44 Donald Burrows, 'Handel in Hanover', in Peter Williams, (ed.), *Bach, Handel, Scarlatti: Tercentenary Essays* (Cambridge University Press, 1985), p. 43.

45 *Documents I*, pp. 277–8.

In England, in his usual way, Handel had gone straight to the heart of things. He had composed and played for the queen's birthday back in February 1711, even before the premiere of *Rinaldo* had made him a public figure in London. And through his friendship with Arbuthnot he soon came to know the group of men who set the cultural tone in those last years of the Stuart dynasty: Pope, Swift and Gay, fellow members with Arbuthnot of the Scriblerus club, and the young Lord Burlington, in whose Piccadilly mansion Handel lived for extended periods between 1713 and 1716, and to whom he dedicated both *Teseo* and *Amadigi*.

While both Burlington and Arbuthnot became warm supporters of Handel's work in the opera house, for the other Scriblerians Italian opera was generally a matter of indifference and often of derision. Handel's first London operas had to fight for a hearing in a theatre which had no established tradition of such works, and which had begun to make tentative experiments in introducing them only in the five years since the opening of the Haymarket Theatre in April 1705. Circumstances in the London theatres still fluctuated chaotically and sometimes riotously; swaggering feuds between those who ran them were commonplace.[46] And the steady support of men of letters, of the intelligentsia, even of the most civilised lovers of music and drama, was not automatically to be counted on.

Obviously this was not because England's theatre life had no space for music; on the contrary, music had held an honoured place in the English theatre since Elizabethan times. The problem rather was this: that music was perceived to have a number of quite specific theatrical purposes; these were important, but they were limited. First, of course, characters, especially minor characters, often sang 'real' songs in the course of the play (music serving as diversion or pastime), and if they were comic characters or mad ones their songs might form an important element in their characterisation; second, music was used to accompany stage processions, ceremonies or rituals (music serving in a quasi-liturgical function); and third, and most typically, music was associated with the supernatural, with the magical or the uncanny (music serving literally to enchant). But the idea of music as heightened declamatory speech, as in the Mediterranean traditions of ancient Greece or Renaissance Italy, was no part of English theatre aesthetics.

In English opera (often described as 'semi-opera' or 'dramatick opera'), music therefore found its proper place in masques, extended episodes of

[46] For a good account of the conditions at the time of *Rinaldo*, see J. Milhous and R. D. Hume, 'The Haymarket Opera in 1711', *EM* 17 (1989).

magnificent spectacle articulated in song, choral singing, dance and symphony; it featured not at all in the unfolding of the dramatic plot. In Purcell's *Fairy-Queen*, for example, an adaptation of Shakespeare's *Midsummer Night's Dream* in the form of an English opera, the music occupies approximately two and a half hours of a four-hour entertainment, but Purcell sets not one line of Shakespeare, nor do any of Shakespeare's characters sing. Music is (to reiterate the three categories I have proposed) pastime or ceremony or enchantment. It takes the form of, for example, a Masque of Night in Act II (performed by the allegorical figures Night, Mystery, Secrecy, Sleep and their attendants) to transport us into Shakespeare's nocturnal forest; or a Masque of Seasons in Act IV (performed by the allegorical figures of Spring, Summer, Autumn, Winter and their attendants) to mark the reconciliation of Oberon and Titania and the re-establishment of due order in the sublunary world; or the comic scene of the drunken poet in Act I.

When one wanted music in the English theatre, this was how it was supposed to work – and it worked very well. That must have been one of the reasons why, for all the enthusiasm for Italian music that was often one of the consequences of a Grand Tour, early attempts to stage opera in the Italian style, and increasingly in the Italian language, seemed to many Englishmen quite superfluous, even an affront to common sense – a sentiment most wittily expressed in some of the essays of Addison and Steele in early numbers of the *Spectator*.[47] In England, only the rarest spirits were beginning to reflect, as Lord Shaftesbury was, that perhaps there might indeed be a kinship between this new Italian opera, with its 'plain and simple' recitatives and its 'more sedately Passionate Parts … of *Reflection*' [he means the arias], and the tragedies of ancient Greece; a kinship which, if understood aright, could bring about a situation in which 'the Opera will every day gain upon the other Theatre, and our best Tragedy at last melt into Opera, which Union will be a kind of reviving the antient Tragedy in all its noble Orders of Musick and continu'd harmony'.[48] This was a kind of opera for which few in the audiences at the Haymarket Theatre were yet ready (and few in Italian opera houses either, if truth be told).

[47] See, for example, the essays that appeared in the *Spectator* on 6 March and 16 March 1711; they are reprinted in *Documents I*, pp. 204–7 and 208–9. A fine line from James Miller's 'Harlequin-Horace' deserves to be as well known: twenty years on from the *Spectator* he is still deploring the vogue for those 'foreign *songsters*' who 'In unknown Tongues mysterious Dullness chant.' See Otto Erich Deutsch, *Handel: a Documentary Biography*, London: A. & C. Black, 1955 (hereafter Deutsch), p. 280.

[48] From a letter of February 1709 to Pierre Coste, quoted in full in T. McGeary, 'Shaftesbury on Opera, Spectacle and Liberty', *ML* 74 (1993), 539–41. See further on these questions in Chapter 3 – the subsections 'Recitative and aria' and 'The Italian *dramma per musica*'.

None of what we might call Handel's 'Queen Anne operas' – though *Amadigi* appeared only after her death – made use of the Italian librettos he had, we assume, brought with him; two, however, *Teseo* and *Amadigi*, were based on French librettos, examples of *tragédie en musique*, the aesthetics of which occupied a position somewhere between Italian opera and English semi-opera.[49] Together with *Rinaldo*, *Teseo* and *Amadigi* formed a trio of operas in which Handel, stimulated by these French models, achieved, with growing refinement, a near ideal fusion of the two styles: Italian and English. They were heroic operas, but theirs was the heroism of classical mythology or mediaeval Romance, so there was ample scope for the 'marvellous': for spectacle and for enchantment; for elements of masque in fact, though the elements were more fragmentary and more randomly broadcast than in English semi-opera.[50]

Quite apart from the fact that it is Handel's first London opera, *Rinaldo* is important because it brought Handel into a collaboration with Aaron Hill, who, of all the colourful figures who flickered around the opera house in those early days, was the one who thought most fruitfully about the possibilities of Italian opera and did his ingenious best to naturalise it for London. His Preface to the *Rinaldo* libretto is worth quoting quite fully: as an essay in aesthetics it is perhaps primitive, but it does usefully summarise the problem and what Hill saw as the solution, and in doing so helps explain why *Rinaldo*, though it may be poor stuff as a drama in music, is nevertheless one of Handel's best-loved operas.

> When I ventur'd on an Undertaking so hazardous as the Direction of OPERA'S [...] I resolv'd to spare no Pains or Cost, that might be requisite to make those Entertainments flourish in their proper Grandeur, that so at least it might not be my Fault, if the Town should hereafter miss so noble a Diversion.
>
> The Deficiencies I found, or thought I found, in such *Italian* OPERA'S as have hitherto been introduc'd among us, were, *First*; That they had been compos'd for Tastes and Voices, different from those who were to sing and hear them on the *English* Stage; And *Secondly*, That wanting the Machines and Decorations, which bestow so great a Beauty on their Appearance, they have been heard and seen to very considerable Disadvantage.
>
> At once to remedy both these Misfortunes, I resolv'd to frame some Dramma, that, by different Incidents and Passions, might afford the Musick Scope to vary and display its Excellence, and fill the Eye with more delightful Prospects, so at once to give Two Senses equal Pleasure.

[49] See checklist at the start of Chapter 2.

[50] See further on this matter Chapter 2, subsection 'Fictions 2: romance'.

I could not chuse a finer Subject than the celebrated Story of *Rinaldo* and *Armida*, which has furnish'd OPERA'S for every Stage and Tongue in *Europe*.'[51]

Hill goes on to commend the librettist Rossi – 'a Gentleman so excellently qualify'd ... to fill up the Model I had drawn, with Words so sounding and so rich in Sense, that if my Translation is in many Places led to deviate, 'tis for want of Power to reach the Force of his Original' – before finally turning to 'Mr *Hendel*, whom the World so justly celebrates, [and who] has made his Musick speak so finely for its self, that I am purposely silent on that Subject.' And if in most respects *Rinaldo* did not quite match up to the expectations Hill raised, Handel's part in the enterprise emphatically did. He had come to London with a dazzling reputation as a virtuoso exponent of the Italian style, and he was determined to provide the city with a cornucopia of the best Italy had to offer. Much of the music he had indeed literally brought with him: a collection of his own choicest numbers, which he proceeded to adapt or revise or rework for their new dramatic context, fully aware of the fact that he was writing for one of the finest teams of singers and orchestral players in Europe. Audiences must have found the energy and emotional range of the music breathtaking: at one moment they might be rapt in enchantment by such seemingly effortless lyricism as we hear in, say, 'Il vostro maggio'; at another flabbergasted by the sheer scale of such a virtuoso aria as 'Sibillar gl'angui d'Aletto', where the orchestral richness, the forcefulness of line and rhythm, the slow unfolding of the harmonies, give the music a spaciousness and a grandeur in which, with the benefit of hindsight, we already catch premonitory glimpses of the vast spreading choral tapestries of the oratorio years.[52] As far as Hill was concerned, though, his moment of glory was brief; it will have given Handel a lively picture of London theatre conditions, when nine days after the premiere his collaborator and manager was thrown out, ostensibly because he could not pay his bills.[53]

The other operas of the period, *Il pastor fido* and the bizarre *Silla*, are not quite such 'sports' as might at first appear. *Silla*, with its historical subject constructed around partly familiar figures from ancient Rome, was in fact the kind of drama (albeit an inexplicably silly specimen) which shortly, with the establishment of the Royal Academy, moved to the centre of Handel's concerns. *Il pastor fido* was what its title suggested: a pastoral.

[51] The whole of the Preface, which is dated 24 February 1711, is reprinted in *Documents I*, p. 200.

[52] More will be said about the music of *Rinaldo* and its links with the music of the Italian years in Chapter 4.

[53] Milhous and Hume, 'The Haymarket Opera in 1711', 525–6.

And pastoral drama had been much in favour on the English stage for some years, especially as a factor in the arguments about the best way of responding to the prestige of Italian opera. Modern critics have discerned little but effete mediocrity in this repertory, but one thread of some interest does run through it, and it leads to Handel's opera.[54]

In 1676 Elkanah Settle had made an English stage adaptation of Battista Guarini's pastoral drama *Il pastor fido*, originally written in 1580–84 and from that day to this a classic of Italian literature. Settle's adaptation, based on what was also a literary classic of its kind, Richard Fanshawe's 1647 translation of Guarini, had virtually the effect of turning it into a Purcellian semi-opera: Guarini's messenger scenes were replaced by the direct on-stage representation of events, and extensive scenes of song and dance were introduced in Acts Three, Four and Five.[55] Settle's *Faithful Shepherd* was regularly revived: in 1694, 1706, 1707, 1711. It would have been possible for Handel to have seen this last revival himself – it took place in Greenwich – though there is no evidence that he did. If *Il pastor fido* seems a bloodless affair compared with *Rinaldo*, it did belong to one quite flourishing strand of English theatre which accorded music generous space.

The Royal Academy of Music

For all the enthusiasm of some English connoisseurs, the Italian opera house was proving a precarious sort of institution, one which certainly could not be supported by box office takings alone; and the art of opera remained a controversial and therefore fragile thing. A significant proportion of those who set the cultural tone in the city was sceptical or downright hostile, finding it absurd that they should be expected, in Addison's words, 'to sit together like an Audience of Foreigners in their own Country, and to hear whole Plays acted before them in a Tongue which they did not understand'.[56] Things had worsened when George I acceded to the throne in 1714, and especially by 1717, because squabbles, continual and sometimes acrimonious between him and the Prince of Wales, split into cliques the patrons of cultural life in the capital. If opera was ever to flourish, it needed to be put on an altogether sounder, more financially stable footing.

54 The operatic charms of the pastoral are discussed further in Chapter 2, subsection 'Fictions 1: mythology and pastoral'.

55 On the background to this opera see D. Chisholm, 'The English Origins of Handel's *Pastor fido*', *MT* 115 (1974).

56 *Spectator*, No. 15, 21 March 1711.

Mainwaring's account of how this happened sets Handel firmly in the centre of the enterprise:

During the last year of his residence at Cannons, a project was formed by the Nobility for erecting an academy at the Haymarket. The intention of this musical Society, was to secure to themselves a constant supply of Operas to be composed by HANDEL, and performed under his direction. For this end a subscription was set on foot: and as his late Majesty was pleased to let his name appear at the head of it, the Society was dignified with the title of the Royal Academy.[57]

In fact a group of music-loving noblemen and aristocrats had decided to avail themselves of the resources of the fast-developing capitalist system to launch the scheme. Those admitted to this corporation as subscribers included most of Handel's first London patrons, among them John Arbuthnot, Lord Burlington and the Duke of Chandos, and their purpose, repeatedly emphasised in the Charter, was to 'carry on Operas and other Entertainments of Musick' for a period of twenty-one years – the twenty-one years in fact during which all Handel's thirty-two remaining operas would be composed.[58] Those who drew up the Charter had learned from earlier experience in running theatres: provision for the expulsion of 'scandalous and mutinous persons' had to be made; and, opera having shown in the past how inordinately expensive it was to put on, the Academy needed the freedom to set its admission prices at whatever level proved necessary; and King George did rather more than 'let his name appear' in connection with the scheme: he contributed a generous 'Bounty', while his Lord Chamberlain, Thomas Holles, Duke of Newcastle, was appointed Governor, with supreme authority over the enterprise. The outcome was what Milhous and Hume call 'an odd amalgam of royal household entertainment and publicly held joint stock company'.[59]

The aspirations and ideals of the new company are best described in the words of a prospectus, possibly drawn up by Vanbrugh, who for two seasons was to serve as one of the directors of the Academy, and who had, of course, fifteen years earlier been the architect of the theatre in the Haymarket that was to be the company's home:

Opera's are the most harmless of all publick Diversions. They are an Encouragement and Support to an Art that has been cherished by all Polite Nations. They carry along

[57] Mainwaring, *Memoirs*, pp. 96–7; in *Documents I*, p. 406.
[58] The Charter is reprinted in *Documents I*, pp. 435–40.
[59] J. Milhous and R. D. Hume, 'The Charter for the Royal Academy of Music', *ML 67* (1986), 57.

with them some Marks of Publick Magnificence and are the great Entertainment which Strangers share in. Therefore it seems very strange that this great and opulent City hath not been able to support Publick Spectacles of this Sort for any considerable time. The reason of which seems to be cheifly that they have been hitherto carryed on upon a narrow Bottom by temporary Contributions Extreamly Burthensome to the People of Quality and entirely unproportioned to the Beauty, Regularity and Duration of any great Designe … As the Operas themselves will be in greater Perfection [than] what have hitherto appeared (Joyning what is excellent both in the French and Italian Theatre) so they will undoubtedly procure better Audiences, And by the Constancy and Regularity of the Performance the Taste rendred more universall.[60]

Day-to-day management remained in the hands of the impresario John Jacob Heidegger, who had been doing the job since 1713; Paolo Rolli was appointed Italian Secretary.[61]

Besides the Governor, Holles, the board of directors comprised 'the cream of the Whig ascendancy'. It was an intelligent and cultivated body of men, as well as a well-connected one.[62] It included at least one skilled musician, Colonel John Blathwayt,[63] and it was genuinely concerned to establish an opera company that would do credit to the nation: that dealt nobly with noble themes, that dressed those dramas in eloquent and expressive music, and that performed and staged them to the highest contemporary standards of excellence. Handel was sent to the continent with a 'Warrant' to procure the best singers money could buy, especially the great castrato Senesino; most of them he found in Dresden. The 'Instructions to Mr Hendel' which accompanied the warrant read:

That Mr Hendel either by himself or such Correspondenc[e]s as he shall think fit procure proper Voices to Sing in the Opera.

The said Mr Hendel is impower'd to contract in the Name of the Patentees with those Voices to Sing in the Opera for one Year and no more.

That Mr Hendel engage Senezino as soon as possible to Serve the said Company and for as many Years as may be.

That in case Mr Hendel meet with an excellent Voice of the first rate he is to Acquaint the Gov[erno]r and Company forthwith of it and upon what Terms he or She may be had.

60 *Documents I*, pp. 421–2 (present author's punctuation).

61 Rolli's work for Handel is discussed in Chapter 3. See particularly pp. 87–91.

62 The Directors' cultural interests are helpfully summarised by Elizabeth Gibson in 'The Royal Academy of Music (1719–28) and its Directors', in Stanley Sadie and Anthony Hicks (eds.), *Handel Tercentenary Collection* (Basingstoke: Macmillan Music Division, 1987), pp. 138–64.

63 Handel's and Blathwayt's paths may have crossed in 1707 when both were in Italy. See Gibson, 'The Royal Academy of Music', pp. 144–5.

That Mr Hendel from time to time Acquaint the Governor and Company with his proceedings, Send Copys of the Agreem[en]ts which he makes with these Singers and obey such further Instructions as the Governor and Company shall from time to time transmitt unto him.

Holles Newcastle[64]

Handel's official post in the Royal Academy of Music was 'Master of the Orchestra', and the orchestra he directed was a large and fine one. It comprised seventeen violins, two violas, four cellos, two double basses, four oboes, three bassoons, a theorbo and a trumpet.[65] It was a cosmopolitan crew, including most of the most famous virtuosos then resident in London, and Handel presided over it from the harpsichord.

But London audiences had long been accustomed to the best instrumental playing. The critical issue for the survival and flourishing of opera was that the Academy should be able to assemble a company of singers, preferably Italian singers, not only consummate enough to satisfy real music lovers, but also sensational enough to pique the curiosity of more trivial and casual and occasional listeners, and perhaps – forlorn hope! – gradually to turn them too into connoisseurs of opera.

As the instructions given to Handel in 1719 made clear, from the first the central figure in this strategy was Senesino; though he did not turn up in London in time for the first season, and made his Handelian debut only in revivals and the composite *Muzio Scevola*, it was for him that Handel was to compose all his greatest castrato roles from Floridante (1721) to Orlando (1733). We have a good account of Senesino's art from Quantz, who, as a member of the court musical establishment at Dresden, heard and saw him in Lotti's *Teofane* in 1719, just at the time Handel was there recruiting singers:

Senesino had a penetrating, bright, even, and pleasing low soprano voice (mezzo soprano), pure intonation and a beautiful trill. At the top he seldom went higher than f''. His manner of singing was masterly, and his diction [*Vortrag*] perfect. He did not too much overload the Adagios with capricious embellishments: on the other hand, he delivered the essential graces with the greatest refinement. He sang the Allegros with much fire, and using his chest [voice], knew how to attack florid passagework, at a pretty fast tempo, in a pleasing manner. His figure was very well suited for the stage and he was a natural actor. The role of a hero suited him better than that of a lover.[66]

64 *Documents I*, p. 430.

65 Winton Dean, and John Merrill Knapp, *Handel's Operas 1704–1726* (Oxford: Clarendon Press, rev. edn, 1995), p. 303, quoting the Portland Papers, which can now be consulted in *Documents I*, pp. 462–5.

66 'Herrn Johann Quantzens Lebenslauf von ihm selbst entworfen', in F. W. Marpurg, *Historisch-kritische Beyträge zur Aufnahme der Musik* (Berlin: Schütz, 1755), p. 213. The accomplishments of Handel's singers are discussed further in Chapter 6.

Senesino was joined by a series of outstanding leading ladies. To begin with the Academy's prima donna was 'old' Margherita Durastanti, whom Handel had first got to know in the salons of Rome in 1707–08, and with whom he had already worked in the opera house as far back as *Agrippina*. She was still a redoubtable artist, and sufficiently respected in society for King George to consent to stand godfather to the child she bore in 1721. But, already perhaps past her prime, she was gradually demoted during the early Academy years 'from principal singer to leading lady to second lady to second man'.[67]

Both Durastanti and the English soprano Anastasia Robinson, who had also enjoyed a long association with Handel, retired at the end of the 1723–24 season.[68] Durastanti graced her farewell with an English cantata in which she praised our 'generous, gay and gallant Nation' and acknowledged that younger 'charmers' were now succeeding her.[69] The younger charmer she doubtless had in mind was a singer who created the kind of sensation that Durastanti had never occasioned. Francesca Cuzzoni's debut in *Ottone* early in 1723 had been preceded by much preliminary puffing, some evidently satirical; and the satirical note was not lacking in many accounts of her powers after she had finally materialised. On 19 January 1723 the *London Journal* reported that she had performed 'for the first Time, to the Surprize and Admiration of a numerous Audience, who are ever too fond of Foreign Performers. She is already jump'd into a handsome Chariot, and an Equipage accordingly. The Gentry seem to have so high a Taste of her fine Parts, that she is likely to be a great Gainer by them.'[70] That she was the focus for much silliness is certain – indeed, she had an ample supply of it herself; but that she was a stupendous artist too cannot be questioned in the light of the roles Handel wrote for her: Cleopatra, Asteria, Rodelinda among them.

Yet scarcely had Cuzzoni arrived in London than rumours were circulating of another singer, Faustina Bordoni, 'the fine Songstress at Venice … whose Voice, they say, exceeds that we have already here'.[71] Cuzzoni maintained her solitary reign as prima donna for 1723–24, and 1724–25 – artistically the two seasons that many a modern critic would view as the climactic phase of the Royal Academy. Then, fatefully, for the seventh season the Directors decided they needed a second prima donna (clearly a contradiction in

67 C. Steven Larue, *Handel and His Singers: The Creation of the Royal Academy Operas, 1720–1728* (Oxford University Press, 1995), p. 83. This didn't discourage her from returning to the opera house for Handel's 1733–34 season.

68 Robinson went back to the 1714–15 season, when she sang Almirena in *Rinaldo* and Oriana in the premiere of *Amadigi*.

69 The text of the cantata is printed in *Documents I*, pp. 679–80.

70 *London Journal*, 19 January 1723, in *Documents I*, p. 618.

71 *London Journal*, 30 March 1723, in *Documents I*, p. 633.

terms) to set alongside her;[72] Faustina made her London debut in *Alessandro* in 1726. To begin with, Handel took great care to write music that matched the different and particular qualities of each artist (predominantly pathetic and tender for Cuzzoni, predominantly brilliant and optimistic for Faustina) and to keep the two ladies in perfect equilibrium – his solicitude for their sensibilities is demonstrated with delicious ludicrousness in the *accompagnato* and duet in Act I of *Alessandro*. But tension between the two divas and their respective factions mounted steadily and led to a scandalous outbreak of hostilities at the close of the 1727 season. This kept the satirists happy for weeks, and in 1728 provided a principal motif for Gay's *Beggar's Opera*.[73]

The hope voiced in the prospectus about joining Italian and French taste in a 'greater perfection' is reminiscent of Aaron Hill's remarks about *Rinaldo* back in 1710–11; and perhaps Vanbrugh, if it was he, dreamed of a repertory of operas that would continue in the manner of *Rinaldo*, *Teseo* and *Amadigi*. But with the company of singers Handel was now assembling, and with Italian opera enjoying a new self-confidence in its homeland, it was inevitable that the Royal Academy operas should soon be more redolent of Naples and Vienna than of Paris.

I shall discuss the artistic qualities of the Royal Academy operas later.[74] In the context of this survey of Handel's operatic career all that need be said is that this was the period when opera in London came closest in style to heroic Italian opera as practised on the Continent; when the vision sketched by Lord Shaftesbury ten years earlier looked as if it just might become a reality; because London-based composers were identifying themselves more fully with the aesthetics of the reformed *opera seria* which Metastasio, beginning with *Didone abbandonata* in Naples in 1724, was just bringing to perfection.[75]

Identification could, however, never be total: *opera seria* was a species of poetic drama, written by the finest poets of the day, generally on a (quasi)-historical subject; the essential elements of the drama (the action, the dialogues, the soliloquies) were set to simple recitative, and the full music (the arias, the rare ensembles) that rounded off the scenes was strictly speaking extraneous to that essential dramatic business. In arias the characters' passions and emotions might be distilled or objectified

[72] For a different perspective, see the article 'Rival Queens, The' in *CHE*.

[73] See the documents collected in Deutsch, starting at p. 210.

[74] See particularly Chapter 3, pp. 78–81.

[75] To be clear about terminology: an *opera seria* is a musical setting of what Metastasio called a *dramma per musica* (not a 'libretto'). In English, 'heroic opera' seems a better translation than 'serious opera'.

(sometimes in music of great intensity); but often, too, the arias were reflections – moral or philosophical – on the action; sometimes they were decorative *jeux d'esprit* in the form of metaphor or simile poems (over which towards the end of the Royal Academy period John Gay also made merry in *The Beggar's Opera*).

Such a genre was evidently impossible in a country where few of the audience could claim any real expertise, any real literary connoisseurship, in the Italian language; inevitably the recitatives had to be radically abbreviated, while the fundamental dramatic issues – the characterisation of the protagonists, the passions that assail them, the atmosphere that envelops them – had in large part to become the responsibility of the composer. All the same, the closeness of the Royal Academy repertory – of Bononcini's operas probably more than of Handel's – to the aesthetics of heroic opera in Italy is unmistakable; and many of them are based on the best Italian authors of the period.

Far from lasting twenty-one years, the Royal Academy survived for only nine seasons: not enough patrons acquired the taste for Italian opera and its finances were therefore never really secure. It remained too much the province of fashion rather than of genuine connoisseurship, and it was too easy for carpers, setting themselves up as devotees of Purcell and his 'old English' music, to mistake – or misrepresent – enthusiasm for foppery.[76] Professional and personal jealousies also played a fatal role.

Handel's high-handed way with singers was not appreciated by some of the biggest stars, particularly not by Senesino; but it would be wrong to blame the singers for all the problems. Handel was not the only composer working for the company. Bononcini was engaged for the start of the second season, and his operas provided the largest share of the repertory for that and the following season (he therefore deserves the greater credit for what was ostensibly the most successful period of the Academy's activities). We must suppose that Handel and Bononcini had a real, if slightly wary or reserved admiration for one another's music. In a less disputatious society it might have been possible to have given each man his due and to find in their different approaches to opera different sources of delight, for it was not only Handel who was indisputably a master. But masterly colleagues engaged in a common enterprise was not, it seems, what London audiences wanted; they wanted competitive rivalry. Writing to Steffani early in the second season, 1720–21, Riva depicts Handel's admirers as hunting for

[76] By 1724 *The Universal Journal* was running a series of articles on this controversy; excerpts are in *Documents I*, at pp. 704–5 and 706–7.

faults in Bononcini's *Astarto*;[77] while Riva himself, though he liked to blame the 'capricious and fickle' English for their wilfully obtuse partisanship, was (being a man who expected music 'to touch the heart', he explained) unable to find anything to admire in *Radamisto*.[78] An enterprise like *Muzio Scevola*, where three different composers wrote the three acts, could not be conceived as a sumptuous gala evening, showcasing the array of varied talents the Royal Academy of Music had at its disposal; it had to be the occasion for one of the composers to trounce his rivals. Audience enthusiasms were as factional as parliamentary debates; views on Handel and Bononcini (or later on Cuzzoni and Faustina) as partisan as Whig and Tory views on the state of the nation.[79]

An edge was given to these sentiments with the exposure of a Jacobite plot in 1722, which caused much suspicion about some of the Italians and catholics in the company. Bononcini and Rolli were temporarily dismissed, and a third maestro, Attilio Ariosti, signed up for the fourth season. His operas, after the encouraging reception of *Coriolano*, aroused rather less enthusiasm in subsequent years, and after Bononcini had left again, Ariosti and Handel sustained the 1724–25 season on very unequal terms. Ariosti continued to compose occasionally for the Academy until its final season; but his music seems not to have been the focus of the partisan enthusiasm that sometimes flared up around Handel and Bononcini. One notes that when, in the course of his ironic essay on the 'reigning diversions of the town', James Ralph attempted to characterise the three composers, he found it impossible to identify the quiddity of Ariosti's music, in the way he partly managed to do with Handel and Bononcini.[80] Increasingly after 1724, Handel dominated the repertory; and as he was the musical commander of the whole enterprise while Heidegger continued to manage the company, the Royal Academy in these last seasons already began to bear a strong resemblance to what has come to be called the 'Second Academy' of 1729–34. Bononcini was readmitted to the team for the 1727 season (it was in his *Astianatte* that the Cuzzoni–Faustina rivalry came to a head), but by this stage nothing could disguise what Haym, in the preface to *Tolomeo*, described as the 'declining vigour' of the whole Royal Academy of Music enterprise.

[77] Letter of 2 December 1720, in *Documents I*, pp. 521–2.

[78] Letter to Steffani, 5 January 1721, in *Documents I*, pp. 525–6.

[79] See, for example, the letter of Friedrich von Fabrice to Count von Flemming, 15 January 1723, in *Documents I*, p. 616.

[80] An excerpt is given in Deutsch, pp. 231–2.

This was such an important phase of Handel's operatic career – so much thought and ambition and goodwill and talent had been invested in it; so much was being learned about the difficulties (financial, personal, philosophical, aesthetic) of running an Italian opera house in a strange land – that it is worth summarising the Royal Academy of Music years in annotated tabular form. I have done this in the Appendix.

The 'Second Academy'

Despite the failure of the Royal Academy, after a fallow interlude in 1728–29 (Handel staged nothing between the *Admeto* revival in May–June 1728 and the *Lotario* premiere in December 1729), what has come to be called a 'Second Academy' was set up for the 1729–30 season. This was to be run by Handel in conjunction with Heidegger, who, already long associated with the theatre, was to continue to manage it through all vicissitudes of patronage, party and taste until 1739.

Beyond the fact that it was launched to provide London with Italian operas for five more years, the Second Academy remains a strangely mysterious affair. Clearly it was in some sense simply a continuation of the Royal Academy, whose effects – 'scenes, machines, clothes, instruments, furniture, etc.' – it continued to use;[81] King George's annual bounty of £1,000 continued to be paid; but Handel, as far as we can see, was now the sole authority in musical matters, and whether he and Heidegger were engaged at the behest of some kind of directing board or whether they worked as independent entrepreneurs, and in either case how the business functioned, simply isn't known. Relationships between Handel and Rolli being prickly, and Haym having died in the summer of 1729, 'the famous Rossi', as Rolli sarcastically reported, became 'Handel's accredited bard',[82] responsible, one presumes, for adapting librettos for Handel's needs. (Rossi will be remembered as Handel's first London collaborator in the days of *Rinaldo*.) From 1729 to 1733 Samuel Humphreys, best known as the author of the texts of some of Handel's first English oratorios (*Deborah*, *Athalia*) acted as the company's English Secretary, a task which entailed the translation of Rossi's (or whoever's) verses, so that Italian and English texts could continue to be presented on facing pages of the printed librettos.

[81] Viscount Percival's Diary, 18 January 1729; in Deutsch, p. 234.

[82] Letter to Riva, 3 September 1729; in Deutsch, p. 245.

The period of the Second Academy was anything but one single straightforward phase of Handel's career. The company he assembled for the first season failed to take, and both the principal castrato and the principal bass had to be replaced urgently for 1730–31 (Senesino for Bernacchi, Montagnana for Riemschneider). Another far more radical rebuilding of the company was forced upon Handel at the end of the fourth season, when the launch of the Opera of the Nobility brought about the defection of most of Handel's Italian stars. The exception, Handel's prima donna from the start of the Second Academy to the end of the Covent Garden years, was Anna Strada del Pò, whose loyalty and dependability were rewarded with an incomparable series of roles, ranging from Handel's most exemplary embodiment of the ideal of an *opera seria* heroine, Fulvia in *Ezio*, to the three wonderfully diverse heroines in his Ariosto operas, Angelica in *Orlando*, Ginevra in *Ariodante*, and Alcina.

The musico-theatrical substance of Handel's operatic seasons was also changing. The Second Academy began with operas, historical or quasi-historical, in that English dialect of the classic *dramma per musica* manner which he had practised for the Royal Academy; in its later years, however, he moved back into the world of romance (*Orlando*, and a reworked *Rinaldo*) and of mythology (*Arianna*, *Parnasso in Festa*, a bilingual *Acis and Galatea*). Some of the stimulus to rethink the *opera seria* format will have come from the apparently growing interest in the possibilities of opera in English. The triumph of the Gay/Pepusch *Beggar's Opera* in 1728 had created a fashion for ballad opera that persisted throughout the Second Academy years.[83] More direct rivalry came from Lampe at the Little Theatre in the Haymarket and Arne at Lincoln's Inn Fields, who both produced English operas, serious and comic, in the Italian style. Between March 1732 and April–May 1733 these two between them staged no fewer than nine English operas, entertainments offered at a fraction of the cost of Handel's operas at the King's Theatre. And though very few of them enjoyed even modest success, they must collectively have played some part in undermining the supposition (which lay behind the setting-up of the original Royal Academy) that heroic opera in Italian was a necessary constituent part of civilised life in a great city.[84]

[83] Handel's own music, operatic and non-operatic alike, was regularly laid under contribution in the ballad operas. For details, see B. Joncus, 'Handel at Drury Lane: Ballad Opera and the Production of Kitty Clive,' *JRMA* 131 (2006), 179–226.

[84] The most illuminating discussion of these English operas in the Italian style is J. Milhous and R. D. Hume, 'J. F. Lampe and English Opera at the Little Haymarket in 1732–3,' *ML* 78 (1997), 502–31.

In the middle of this spasm of activity, one of the central figures in the English opera party, his old collaborator Aaron Hill, wrote to attempt to engage Handel for the cause.

Having this occasion of troubling you with a letter, I cannot forbear to tell you the earnestness of my wishes, that, as you have made such considerable steps towards it, already, you would let us owe to your inimitable genius, the establishment of *musick*, upon a foundation of good poetry; where the excellence of the *sound* should be no longer dishonour'd, by the poorness of the *sense* it is chain'd to.

My meaning is, that you would be resolute enough, to deliver us from our *Italian bondage*; and demonstrate, that *English* is soft enough for Opera, when compos'd by poets, who know how to distinguish the *sweetness* of our tongue, from the *strength* of it, where the last is less necessary.

I am of opinion, that male and female voices may be found in this kingdom, capable of every thing, that is requisite; and, I am sure, a species of dramatic Opera might be invented, that, by reconciling reason and dignity, with musick and fine machinery, would charm the *ear*, and hold fast the *heart*, together.[85]

Handel did not respond to this challenge directly: but Hill's reference to the 'considerable steps' Handel had already made must refer to the fact that, towards the close of the 1731–32 season, presumably prompted by the activities of Lampe and the other exponents of English opera, he had put on revivals of both *Esther* and *Acis and Galatea*. The following year, for the first time, he was to make a principal attraction of the season a new English oratorio, *Deborah*, with a text by the Academy's English secretary, Humphreys. The linguistic challenge of performing such works of course exercised his Italian singers most disagreeably, and it was at this juncture that a lively account of the confusions of taste, style and performance practice appeared in a satirical pamphlet purporting to be sent by Lord Burlington to Aaron Hill.

I left the *Italian* Opera, the House was so thin, and cross'd over the way to the *English* one, which was so full I was forc'd to croud in upon the Stage …

This alarm'd *H-l*, and out he brings an *Oratorio*, or Religious *Farce*, for the duce take me if I can make any other Construction of the Word, but he has made a very good *Farce* of it, and put near 4000£ in his Pocket, of which I am very glad, for I love the Man for his Musick's sake.

This being a new Thing set the whole World a Madding; Han't you be at the *Oratorio*, says one? Oh! If you don't see the *Oratorio* you see nothing, says t'other; so away goes I to the *Oratorio* … before [Handel] stood sundry sweet Singers of this poor *Israel*, and *Strada* gave us a *Halleluiah* of Half an Hour long; *Senesino* and *Bertolli* made rare work with the *English* Tongue you would have sworn it had been

[85] Hill to Handel, 5 December 1732; in Deutsch, p. 299.

Welch; I would have wish'd it *Italian*, that they might have sung with more ease to themselves, since, but for the Name of *English*, it might as well have been *Hebrew*.[86]

Other changes were afoot. As in 1719, so in 1729; before launching a new operatic enterprise, Handel had gone to the Continent in search of singers. The new music he heard there interested him keenly, especially, we must suppose, that of Vinci, from whose operas had been chosen the bulk of the music of the Royal Academy pasticcio *Elpidia* back in 1725. He would soon begin 'borrowing' from Vinci as he had twenty or twenty-five years earlier from Keiser and his Hamburg colleagues.

Whatever Handel may have learned from the younger Italians, his own musical language remained rooted in the venerable traditions of contrapuntal workmanship, which he had mastered in his youth. But, as the city's taste had grown so capricious, it did seem an opportune moment to introduce to his repertory a number of pasticcios, that is to say operas for which the music was selected by Handel himself from the best contemporary masters and linked together by recitatives of his own composition. He was reviving a practice that had been usual in the London opera house before *Rinaldo*, and it seemed to offer obvious advantages now: in a pasticcio his patrons could hear select examples of music in the latest fashion, set to words in the best Italian literary taste by Zeno and Metastasio. It was a convenient way of introducing new singers, giving them every chance to ingratiate themselves with their public by allowing them – to some extent at least – to sing favourite items out of their suitcases when they made their London debuts.[87] What is more, according to Rolli, Handel was paid the same for arranging a pasticcio for composing a new opera,[88] though the labour would surely have been less (if also appreciably less interesting). Pasticcios were to form a regular ingredient of his seasons during the Second Academy, and he continued with them more intermittently for the rest of his operatic career.

But neither pasticcios, nor English oratorios, nor a new romantic-legendary repertory of operatic subjects could help the Second Academy flourish as, in its few best years, the first Royal Academy had looked like doing. There were no rival prima donnas now on the books, but Handel, in his mid forties, had grown no more diplomatic in his dealing with singers' sensibilities, and some of them took it ill. The first stirrings of discontent

[86] *See and Seem Blind: or a Critical Dissertation on the Publick Diversions, &c ... in a Letter from Lord B– to A– H–. Esq*; in Deutsch, pp. 300–1.

[87] Reinhard Strohm, *Essays on Handel and Italian Opera* (Cambridge University Press, 1985), p. 166.

[88] See Rolli's letter to Senesino, 25 January 1729; in Deutsch, p. 235.

had made themselves felt at the end of the 1731–32 season, and matters came to a head at the end of the next. Early in June 1733 two London journals, the *Bee* and the *Craftsman*, carried virtually identical reports:

> We are credibly informed, that one Day last Week Mr *H-d-l*, Director-General of the Opera-House, sent a Message to Signior *Senesino*, the famous *Italian* Singer, acquainting Him, that He had no farther Occasion for his Service: and that *Senesino* replied, the next Day, by a Letter, containing a full Resignation of all his Parts in the *Opera*, which He had performed for many Years with great Applause ... *the World seems greatly* ASTONISH'D at *so unexpected an Event ... all true Lovers of Musick GRIEVE to see so* fine a Singer *dismissed, in so critical a Conjuncture.*[89]

One wonders how astonished 'the World' really was. Senesino was certainly confident that he had the support of enough noble and aristocratic patrons, for many of them too had the feeling that the 'Dominion of Mr. Handel' had made it impossible to enjoy operas 'on a good foot', or to help 'carry on the Undertaking comme il faut'.[90] And so he led off most of his fellow Italians to set up a rival opera company, known at first simply as Senesino's Opera, but soon as the Opera of the Nobility. Since Hasse, who would have been their first choice, was unwilling to set himself up against Handel, Porpora was to be the principal composer. During 1733–34, the fifth season of the Second Academy, this Opera of the Nobility ran a rival programme of opera at Lincoln's Inn Fields.

The financial position of the Handel–Heidegger scheme was already precarious: in 1732–33 the number of their subscribers sank from 170 to 122,[91] and the frenetic activity on the English opera front already constituted a challenge for them. But it was the setting-up of the Opera of the Nobility to perform a repertory of the best contemporary Italian operas, with most of Handel's biggest stars engaged to sing them, and with the promise that Farinelli, the biggest star of them all, would be added to the company the following year, that made the fifth season of the Second Academy quite ruinous. Five of the operas staged that year failed to achieve more than four performances, and Handel's losses have been judiciously calculated at between £2,500 and £4,000.[92] For the next season the King's Theatre in the Haymarket, the scene of all Handel's earlier operatic triumphs in London, had to be yielded to the Opera of the Nobility.

[89] This is the version from the *Bee*, 2 June 1733; in Deutsch, pp. 315–16.

[90] The phrases are from a letter of the Earl of Delaware to the Duke of Richmond, 16 June 1733; in Deutsch pp. 303–4 (where it is wrongly dated).

[91] J. Milhous, 'Händel und die Londoner Theaterverhältnisse im Jahre 1734', *VIHAK* 4 (1992), 122.

[92] *Ibid.*, p. 131.

The Covent Garden years

Handel was not disposed to give up on seasons of opera. In fact, he obviously intended that they should continue to be the principal focus of his career as a freelance composer in London; and very promptly he was in discussion with John Rich (1692–1761) about taking his company into a racier part of town to perform in the theatre Rich had recently built (1732) at Covent Garden. Actor manager, pantomime star, impresario-entrepreneur, Rich was one of the great characters of eighteenth-century London theatre life. He is commonly said to have been parsimonious, perhaps even philistine; he will certainly have been hard-headed in deciding what should and what should not be admitted to his new theatre. Some commentators have been surprised at his welcome for Handel, especially as he was an avowed sceptic about how congenial English audiences could be expected to find Italian opera. 'I confess', he had written a few years earlier in the dedication of Lewis Theobald's *Rape of Proserpina*, 'it is not in the Power of the present Excellent Performers [of Italian opera] to prevent my falling into the very common Opinion, that there are many essential Requisites still wanting, to establish that Entertainment on a lasting Foundation, and to adapt it to the Taste of an English Audience.'[93]

This 'opinion' he proceeds to explain in a way which, far from being evidence for his philistinism, is eminently sensible: the language is not understood; the subjects are often ill-chosen; the vast expense of procuring 'foreign voices' leaves insufficient cash in the kitty to invest in machines and stage-sets and dancing and good poetry – all of which 'have been always esteemed … Auxiliaries absolutely necessary to the Success of Musick'. Even so, says he, 'my Inclination to Musick frequently leads me to visit the *Italian* Opera'. He was partial enough to Handel's music in particular to subscribe to the printed editions of it, from *Rodelinda* onwards.

So Rich is likely to have been at least sympathetic to any approach from Handel, not least in view of the generous supply of royal patronage which Handel would bring with him. While it is true that the Prince of Wales was continuing to support only the Opera of the Nobility during the first Covent Garden season, King George remained an ardent Handelian, whose £1,000 royal bounty was – the Treasury Minutes Book expressly instructs – to be paid, not to any 'Academy of Music', but to Handel personally. The frequency with which Covent Garden performances were advertised as 'By Royal Command' will have served to underline publicly and conspicuously

93 R. D. Hume, 'Handel and Opera Management in London in the 1730s', *ML* 67 (1986), 354.

the king's support for the Handel–Rich venture, and perhaps also the legitimacy of Italian opera (a form hitherto exclusive to the King's Theatre in the Haymarket) now being sung in a different theatre.

Be that as it may, it is surely admissible – to return for a moment to Rich's *Rape of Proserpina* dedication – to infer that the arrangement he made with Handel would not have come about unless he had been satisfied that the composer shared something of his own aspirations: that they could together make a fresh attempt 'to adapt [Italian opera] to the Taste of an *English* Audience', in the spirit he had outlined. It was to be rather like going back to *Rinaldo* and starting again. With so much clarified and agreed, Covent Garden became the base for the remaining three seasons of Handel's rivalry with the Opera of the Nobility.

Rich's Covent Garden had been built not as an opera house but as a general purpose theatre. That meant primarily a playhouse, though the plays were commonly decked out with musical, balletic, pantomimic and in other ways spectacular interludes, entr'actes and afterpieces. Some manoeuvring around the licensing laws may well have been necessary (as it will have been at Lincoln's Inn Fields for the Opera of the Nobility the previous year) to allow Rich to stage operas at all. And considerable manoeuvring will certainly have been necessary to solve the complicated logistics of fitting two performances a week of Italian opera around a repertory of theatrical entertainments of various other kinds on the other four nights the theatre was open.

After his move to Covent Garden, a theatre more democratic in its physical layout than the Haymarket, and with a repertory which suggested a more flexible, multimedia approach to the theatrical arts, Handel found himself more dependent on English or, more correctly, non-Italian singers than heretofore: John Beard, Thomas Reinhold, Gustavus Waltz, Cecilia Young. This was by no means to be regretted, for with fewer singers in the company with hidebound notions about the kind of music appropriate in a theatre, Handel was encouraged to make oratorio and ode regular ingredients of his opera seasons. Beard was to play a distinguished part in Handel's later career. He was only a teenager when he was engaged for the Covent Garden company to sing in the third version of *Il pastor fido* in November 1734, but Handel was 'full of his Praises', and confident that he was already artist enough to 'surprise the Town'.[94]

[94] Lady Compton to the Countess of Northampton, letter of 21 November 1734; in Deutsch, p. 375.

Of course the leading roles continued to depend on Italian virtuosos. The peerless Strada remained Handel's *prima donna assoluta* throughout the Covent Garden years, while a succession of brilliant castratos supplied the place of Senesino. If we may judge from the quality of the music written for him in *Ariodante* and *Alcina* – its sensational technical demands and its vast expressive range – Carestini was, of all the castratos Handel ever composed for, the one whose art he found most stimulating. But Carestini was apparently uncomfortable singing in English and, if the 'Verdi prati' anecdote is to be credited, may not have been the easiest of colleagues.[95] He remained only two seasons in London. After his departure Handel engaged two castratos of a younger generation, the alto Annibali and the soprano Conti. Trustworthy contemporary tributes, not to mention Handel's music, suggest that they were first-rate artists. Both of them – Conti in the 1736 revival of *Ariodante*, Annibale in the revival of *Poro* at the start of the 1736–37 season – were allowed to make their London debuts singing *arie di baule* ('suitcase arias') – a unique circumstance in Handel's career. This could be seen as a way of helping young singers find their feet in an unfamiliar world by allowing them to bring with them something familiar, trusted and comfortable. But might it not also have been a way of helping himself, of hearing for himself how dramatically effective the latest operatic styles could be when sung by artists trained and thoroughly at home in them, and from that judging how useful they might be in his own music?

The Covent Garden orchestra was probably smaller and may have been a little less accomplished than the ones he had been accustomed to work with at the King's Theatre. But there were new sources of stimulation to compensate for any such tailing off. When Rich agreed to instal an organ in the theatre early in 1735, Handel composed and performed organ concertos, providing a sparkling adornment to the relatively sober oratorio 'entertainments' offered during Lent. For an opera composer more to the point, he also had at his disposal a small chorus and, during the 1734–35 season, a troupe of ballet dancers. Moreover, these dancers were no mere routineers: their leader Marie Sallé (who as a child had taken part in the 1717 revivals of *Rinaldo*) was one of the great dance innovators of the eighteenth century. At this very period, casting aside the traditional ballet masks and the 'cumbersome regalia of baroque stage costume',[96] she was coming to the peak of her reputation as an exponent of expressively

95 The anecdote is recorded by Burney; see Deutsch, p. 386.

96 W. Thompson, 'Sallé', in *The New Grove Dictionary of Music and Musicians*, Stanley Sadie (ed.), London: Macmillan, 1980.

characteristic and dramatically purposeful dance – dance as '*poëme muet ... vive peinture*'.[97] In terms of dance history, these ballet scenes were novel – scandalously so in the case of *Alcina*, when Sallé performed as Cupid; but purely in terms of Handel's own operas they also marked an important step, away from, and to some extent backwards from, the aesthetics of the Metastasian *opera seria* into a more kaleidoscopic world, akin to that of seventeenth-century opera.

The three seasons at Covent Garden were so interestingly different from one another that they are worth discussing separately.

1734–35

The happy combination of circumstances I have been describing made this season artistically the most sumptuous of Handel's entire operatic career. The two new operas, *Ariodante* and *Alcina*, brought to a glorious climax what one might call the Romance–Enchantment strain in Handelian opera; a new mythological pasticcio, *Oreste*, gave further scope to Sallé's troupe; revivals of *Arianna* and *Il pastor fido* were gorgeously enriched with pageants of dance and choral song; the oratorios in the latter part of the season were decked out with Handel's own inimitable performances of his new organ concertos. Before the season even started, a notice in the *London Daily Post* reported that Handel had 'waited on their Majesties with his New Opera of *Ariodante*' and that 'his Majesty express'd great Satisfaction with the Composition, and [giving the stamp of royal approval both to the commercial ambitions and the address of the new ensemble] was graciously pleased to Subscribe 1000£. towards carrying on the Operas this Season at Covent-Garden'.[98]

Yet it seemed that nothing Handel offered could induce fashionable London to leave flocking to the Haymarket, where Farinelli had newly arrived. As the *Old Whig* for 20 March 1735 reported:

> In the flourishing State of this Opera [of the Nobility], 'tis no Wonder that the other Theatres decline. *Handel*, whose excellent Compositions have often pleased our Ears, and touched our Hearts, has this Winter sometimes performed to an almost empty Pitt. He has lately reviv'd his fine *Oratorio* of *Esther*, in which he has introduced two Concerto's on the Organ that are inimitable. But so strong is the Disgust taken against him, that even this has been far from bringing him crowded Audiences; tho' there were no other publick Entertainments on those Evenings.

[97] S. Henze-Döhring, 'Zur Gattungs-Tradition von Händels "Ariodante"', *VIHAK* 4 (1992), 62.

[98] *London Daily Post*, 4 November 1734; in Deutsch, p. 372.

His Loss is computed for these two Seasons [since the launch of the Opera of the Nobility] at a great Sum.[99]

1735–36

Urgent retrenchment was called for, and at first Handel seemed to be steering clear of opera altogether. In fact he did not launch his season at all until February, and when he did, it was with a radically different kind of work, a setting on the grandest scale of one of the grandest classics in English verse, Dryden's *Alexander's Feast*. This was followed by revivals of *Acis and Galatea* and *Esther*. But Handel continued to keep an eye on the Opera of the Nobility, and in November had been observed at one of their performances of Veracini's *Adriano in Siria*. The reporter was Lord Hervey. His lordship's satirical, partisan and gossipy pen cannot be depended upon for the unvarnished truth; but one passage from a letter to Mrs Charlotte Digby is so interesting it is worth taking the risk with:

Handel sat in great eminence and great pride in the middle of the pit, and seemed in silent triumph to insult this poor dying Opera in its agonies, without finding out that he was as great a fool for refusing to compose [opera], as Veracini had shown himself by composing … And what his understanding must be, you may easily imagine, to be undone by a profession of which he is certainly the ablest professor, though supported by the Court: and in a country where his profession is better paid than in any other country in the world. His fortune in music is not unlike my Lord Bolingbroke's in politics. The one has tried both theatres, as the other has tried both Courts. They have shone in both and been ruined in both; whilst everyone owns their genius and sees their faults, though nobody either pities their fortune or takes their part.[100]

Then, rather hastily, a marriage was arranged between Frederick, Prince of Wales and Augusta, Princess of Saxe-Coburg; and this absolutely demanded that Handel's company, with such reinforcements as might prove necessary, again address itself to the staging of an Italian opera. *Atalanta*, with the partial exception of *Riccardo primo*, the only opera Handel ever composed primarily to celebrate a public event, was completed less than a week before the marriage ceremony (for which he had also produced a substantial wedding anthem). Because relationships between Frederick and the king had broken down, the prince 'could not be persuaded' to go to any of the eight performances of *Atalanta* staged in his honour;[101] but he did command two

[99] In Deutsch, p. 384.
[100] 25 November 1735; in Deutsch, p. 396.
[101] Winton Dean, *Handel's Operas 1726–1741* (Woodbridge: The Boydell Press, 2006), pp. 343–4.

subsequent performances at the start of the 1736–37 season when, King George being still in Germany, he and Augusta could have the royal box to themselves.

Modern revivals show *Atalanta* to be a charming and touching opera. In the terms that were required of it in 1736 it also proved a success. The *London Daily Post* for 13 May 1736, having described it as 'composed by Mr. Handel on the joyous Occasion of the Nuptials of their Royal Highnesses the Prince and Princess of Wales', continued:

> In which was a new Set of Scenes painted in Honour of the Happy Union, which took up the full length of the Stage: The Fore-part of the Scene represented an Avenue to the Temple of *Hymen*, adorn'd with Figures of several Heathen Deities. Next was a Triumphal Arch on the Top of which were the Arms of their Royal Highnesses, over which was placed a Princely Coronet. Under the Arch was the Figure of *Fame*, on a Cloud, sounding the Praise of this Happy Pair. The Names *Fredericus* and *Augusta* appear'd above in transparent Characters.[102]

And there was much more in the same vein. *Atalanta* was received, concluded the report, 'with unusual Acclamations'. There was, unfortunately, no place in the new opera for Sallé and her troupe; having outraged English proprieties with her contributions to *Alcina*, she had now returned to Paris where her career was to continue in the *tragédies lyriques* and opera ballets of Rameau.

Whatever the pleasures afforded by *Atalanta*, it was clear to any objective view that both opera companies were struggling to survive. Once the novelty of Farinelli had worn off, even he regularly 'exhibited to empty benches'.[103] To those who loved Handel's music, especially his Italian operas, the tastes of London theatre-goers were proving lamentably perverse. Jennens' friend Edward Holdsworth was soon to suggest it was time the greatest poet of the age, Alexander Pope, exercised his satirical genius on Handel's behalf.[104]

1736–37

After the meagre operatic harvest of 1735–36 Handel's third season at Covent Garden could not have offered a stronger contrast. In November it started earlier than usual, with the two command performances of *Atalanta* for Frederick and Augusta; these inaugurated what proved to be 'the most

[102] In Deutsch, p. 407.

[103] Letter from Benjamin Victor to Matthew Dubourg, *c.*15 May 1736; in Deutsch, p. 409.

[104] For his letter, see *HHB 4*, p. 275.

ambitious season [Handel] had ever attempted single-handed'.[105] He composed, rehearsed and staged three new operas; he prepared a part-pasticcio version of Vinci's *Didone abbandonata*; and he revived no fewer than eight works – operas, odes, oratorios. He even contrived to get a special licence to continue performing oratorios (a term indulgently understood) during Holy Week.

It may indeed be, as Burrows goes on to suggest, that Handel now felt he had the Opera of the Nobility 'on the run'. But there was surely more than characteristic Handelian energy in the way he launched himself at his public this season: a touch of feverishness, even of frenzy. It was not a good sign. Had any of his productions really taken, he would not have needed so extensive a repertoire. More ominous still, by the early part of March rumours were to be heard in London that Handel, 'indisposed with the rheumatism', was retiring from composition.[106] Early in April he had a stroke – that at least seems the likely diagnosis – and when *Berenice*, the last of his Covent Garden operas, was premiered in May, it was the younger John Christopher Smith who presided at the harpsichord.[107]

Berenice had fewer performances than any other of Handel's London operas except (it is presumed) *Silla*. One is bound to wonder whether it would have fared better under Handel's own direction; but given the public mood in the London theatres in that early summer, it seems unlikely that it would have made much difference.

The final phase

So after a deeply unsatisfactory final season, the Covent Garden years ended sombrely with a career-threatening illness. But instead of putting a decisive stop to Handel's operatic career, the summer of 1737 marked the start of a four-year period during which it gradually petered out. Over four seasons, with differently constituted companies performing under very different conditions in three different theatres (the King's Theatre, Lincoln's Inn Fields, the Little Theatre at the Haymarket), Handel produced just four operas. It has been disputed whether this desultory pattern was the outcome of

[105] Donald Burrows, *Handel (The Master Musicians)* (Oxford University Press, 1994), p. 194.

[106] See the letters of Miss Ann Granville to her mother (8 March 1737), in Deutsch, p. 428; and of Holdsworth to Jennens (15 March 1737), *HHB 4*, p. 277; also the report in the *London Daily Post* (30 April 1737), in Deutsch, pp. 432–3.

[107] Donald Burrows and Rosemary Dunhill (eds.), *Music and Theatre in Handel's World. The Family Papers of James Harris 1732–1780* (Oxford University Press, 2002), p. 29.

his reluctance to abandon his favourite art form in even the most discouraging circumstances, or of a residual commitment from which he could not easily escape despite his eagerness to move on to other things,[108] or whether indeed it simply amounted to a series of duckings and weavings and retaliatory strokes of opportunism as circumstance demanded. Every new document that scholarship uncovers seems to make the picture more confused.

One suitable point from which to try to take our bearings might be the enforced rest, of six weeks according to Mainwaring, which Handel took in Aachen (Aix-la-Chapelle) in the autumn of 1737. When all due allowance has been made for the fancifulness with which Mainwaring and his sources may have embellished this episode, it is clear that Handel did not spend the weeks sipping water in a condition of faded lethargy: he was raring to go, and his intelligence and his imagination will have been teeming with questions and new plans. He must also surely have sensed that his powers as a composer were still growing. The two or three seasons that followed the Aachen interlude were the seasons of two of his mightiest oratorios, *Saul* and *Israel in Egypt*; of his greatest instrumental music, the twelve Concerti Grossi op. 6; of the Funeral Anthem for Queen Caroline; and of his most glorious setting, in any language, of great poetry, *L'Allegro ed il Penseroso*. And if the operas of the period seem for the most part rather slight affairs in comparison, they do include, in *Serse*, one of his most deliciously inventive scores.

One of the matters about which, while he was in Aachen, Handel will have thought a great deal was the collapse of the Opera of the Nobility only a few weeks after the breakdown of his own health. Since there had also been in the meantime an attempt to bring about some improvement in the relationship between King George and the Prince of Wales, the time seemed opportune to effect – under the management of Heidegger and with patronage now consolidated – what Shaftesbury called a reconciliation between Handel and the Goths. It had much to attract Handel, who would be able to shed the administrative burdens associated with repertory planning and contracts with singers and instrumentalists. It need not have been a disadvantage that he would have to work with a company of singers of whom the principals (Francesina, Chimenti, Lucchesina, Montagnana) had been selected not by himself but by the Opera of the Nobility, and consequently to part from most of those on whom he had depended in the Covent Garden years. The severest loss, that of Strada, was compensated for

[108] The original patent for the Royal Academy of Music expired only in July 1740.

by the acquisition of Francesina (Elisabeth Duparc), for whom Handel took 'great pleasure in displaying [her] natural warble and agility of voice';[109] and the prospect of composing for Farinelli, at least Senesino's equal as an artist and perhaps more agreeable as a man, was a further lure. He would be well paid for composing two operas, *Faramondo* and *Serse*, and arranging one pasticcio, *Alessandro Severo*, the music of which was largely taken from the failed operas of his final Covent Garden season – evidently neither Heidegger nor Handel felt that it would be a good idea to try to revive them. The proposal also allowed him time to supervise the publication of a number of important compositions.

Whatever high hopes Handel, his supporters and his former rivals may have had for the 1737–38 season, it was ill-fated from the start, indeed before the start; for Farinelli broke his contract and failed to return to London after the summer. Then, after only a handful of performances, none of them of Handelian works, the season was interrupted by the death of Queen Caroline on 20 November, which demanded several weeks of public mourning.[110] It was not until the New Year that Handel's operas could be staged. None of them proved a lasting success, so that, looking at the matter simply from an operatic perspective, Burney could conclude that the season ended 'very calamitously'. When it was over, Heidegger failed to raise sufficient interest among subscribers to be able to contemplate an opera season for 1738–39; this failure followed an attempt by 'twenty ladies of distinction' to take over the directorship of the opera, a task of which the gentlemen of the continuing Opera of the Nobility board had by now had enough.[111]

But Handel's seasons could no longer be viewed simply from an operatic perspective, and it has been persuasively argued that, in other respects 1737–38 'must have been Handel's most rewarding season to date'.[112] Working for the opera company only to commission, he will, with far less strain on his nerves and his patience, have made a substantial sum of money; his Funeral Anthem for Queen Caroline had been universally admired; members of the royal family and the nobility and most of the best musicians in the land had enthusiastically subscribed to the handsome

109 Charles Burney, *A General History of Music from the Earliest Ages to the Present Period* (London: 1776–89), in 2 vols., Frank Mercer (ed.), London: G. T. Foulis & Co, 1935, vol. II, p. 819, in his discussion of *Faramondo*.

110 King George remained absent from the opera house for the rest of the season, though his subscription continued to be paid.

111 See I. Chrissochoidis, 'Handel at a Crossroads: His 1727–1738 and 1738–1739 Seasons Re-examined', *ML* 90 (2009), 600–1.

112 *Ibid.*, 610.

full score of *Alexander's Feast*, published by Walsh early in March; a few weeks later (28 March) he had enjoyed a heart-warming display of generosity at his benefit concert; in April was installed and in May unveiled Roubiliac's statue of Handel in Vauxhall Gardens, where 'his Harmony has so often charm'd even the greatest Crouds into the profoundest Calm and most decent Behaviour'.[113] And before Heidegger gave up on the opera subscription, Handel had already begun work on *Saul*, the most tangible evidence for the likelihood that, partly under the influence of a new group of intelligent and cordial patrons in the Harris circle (which included Charles Jennens, the librettist of *Saul*), he was, with unusually cautious deliberation, gradually making up his mind to dedicate future seasons wholly to English oratorio and ode.

It was for such an opera-free season that, from January to April 1739, Handel hired the King's Theatre from Heidegger, presenting performances of the two new oratorios *Saul* and *Israel in Egypt*, and a revival of *Alexander's Feast*. But his strategy was spoiled when an anti-Handelian faction, probably led by his 'persevering enemy' (Burney) Lady Margaret Brown (one of the twenty disappointed ladies of distinction of the previous season's failed subscription scheme), decided to sponsor an Italian opera – Pescetti's *Angelica e Medoro* – at Covent Garden in early March, and poached a number of Handel's best performers to do so. If Pescetti seems scarcely a formidable rival for Handel, this pasticcio-opera was nevertheless enough to oblige him to make a part retreat from any great English-language oratorio project. *Il trionfo del tempo* was resurrected in its bilingual, heavily choral 1737 transformation, with some further revisions, and the season ended, if not ignominiously, certainly ingloriously, with the hasty assembling of the pasticcio *Giove in Argo*.

Except for one unsuccessful oratorio season in 1744–45, this was Handel's farewell to the King's Theatre. For the next two seasons he hired the Lincoln's Inn Fields Theatre from Rich. In 1739–40 only English works were performed, leavened by concertos from the Op. 6 set he had composed in the autumn; in 1740–41, for the last time in his career, he staged two new Italian operas, *Imeneo* and *Deidamia*. It can hardly be coincidence that this was the season in which the original Royal Academy charter had been expected to expire. At least one supporter regretted that Handel seemed to be 'leaving English and good chorus's for any thing of that kind'.[114] Why the

[113] *London Daily Post*, 18 April 1738; in Deutsch, p. 456.

[114] Thomas Harris, 18 October 1740; in Burrows and Dunhill, *Music and Theatre in Handel's World*, p. 106.

third and last performance of *Deidamia* was given in the Little Theatre in the Haymarket rather than Lincoln's Inn Fields remains a mystery.

The charming *Imeneo* is the work that best exemplifies the hithers and thithers of this period of his operatic career. He began work on it in the autumn of 1738, drafting it in the form of a relatively short three-act pastoral opera. It was abandoned with the abandoning of any operatic ambitions for that season, and much of its music was worked up or adapted for *Saul* or *Giove in Argo*. For the 1739–40 season he thought to return to it, and since this was to be an English-language season, began adapting it as an English serenata, condensing it into two acts, but at the same time expanding it with choruses. Before the task was completed, however, he changed his mind again, and eventually *Imeneo* – now once more a three-act Italian piece – was staged, or perhaps semi-staged, as an 'operetta' at Lincoln's Inn Fields as part of the 1740–41 season. A little later, in 1742, Handel performed it in Dublin; now described as a 'serenata', it was presumably done without staging. This was the last occasion on which he conducted one of his own operas.

In the meantime a new figure had appeared on the operatic scene in London in the person of Charles Sackville, Earl of Middlesex. Arriving in London in January 1739 from a second instalment of his Grand Tour, the young Middlesex found the city's traditional Italian opera house occupied by Handel, on the point of launching an English oratorio season. Middlesex was moved to assume responsibility himself for staging some Italian opera, an art form he had, one imagines, come to love and understand better during his years in Italy, particularly since he had in tow an Italian mistress who aspired to sing in such operas. He has generally been supposed, even if there is no explicit proof of the matter, to have involved himself in the Pescetti enterprise at Covent Garden in March, which so tiresomely deflected Handel's own programme. It is certainly the case that for the following 1739–40 season Middlesex took over and revamped the Little Theatre in the Haymarket so that he could stage Italian opera there.

For the next few years Middlesex's efforts to encourage Italian opera in London and Handel's gradual disengagement from it interconnected in messy and what must at the time have been uncomfortable ways. Middlesex was keen to have Handel compose for him; Handel prevaricated in a fashion that was felt to be discourteous, even 'proud and saucy'. Nothing came of their negotiations except a great deal of ill-feeling, and much later, in 1743, the loan to Middlesex's company of a performing score of *Alessandro*, which, that year, and for several revivals later in the 1740s, they staged under the name *Rossane*. By the autumn of 1741 Pescetti had been joined in the musical leadership of the company by Galuppi, and it was a pasticcio and an opera by Galuppi which were the last Italian operas heard by Handel before he set out for Dublin in November. The thought of Lord Middlesex, with the composers at his disposal, endeavouring to put on a season of Italian opera in 1741–42 made Handel very merry all the way to Dublin, he told Jennens.[115] A holiday mood, relief to have left that opera world behind, scorn for the quality of the music now being offered in the opera house, probably all contributed to Handel's mirth. Perhaps something else too: the confidence of one who sensed that he was on to something new and something good, and that his last operas had shown he had all the musical resources to deal with it.

Those resources were in flux again. If it is a little surprising to find *Imeneo* described as an operetta, it is still odder to find Lord Shaftesbury reporting of *Serse* that 'tis called a ballad [opera]'.[116] But indeed there is new flavour to the last operas, and it marks a retrenchment both from the high-mindedness of the Royal Academy masterpieces and from the glorious opulence of the best Covent Garden days. New sounds were in the air. Even the Opera of the Nobility had been experimenting with burlettas during the 1736–37 season; Handel himself is known to have enjoyed ballad opera, and still more Lampe's burlesque *Dragon of Wantley*; and he is unlikely to have been indifferent to the charms of Arne's new 'English' lyricism, which made *Comus*, first staged at Drury Lane in March 1738, one of the most popular theatre pieces of the middle decades of the century.

As always he was alert to the new types of music coming from Italy, even if he didn't particularly admire it. Handel had never lacked lightness of touch when it was called for, but in the last operas it became more all-pervasive: the symmetrical phrase-structure, the easy tunefulness, the dancing rhythms.[117] And this more relaxed manner harmonised well with the types of libretto he now favoured, which were more smiling, more old-fashioned and flexible than those of the Metastasian *dramma per musica*. It lent itself better, too, to the English language. As he drew to the end of his operatic career, the 'colossal' Handel was to be sought in other fields.

115 Letter of 29 December 1741; in Deutsch, pp. 530–1.

116 Letter to James Harris, 4 May 1738; in Burrows and Dunhill, *Music and Theatre in Handel's World*, p. 49. Some of the musical characteristics of *Serse* will be discussed further in Chapter 5.

117 Jennens complained that there were 'too many minuets' in *Giove in Argo*: letter of 8 May 1739; in Burrows and Dunhill, *Music and Theatre in Handel's World*, p. 70.

2 | The libretto (1): argument – *dramatis personae*

Checklist of operas

Handel's operas, with few exceptions, use librettos originally written in other places for other composers. The checklist in Table 2.1 gives, in chronological order of the operas' stagings, their full titles, the name of the librettist who assisted Handel in making his version, and (in the right-hand column) the place, date and names of author and composer of the original version of the libretto.

As it is intended simply for ready reference, the list does not include (except in a handful of particularly interesting cases) dates of revivals, second versions and so on, either of Handel's operas or of the operas and librettos on which they were based. Where no source libretto has been identified, I have tried to indicate the more important literary source(s) for the opera.[1]

Provenance: histories and fictions

As the checklist in Table 2.1 shows, the majority of Handel's operas have librettos whose provenance stretches some way back in operatic history. At the start of his career he composed a number of operas on librettos expressly written for him: the lost Hamburg works, *Nero*, *Florindo* and *Daphne; Agrippina* for Venice; *Rinaldo* for his London debut and, seemingly, *Il pastor fido*, its wilfully contrary sequel. Thereafter, until his very last Italian opera, *Deidamia*, he never again set original librettos; rather, he chose pre-existing ones which had in some way already proved their worth and which, for some quality or another, had already ignited a spark in his own imagination. In several cases there is a good likelihood that he had seen the opera staged, either during his Italian years or on his talent-spotting

[1] For fuller details see Dean and Knapp, *Handel's Operas 1704–1726*; Dean, *Handel's Operas 1726–1741*; Strohm, *Essays on Handel and Italian Opera*; *CHE*; and the volumes of *HHA*, where applicable.

Table 2.1 Checklist of operas

Date of staging/title/Handel's librettist and/or adapter	Original source of libretto: place and date/librettist/composer
1705 *Der in Krohnen Erlangte Glücks-Wechsel, oder: Almira, Königin von Castilien* (Feustking)	Venice 1691/Pancieri/Boniventi
1705 *Die Durch Blut und Mord Erlangete Liebe, oder: Nero* (Feustking)	(Literary source: unknown)
1707 *Vincer se stesso è la maggior vittoria* (*Rodrigo*) (anon [?Salvi])	Venice 1700/Silvani/M. A. Ziani
1708 *Der Beglückte Florindo* (Hinsch)	(Literary source: unknown)
1708 *Die Verwandelte Daphne* (Hinsch)	
1709 *Agrippina* (Grimani)	(Literary source: Tacitus, *Annals*; Suetonius, *Lives of the Emperors*)
1711 *Rinaldo* (Hill and Rossi)	(Literary source: Tasso, *Gerusalemme liberata*)
1712 *Il pastor fido* (Rossi)	(Literary source: Guarini, *Il pastor fido*)
1713 *Teseo* (Haym)	St Germain-en-Laye 1675/P. Quinault/Lully
1713 *Lucio Cornelio Silla* (Rossi)	(Literary source: Plutarch, *Lives*)
1715 *Amadigi di Gaula* (?Haym)	Fontainebleau 1699/Houdar de la Motte/Destouches
1720 *Radamisto* (Haym or Rolli)	Venice 1710/Lalli/Gasparini
1721 *Muzio Scevola* (Rolli)	Vienna 1710/Stampiglia/Bononcini
1721 *Il Floridante* (Rolli)	Venice 1696/Silvani/M. A. Ziani

(*continued*)

Table 2.1 (*cont.*)

Date of staging/title/Handel's librettist and/or adapter	Original source of libretto: place and date/librettist/composer
1722 *Ottone, Re di Germania* (Haym)	Dresden 1719/Pallavicini/Lotti
1723 *Flavio, Re de' Longobardi* (Haym)	Venice 1682/Noris/Partenio
1724 *Giulio Cesare in Egitto* (Haym)	Venice 1677/Bussani/Sartorio
1724 *Tamerlano* (Haym)	Venice 1711/Piovene/Gasparini
1725 *Rodelinda, Regina de' Longobardi* (Haym)	Florence 1710/Salvi/Perti
1726 *Publio Cornelio Scipione* (Rolli)	Livorno 1704/ Salvi/ anon.
1726 *Alessandro* (Rolli)	Hanover 1690/Mauro/Steffani
1727 *Admeto, Re di Tessaglia* (?Haym or Rolli)	Venice 1660/Aureli/P. A. Ziani via Hanover 1681/Mauro/Trento
1727 *Riccardo Primo, Re d' Inghilterra* (Rolli)	Venice 1710/ Briani/ Lotti
1728 *Siroe, Re di Persia* (Haym)	Venice 1726/Metastasio/Vinci
1728 *Tolomeo, Re di Egitto* (Haym)	Rome 1711/Capece/D. Scarlatti
1729 *Lotario* (Rossi)	Munich 1722/Salvi/Torri
1730 *Partenope* (anon.)	Naples 1699/Stampiglia/Mancia via Venice 1708/Stampiglia/Caldara
1731 *Poro, Re dell' Indie* (anon.)	Rome 1730/Metastasio/Vinci
1732 *Ezio* (anon.)	Rome 1728/Metastasio/Auletta
1732 *Sosarme, Re di Media* (anon.)	Florence 1707/Salvi/Perti

Table 2.1 (*cont.*)

Date of staging/title/Handel's librettist and/or adapter	Original source of libretto: place and date/librettist/composer
1733 *Orlando* (anon.)	Rome 1711/Capece/D. Scarlatti
1734 *Arianna in Creta* (anon.)	Vienna 1715/Pariati/F. Conti via Rome 1729/Pariati/Leo
1735 *Ariodante* (anon.)	Florence 1708/Salvi/Perti
1735 *Alcina* (anon.)	Rome 1728/anon./R. Broschi
1736 *Atalanta* (anon.)	Ferrara 1715/Valeriani/Chelleri
1737 *Arminio* (anon.)	Florence 1703/Salvi/A. Scarlatti
1737 *Giustino* (anon.)	Venice 1683/Beregan/Legrenzi via Rome 1724/Pariati/Vivaldi
1737 *Berenice, Regina d'Egitto* (anon.)	Florence 1709/Salvi/Perti
1738 *Faramondo* (anon.)	Venice 1699/Zeno/C. F. Pollarolo
1738 *Serse* (anon.)	Venice 1665/Minato/Cavalli via Rome 1694/Stampiglia/Bononcini
1740 *Imeneo* (anon.)	Naples 1723/Stampiglia/Porpora
1741 *Deidamia* (Rolli)	(Literary source: unknown)

returns to the Continent in 1719 and 1729 (*Ottone*, *Lotario* and *Sosarme* are likely examples). Such librettos now needed to be thoroughly revised, for his own purposes and for the needs of his London audience; and that proves a stimulating state of affairs. For while it would be foolish to presume that we can always understand the reason for the revisions, the sheer profusion of the rewritings and substitutions, the cuts and the insertions, the reorganisations of plot and the rebalancings of character do certainly provide tangible evidence of the kinds of thing Handel valued, and the kinds of thing he felt he could or must do without.[2]

But we should begin with the Arguments. Most of the types of subject tried and tested during the hundred years between the beginning of opera as an art form in Italy around 1600 and the beginning of Handel's own operatic career are to be found in the Handelian repertory. Not quite everything is here, for there is no place for biblical or hagiological opera, and there are no purely comic operas. With those exceptions, we find virtually everything. Several operas are based on subjects from classical mythology, traditionally the most dependable source for opera librettos (for example, *Teseo*, *Admeto*, *Arianna in Creta*, *Deidamia*). Of these mythological operas, some have extensive pastoral episodes; one or two of them indeed, like *Atalanta*, come close to being purely pastoral operas. These form perhaps another genre, such as we find in the lost Hamburg pieces *Der beglückte Florindo* and *Die verwandelte Daphne*, and in the various workings of *Il pastor fido* between 1712 and 1734. In another direction, however, the mythological operas tend toward legend: their subjects are the wonderful tales told of great heroes, and in that respect they resemble a further group, in which the legends are of more modern provenance, from the great chivalric epics of the Middle Ages and Renaissance: *Rinaldo*, *Amadigi*, and the trio of Ariosto-inspired operas from the 1730s, *Orlando*, *Ariodante* and *Alcina*.

The rest, a clear majority of them, have historical themes, sometimes based on the titanic figures of ancient history (*Giulio Cesare in Egitto*, *Alessandro*, *Poro*, *Serse*), sometimes on exceedingly obscure episodes – or indeed completely bogus ones – from the Gothic Dark Ages (*Almira*, *Rodrigo*, *Flavio*, *Rodelinda*, *Lotario*). Very occasionally (*Tamerlano* and *Riccardo primo*), the stories are taken from more recent history. While many of these historical operas treat their themes in heroic, high-minded fashion, their variety of tone is in fact remarkable, on occasion emphatically un-heroic (*Flavio*, *Serse*), and at least once (*Agrippina*) broadly comical.

In sum there are three constellations: history, which provides operas with such essential and worldly themes as how the noble hero is to earn his glory, or what constitutes rectitude and justice; myth, which brings into the opera house Golden Age pastoral and the divinities of the pagan world; and hovering between them, romance – chivalric epic – where the heroic is subject to, and often the plaything of, magic and enchantment. So fluid, however, are the boundaries between these various categories, especially the latter two,

[2] This matter is discussed in Chapter 3, particularly in the subsection 'Librettist colleagues in London'.

that systematic classification proves elusive. It may be better to take a leaf from so many libretto prefaces of the period and simply make a distinction between that which is historical (however indulgently defined) and that which is fictional: then we have a variety of histories and a variety of fictions.

Although most kinds of opera are to be found in most phases of Handel's career, his perspective on this range of subjects did shift over the years, and the nature of the shift comes most clearly into focus if we start from the operas of the Royal Academy period, 1720–28. At that time, the particular interest of Handel's patrons, and therefore of his librettists and himself, was in heroic themes taken from historical sources. As I have already indicated in Chapter 1, this was part of a programme to reform English dramatic taste by aligning the Royal Academy in London with the best contemporary practice in Italy, and in such European centres of Italian operatic activity as Vienna and Dresden. It was a tendency which, briefly, brought Handelian opera quite close, if never very close, to the Italian genre that was ripening towards perfection in those years, and which has come to be called *opera seria.*

Before that Royal Academy phase, in the early London years, Handel's choice of subject was more varied. An array of fictions was attempted: romance, pastoral, myth. History appeared only in the very peculiar case of *Silla*. In fact, as far as subject matter was concerned, the years 1710–15 seem almost like a replay of the founding years of Italian opera at the turn of the sixteenth to the seventeenth century; and in a sense they were. Like the operatic pioneers in Florence and Rome a hundred years earlier, Handel and his librettists were experimenting; not so much trying out what kinds of dramatic theme lent themselves best to musical dress, as what kinds might best persuade sceptical audiences – who were accustomed to fine theatre and fine music and to the English way of combining them – to be less sceptical in the face of fully-fledged Italian opera. Myth, pastoral and romance seemed the most promising fields.

During the Second Academy years, as it became ever clearer that Italian opera was not really taking, and that London society's enthusiasm for it was limited; when the opera company itself was riven by faction, and when the very rationale of Italian opera was again being called into question, Handel returned to those same types of dramatic theme with which, twenty years earlier, he had first tried to lure English music lovers into the Italian opera house. From *Orlando* onwards, this was a continuing tendency; but it was part of a more complicated and untidy picture, in which most of his operas bore ever less resemblance to *opera seria*, and were more and more fruitfully contaminated by the English-language odes, masques and oratorios with which they shared his theatre, perhaps even by the ballad operas and burlesques at rival theatres.

History

Operas based on historical subjects were Handel's chief concern during the years of the Royal Academy of Music. There is no reason to doubt that he was happy composing such works, but certainly the main reason for this shift of emphasis will have been the expectations and requirements of his most important patrons. It is very likely that the Directors themselves chose some of the texts he set,[3] and they may sometimes have done this in order to flatter or provoke their audience. For instance, Rolli was surely acting with the encouragement of the directorate when he remarks, in the dedication of his libretto for *Muzio Scevola*, that an opera which depicts 'the birth of Roman liberty' finds its proper home in the one country where Roman liberty is still preserved: where 'the people possess it, the politicians *[i tribuni*] watch over it, the patricians defend it, the sovereign protects it.'[4]

According to Voltaire, no reading gave Handel's English contemporaries greater delight than the reading of history.[5] It was a branch of literature to be enjoyed and admired both for its literary and its ethical qualities; in particular the great historians of the ancient world, Greek and Latin, whose books were as integral to an eighteenth-century education as those of the classical poets, were read for their narrative and rhetorical power, and for the wisdom of the reflections that punctuated them. Such reflections provide a parallel to the use of moralising arias in opera; and eighteenth-century writers and composers would have felt that they supplied an appropriate and adequate retort to Aristotle's scruple: that history was one of the lesser literary forms because it lacked universality. They were confirmed in their view by Cicero's precepts for the historian: tell your tale in a clear but elevated style; introduce plentiful and varied literary graces; and especially stress the moral lessons of history. Thanks to the educational background shared by Handel's patrons, several of his operas are peopled by characters well known to their audiences; they knew perfectly well what Caesar and Alexander and Xerxes were reported to have done. Moreover, all such heroes were indelibly connected with certain set-pieces in the classical historians – Caesar weeping over the severed head of Pompey; Xerxes and his plane tree and his bridge of boats, and so on – which the dramatist would be expected to turn to good effect. It is again in the libretto to *Muzio Scevola* that Rolli specifically mentions such familiar incidents as being the pivots of his drama.

[3] In at least two cases, *Flavio* and *Tamerlano*, the librettos tell us as much.

[4] Rolli's dedication, from which these words come, is included in *Documents I*, pp. 538–40.

[5] He is cited in R. G. King, 'Classical History and Handel's *Alessandro*', *ML* 77 (1996), 35.

The pleasures and also the purposes of historical writing, and surely of historical drama too, are charmingly evoked in the preface to Isaac Littlebury's translation of Herodotus (1709):

> nothing can be more delightful than by means of History to enter the Athenian Areopagus and the Roman Senate: To be present with Leonidas at Thermopylae, with Aristides at Plataea, with Scipio at Carthage, and with Alexander at Arbela: To be plac'd as a Spectator out of all Hazard, to learn Wisdom from the Dangers of others; to take a distinct View of past Governments, Customs, and Manners; and by applying former Examples to our own Use, reap the Advantage of other Mens Experience, and of Tryals already made in every kind.

'Applying former examples to our own use' is an especially pertinent phrase. Besides reminding audiences what was known of these famous characters, the task of the poet-dramatist was to use 'the silent gaps of history' (Muratori) effectively. In mid seventeenth-century Venice Niccolò Minato had been the first librettist to differentiate explicitly between 'those things we know from history', and 'those things which have been feigned'[6] (in his version of the Xerxes story, which was eventually to furnish the libretto for Handel's *Serse*); and thereafter Minato's became the accepted frame of mind for librettists writing historical operas. What they particularly wished to 'feign' were not necessarily extravagant fantasies; it was more likely to be such crises, emotional and psychological, as would demonstrate the 'unity of all human history', the essential identity of peoples of all ages and all places, including the identity of those depicted on stage and those sitting in the theatre observing the depictions. The interest in humankind that is so fundamental in early eighteenth-century opera is a topic that will recur later in this chapter. It is no accident that the two ancient historians to whom librettists turned most frequently, Livy and Plutarch, were those who placed the psychology of great men at the heart of their narratives: not just what they did, but the dilemmas they pondered, the rhetoric with which they carried the day, and the morals they drew when the day was ended.[7]

But all these considerations do not explain a further group of historical operas in which Handel and his librettist colleagues chose to concern themselves with real characters from the past about whom it would be safe to surmise that almost no one in his audience would know anything: *Rodrigo*, *Rodelinda*, *Lotario*, *Sosarme* and several others. I name four that have either certain or suspected links with the Florentine physician and dramatic poet

6 Following a hint in the fourteenth chapter of Aristotle's *Poetics*.

7 'To understand the course of history through character represents Livy's great achievement.' R. Ogilvie, 'Livy', *Encyclopedia Britannica* 15th edition (1978), vol. XI.

Antonio Salvi. Will this be coincidence? Or does the Salvi link, a link to a man deeply interested in French classical drama, perhaps provide a clue to what Handel was up to here?[8] If the historical figures are themselves unknown, there will be no historically familiar situations or incidents in which the librettist is constrained to place them; the close speculative analysis of character can then prevail wholly.

Fictions 1: mythology and pastoral

Mythological characters were not in principle treated differently from other types of character: they were provided with the same resources of heroism and the same depths of sensibility; and librettists presented their chosen mythological themes and explained what they were up to in their adaptations with the same well-tried formulas. In the libretto for *Admeto*, for instance, we read, 'This [story] is collected out of the Fables of the Ancients: The rest is a Work of Fiction, purely for the ornamenting the Drama.' But since the source of the story was now 'fable', not history, the freedom and imaginativeness with which it could be ornamented was greater: divine and allegorical figures might direct the hero's path; monsters might haunt his dreams; marvels or miracles might transform or reverse or undo the work of nature. Such irruptions from the world of super-nature were just the thing to make mythological themes seem more properly operatic to anyone who, brought up on a repertory of English 'semi-opera', remained doubtful about the all-sung Italian variety.

Pastoral, too, was felt to be peculiarly adapted to music, for, as Giovanni Battista Doni had remarked in an important early treatise on opera (1635), the language was 'flowery and sweet … one may even admit that it has melody in its every part, since there are shown deities, nymphs, and shepherds from that most remote age when music was natural and speech like poetry.'[9]

8 One detail that is perhaps of interest is that behind the Italian sources of the librettos Handel composed during the Royal Academy years there are, in several cases, seventeenth-century French prototypes, as follows:
Radamisto, G. de Scudéry *L'amour tyrannique* (1639)
Flavio, P Corneille, *Le Cid* (1637)
Tamerlano, J. Pradon, *Tamerlan* (1672)
Rodelinda, P. Corneille, *Pertharite, roi des Lombards* (1651)
More tenuous and questionable links have been suggested for *Muzio Scevola*: P. Du Ryer, *Scévole* (1647); *Giulio Cesare*: P. Corneille, *La mort du Pompée* (1644); *Siroe*: J. de Rotrou, *Cosroes* (1649).

9 Quoted in D. J. Grout, *A Short History of Opera* (New York: Columbia University Press, 1947), p. 36.

For English readers Dryden made the point more mordantly, in the preface to *Albion and Albanius*: if you wished to add some 'meaner characters' to the supernatural characters who are most proper to opera, he advised, then you should set your drama in some golden age where 'Shepherds might reasonably be admitted, as of all Callings, the most innocent, the most happy'; they were particularly well adapted to opera because they had, 'in their almost idle Employment, most leisure to make Verses, and to be in Love, without somewhat of which Passion, no *Opera* can possibly subsist'.[10]

Handel had early and plentiful experience of how fruitful for music pastoral could be. Two of his four Hamburg operas had been pastorals. Then, during the years he spent in Italy, he was regularly involved with the activities of the Arcadian Academy at the period of its greatest influence and prestige. Aristocrats and churchmen, including Handel's patrons Ruspoli, Pamphili and Ottoboni, the finest poets and musicians of the age, foregathered under assumed pastoral names in a paradisean garden, recited poetry and made music so sweet, so harmonious, that a Golden Age of Italian culture seemed restored. Handel attended. Indeed, he acquired his mastery of the modern Italian style in those dozens of cantatas, sometimes intimate and sometimes grandiloquent, which, almost without exception embraced the values and the sensibility of the Arcadians in the forms and styles which they cultivated. When he arrived in London, he found that pastoral episodes were often used to provide masques of dance and song in English semi-opera; some of these masques had begun to take on an independent theatrical life of their own. It is no surprise, therefore, to find that pastoral was one of the first matters he turned to as he began to think about a repertory of Italian operas for his new London audiences.

After the sensation occasioned by *Rinaldo*, the result was disappointing: *Il pastor fido*, based on Guarini's dramatic poem of the same name (1589), was, in this early 1712 form, one of the least enjoyed of Handel's operas. It may have shown due respect to a classic of Italian literature, but it paid too little attention to how pastoral scenes had been handled on the English stage since the Restoration, and was too much like a Roman chamber cantata to please a London theatre audience. Not even the spectacle delighted: 'The Scene represented only the Country of Arcadia. the Habits were old. – the Opera Short', 'Francis Colman' grumbled.[11] There seemed little point in transporting a drama to Arcadia if the nymphs and shepherds were going to have no scope for choral song and dance.

[10] Quoted in E. J. Dent, *Foundations of English Opera* (Cambridge University Press, 1928), p. 161.

[11] *Opera Register*, November–December 1712; in *Documents I*, pp. 248–9.

The opportunity wasted in 1712 was, however, seized when, in 1734, Handel twice again took up *Il pastor fido*. First, in the early summer revivals that year, he introduced, among many other changes, festive choruses to close each act. They were borrowed from the serenata *Parnasso in festa*, composed a few months earlier to celebrate the wedding of Princess Anne and Prince William of Orange. In the autumn, in a third version of *Il pastor fido*, dance was added to the melange. The opera was now preceded by a Prologue, *Terpsicore*, a celebration of the Muse of Dance, and since Marie Sallé, the most thrilling theatrical dancer of the age, was involved in it, further suites of dances were added to each of the acts. In this way Handel turned what had begun as an unduly demure pastoral opera into an opera-ballet, and *Il pastor fido* became an Arcadian or Utopian idyll, a vision of a Golden Age in which poetry, song, dramatic action, dance and spectacle were all harmonised in a single work of art. On such great dynastic occasions – in this case the union of the Houses of Hanover and Orange – pastoral opera could serve as a perfect symbol of the hopes, aspirations and wishful thinking of its audience.

Fictions 2: romance

Surveying the operatic harvest it yielded for Handel, it is easy to feel that romance proved the most congenial field of all. But since 'romance' is a slippery term, I must explain what I mean by it.[12] Romance is the literary retelling of traditional tales of love and chivalry (the link between the two is crucial) taken originally from the 'matter of France' (Charlemagne and his paladins) or the 'matter of Britain' (King Arthur and his Knights of the Round Table). For our Handelian purpose the Italian Renaissance outgrowth from these romances, specifically Matteo Maria Boiardo's *Orlando innamorato*, supplies the key. Boiardo's romantic epic (left incomplete at his death in 1494) added two new motifs to the matter of France (and indeed of Britain): first, its central character, Orlando (Roland), eventually to become the hero of Handel's opera of that name, has been driven mad by love; but second, to balance or counter that destructive force, the creative power of love is embodied in the person of Ruggiero (the hero-to-be of Handel's *Alcina*), to whom is entrusted the destiny of his family and his nation (Ferrara). Many, for the most part minor poets attempted to

[12] What follows is indebted to the *Cambridge Companion to Medieval Romance* (Cambridge University Press, 2000) and, more particularly, to the contribution of Peter Marinelli to *CHIL*.

complete Boiardo's work; one greater poet, Ludovico Ariosto, eventually did so, and it was his *Orlando furioso* (1532) that in due course provided the plots for three of Handel's finest operas.

But we must go back a little. *Rinaldo*, Handel's first opera for London, was also the earliest of his romance-based operas and, as we have seen in Chapter 1, Aaron Hill's polemical preface offered a frank admission of the chief attractions of the genre. While earlier operas staged in London, whatever their merits, were 'wanting the Machines and Decorations, which bestow so great a Beauty on their Appearance', the story of Rinaldo and Armida, on the other hand, could by its 'different Incidents and Passions … afford Music Scope to vary and display its Excellence, and fill the Eye with more delightful Prospects, so at once to give Two Senses equal Pleasure'.[13] It is clear from the libretto which Hill planned for Handel that the incidents and prospects he had particularly in mind were those that exploited the recently enhanced facilities at the Haymarket Theatre for effects of magical transformation, supernatural visions and in other ways spectacular happenings – episodes which linked the new Italian opera with the well-established English masque. Handel had been brought up on grand theatrical displays in Hamburg, and Lowell Lindgren has suggested that the beauty and the magnificence of the spectacle on show in his operas remained an enduring concern for him too.[14]

The two finest of Handel's early London operas, the mythological-legendary *Teseo*, and *Amadigi*, the plot of which originates in mediaeval Spanish romance, are surely looking for the same assets as are found in *Rinaldo*. But they approach the challenge from a different perspective, both being modelled on French *tragédies lyriques*, in which each act reached its climax in a spectacular divertissement. 'There is more enchantment and machinery in this opera' – remarked Burney of *Amadigi* – 'than I have ever found to be announced in any other musical drama performed in England';[15] but it is an odd observation, for there is certainly less than is to be found in *Rinaldo*. Given the musical resources of the Haymarket Theatre in 1715, there was no obvious way for Handel's *Amadigi* music to be fertilised chorally and balletically by memories of French divertissements, as *Il pastor fido* was later to be. It remains, nonetheless, a curiously suggestive fact that, at the point where Houdar de la Motte and Destouches celebrated the joy of Niquée (Oriana) and the heroism of Amadis (Amadigi)

[13] See Chapter 1, footnote 51.

[14] See L. Lindgren, 'Handel's London – Italian Musicians and Librettists', *CCH*, p. 85.

[15] Burney, *A General History of Music*, vol. II, p. 697.

in choral song and dance, Handel's parallel scene comprises a sequence of dance-style arias: 'Gioie venite in sen', 'È sí dolce', 'Oh, caro mio tesor'; even Melissa's interruption of the lovers' idyll is a gigue.

The great phase of Handel's interest in romance came with the Ariosto-inspired operas *Orlando*, *Ariodante* and *Alcina*, the choicest fruits of his partial turning away from *opera seria* in the 1730s. *Ariodante* is based on one of several more-or-less self-contained episodes (they have been called *novelle*) in the course of the poem. But in *Orlando* and *Alcina* Handel produced, if not quite a symmetrical diptych, certainly two operatic masterpieces concerning the two contrasted chivalric lovers around whom so much of Ariosto's epic is built. The three grand themes of the poem – war, love and dynastic destiny – become in the operas (where, by the eighteenth century, destiny was no longer to be confined to the House of Este at Ferrara) war, love and the destiny of Enlightenment man. In both cases a magician-sage guides any faltering steps. Aaron Hill would have noticed Handel's move back into a *Rinaldo*-like world with sympathetic interest, for it was in 1732, at a time when Handel was already at work preparing *Orlando*, that that inveterate 'projector' had made his most determined effort to lure him across into the field of English opera, proposing that, 'a species of dramatic Opera' (perhaps Hill is using the term with deliberately Purcellian overtones) 'might be invented, that, by reconciling reason and dignity, with musick and fine machinery, would charm the *ear*, and hold fast the *heart*, together'.[16]

From a very different aesthetic perspective Rolli was, at about the same time, making a rather similar observation. While Rolli is not known to have collaborated on anything with Handel during this period, it is interesting to note what is implied about English taste by the activities in which he was engaged. In a riposte to Voltaire's 'Essay on Epic Poetry' (1728) he invokes Spenser's *Faerie Queene*, and Shakespeare's *Macbeth* and *Tempest*, to underline his conviction that English audiences took especial delight in 'machinery grounded upon Enchantment'.[17] He is citing the two Shakespeare plays which had responded most successfully to treatment as masque and 'Dramatick Opera' in the English style. In the romance-based operas of Handel, masque-like episodes are always ready to break in. Capece's original Italian libretto for *Orlando* was adapted to English taste by the addition of magic scenes supervised by Zoroastro; dream visions,

[16] Letter of 5 December 1732; in Deutsch, p. 299.

[17] George E. Dorris, *Paolo Rolli and the Italian Circle in London, 1715–1744* (The Hague, Paris: Mouton & Co., 1967), p. 201. Rolli's essay is particularly concerned to proclaim the glory of Ariosto.

pastoral enchantment and rough magic prompt the involvement of chorus and ballet in *Ariodante* and *Alcina*. Perhaps this partiality affects other types of opera too: Gronda notes that, of all the myriad operatic versions of the *Arianna* (in Crete) story, only Handel's version for England has a sleep scene, complete with allegorical figures on machines to play out the hero's prophetic dreams.[18]

Dramatis personae – character

When, in one of the eighteenth century's most familiar couplets, Dr Johnson urged his readers to 'Let observation with extensive view / Survey mankind, from China to Peru', he was not commending the casual inquisitiveness of the modern tourist mentality. Tolomeo may have been an Egyptian hero, Poro an Indian one, Arminio a German; but where they were at home was the least interesting thing about them, and there is not the faintest sign in Handel's operas of the kind of atmospheric local colouring that a nineteenth-century composer would have been expected to lavish on them. The enlightened eighteenth-century humanist travelled (in imagination only) from China to Peru not because he was bored with London, and was hunting out exotic thrills for his jaded sensibility, but because to travel thus was to confirm that at root human nature was everywhere the same – the passions of the human heart, the virtues that guided them, the vices that perverted them, could (beneath any superficial strangeness) be observed in essentially the same forms everywhere. Rameau's *Les Indes Galantes* pays supremely eloquent testimony to this world view.

Human nature was not only uniform, it was permanent: what was true of peoples geographically remote was therefore also true of the historically remote. Alexander the Great and King Porus became operatic protagonists not because Metastasio and Handel were fascinated by the almost unimaginably strange worlds evoked by Mary Renault or Valerio Massimo Manfredi, but because they provided timeless universal patterns of noble behaviour and, of course, of noble misbehaviour, and of how nobly to escape the latter in the interests of the former. Human behaviour, human nature, the traits that constitute character had become, for early eighteenth-century poets and philosophers, topics of urgent fascination, and it is a fascination that Handel could not have escaped.

[18] G. Gronda, 'Das Arianna-Libretto und seine Vorlagen', *VIHAK* (1992), 146.

Radamisto, a new start for a new age of opera in England, marks the point in the Handelian repertory where this interest in character first becomes supremely important: where, putting it perhaps a little roughly, we may say that operas of action and spectacle – operas taking up from the English semi-opera – give way to operas of action and character. With its claustrophobically enclosed family group of emotionally and politically entangled principals acting out a well-focussed action, narrowly restrained in place and time, *Radamisto* is the first Handel opera to show clear marks of the influence of French classical drama, from which he was to derive so much in the coming years.[19] But quite certainly, character is a matter that would have interested him from the beginning of his operatic career, and it is worth considering how he might have understood character, and what kind of help his librettists might have been expected to provide.

The assumption that Handel was educated at the Stadtgymnasium in Halle would mean that, in his schooldays, he will have had cause and opportunity to reflect on character as it was depicted in Livy and Tacitus and Plutarch – the authors from whom so many of his operatic plots ultimately derive. In this context the most interesting of them is Plutarch, because although he wrote about great historical figures, he was a biographer rather than a historian; and his *Parallel Lives* are punctuated by reflections on the relationship between historical narrative and the men who drive it. In the first paragraph of 'Alexander' (for Handel one of the most important of his writings) Plutarch explains that:

> it is not Histories that I am writing, but Lives ... a slight thing like a phrase or a jest often makes a greater revelation of character than battles where thousands fall ... or sieges of cities. Accordingly, just as painters get the likenesses in their portraits from the face and the expression of the eyes, wherein the character shows itself, but make very little account of other parts of the body, so I must be permitted to devote myself rather to the signs of the soul in men.[20]

That explanation of the need to select judiciously the little incidents, the momentary impulsive reactions that furnish 'the signs of the soul in men' might almost serve as a lesson in the mechanics of eighteenth-century heroic opera, and, by extension, suggest what its real priorities were.

In Hamburg Handel will have been unsurprised to find that, at least for the better librettists and composers, an interest in character was a consideration. The best illustration is provided by Keiser's *Octavia*, an opera which

[19] See the discussion in M. Bucciarelli, '*Radamisto*'s Theatrical Sources and their Influence on Handel's Creative Process', *GHB* 7 (1999).

[20] Tr. B. Perrin, Loeb Classical Library, vol. 99 (1919), p. 225.

left an indelible impression on him. Its libretto was by Feind, who in the Preface had this to say about his leading figures: 'If I consider [Nero's] disposition or temper, I would say he was a sanguino-phlegmatic, with a slight admixture of the choleric, and that is the temperament I have particularly attributed to him in this drama.' Then, after a brief consideration of how such temperaments react to adversity, Feind continues, 'It is for the judicious critic to decide how far I have succeeded in depicting in Octavia that character of a noble spirit in happiness and in adversity, and in giving to Seneca a wise man's serenity of temper; but at least I know that that was my intention.' His description, we see, is couched in terms of temperaments and types. But what made this such a stimulating age for anyone who had cause to interest himself in such matters was the fact that these traditional temperaments and types had all but outlived their usefulness. To be credible or interesting now, they needed to be qualified or enriched by more changeable and capricious impulses; and these, most commonly, were released by the passions. To examine and reflect upon the workings of the passions became an enthralling pursuit for poets and philosophers alike; some of them, indeed, dreamed that it might soon be possible to master the passions and redirect them 'to the service of a rationally planned vision of the good life.'[21]

There are not in the librettos of Handel's London operas examples of the kinds of reflection found in Feind's *Octavia*; nor can it be demonstrated conclusively that he read or discussed any of the many English writings on the matter. But given his involvement in so many aspects of London's cultural life, it would seem dull of him if he had not taken some interest in the thoughts about human nature expressed by, for example, his occasional collaborator Pope, who was, more than almost anyone, fascinated by the question;[22] or by the philosopher father of his friend, the fourth Earl of Shaftesbury, who, in Herder's words (1794), 'signally influenced the best heads of the eighteenth century'.[23]

Opera was a public art form designed for what was believed, or hoped, or claimed to be a well-ordered society. However extraordinary the historical events in which operatic characters were involved, whatever idiosyncratic impulses may occasionally have shaken them, the dramatist's task was ultimately to restore them in the fullness of their true selves to their proper

21 J. Cottingham, *Descartes (The Great Philosophers)* (London: Blackwell 2000), pp. 54–5.

22 It is interesting to note that in Mainwaring's *Memoirs* a passage praising Pope's unique gifts as an explorer of character is prompted by a discussion about the association of the poet with Handel. See Deutsch, p. 65; *Documents I*, p. 307.

23 Quoted in B. Willey, *The Eighteenth-Century Background* (1940); reprint (Harmondsworth: Penguin, 1962), p. 61. The philosopher third Earl had died in 1713.

place in the order of things. In essence, the plot of the opera was an ordeal subjecting the wholeness of their personalities to a series of trials. What primarily threatened them was passion, particularly erotic passion on the one hand, and the passion for domination or power on the other. And therefore the fundamental dramatic crux in heroic opera of this period was not the unforeseen *peripeteia* of some fresh or ingeniously novel storyline, but the threatened destruction by the passions of the *musica humana* – that ideal of human harmony in the individual soul and in society – and the finally achieved re-establishment of such a harmony.

For a dramatic theme of this kind opera proved the ideal medium, partly because the expression of those corroding passions had in the century since Monteverdi become one of music's proudest accomplishments; but still more because, at a deeper level, it was the *musica humana*, the human and social order, that was to be made to sound and to sing. In *opera seria* (in Handel's reinterpretation of it scarcely less than in the pure Metastasian form), notwithstanding the rationalistic dialogues and philosophical reflections of which it was so full and which can so easily distance it from modern sensibilities, the mechanisms were not really intellectual at all, but imaginative. It was didactic, not in presuming to teach us what human nature is like, but in inviting us, beyond the typical crises and dilemmas and temptations that occupy so much of the opera, to imagine what it might be like. If, as Sir Joshua Reynolds was to declare, human character is in large part the product of our own human imaginations, and if it is to realise its full glorious potential, it must be inspired by examples of the heroic in all its dimensions: courage, magnanimity, self-discipline, love, beauty. Heroic opera did that. A Handelian opera is not a report on historical or legendary events, not even an interpretation of them; it is an imaginative vision.

So the operas commonly enact the stories of heroes and heroines with whom their well-educated audiences will have been familiar – Theseus, Alexander, Julius Caesar, Cleopatra, Agrippina and so on – and the action is woven around a number of crises or incidents which will have been remembered as high points in the traditional accounts. Because solo song is the primary medium of the drama, it is the heroes and heroines themselves who are the chief concern, and because the world for which they were singing was an orderly and optimistic one, the dramatic objective was, with only rare exceptions, to show these characters, after having been tested and tempted, bruised and tormented, finally and deservingly achieving their due place. And because, in some measure, all the characters except the very minor ones have to be similarly tested and tormented, the operas tend to proceed in an erratic, moody way, to be full of inconsequential twists and preposterous accidents which bring them close to the manner of comedy. There is no single-minded, Gluck-like drive to the final issue; rather a compassionate and even smiling sympathy for mortals tossed, as so many arias remind us, on the stormy ocean of life.

Moral – allegory – topicality

It is perhaps startling to find that the early eighteenth century still drew on Pythagorean–Platonic–Boethian tradition to explain the place of music in the order of things. The thought of the world as a harmony was, for example, an inspiring motif in Shaftesbury's writings. Since our aesthetic sense was believed to be closely related to our moral sense, since we most easily recognised what was virtuous by experiencing its harmoniousness, it was perfectly clear to those who took Italian *opera seria* at all seriously that it had, or ought to have, a purpose beyond that of being mere entertainment, even beyond that of being a joy or a solace. Every conscientious librettist would have endorsed what Haym wrote in the preface to his last opera, *Tolomeo*: 'in the beginning [Music] was instituted for praising the Gods, for instructing mankind in morality, and for affording relief from distressful care; so that it is not, as some maintain, of no usefulness in life. The greatest of these blessings comes from musical dramas.'[24] That, albeit in a rather loose way, says it all. We are dealing with the triad *musica instrumentalis*; *musica humana*; *musica mundana*: fine music-making helps our minds to become more harmonious, and in that way brings them closer to enacting the praise of God.

If you were really at home in this particular musical world, a connoisseur of both Handelian opera and of Italian *opera seria* proper, as such a man as Burney was, you would quite naturally wish to go beyond a vague sense of pleasing wholesomeness and find yourself experiencing each opera in terms of a particular character-forming display. At the end of his *Memoirs of the Life and Writings of the Abate Metastasio* Burney appends what at first sight looks like a standard list of works: it contains, as we would expect, basic information about who composed the opera, and when and where it was staged. But there is something else: to the 'Chronological List of Metastasio's ... Operas, specifying the time, and place, where they were first performed, by whom set to music', Burney adds 'the moral object of each'. This is what he chooses to say about the

[24] Tr. T. Best, HHA XI/22, *Tolomeo*, p. xii.

three Metastasio texts set by Handel: *Siroe*: 'A parent's *blind partiality* for one unworthy son, and ill-treatment of another, whose *filial duty* and *affection* are proof against disgrace and suffering, are the vice and virtue chiefly displayed in this opera.' *Ezio*: '*Valour* and *Fidelity* to the hero's sovereign, in spite of ill-treatment, are the principal virtues of the Protagonistes in this drama.' *Alessandro nell'Indie* [= *Poro*]: 'The *magnanimous Generosity* and *Clemency* of Alexander the Great, are the most prominent virtues in this drama.'[25] Presenting the information in this place and in this way suggests that for Burney these 'moral objects' were as integral to the opera as the questions of when and where and by whom.

That does not mean that everyone noticed them. A critic in the *Universal Spectator*, 5 July 1735, deplored the insufficient perceptiveness of one gentleman who failed to observe that 'the Opera of *Alcina* affords us a beautiful and instructive Allegory ["The Character of Alcina's Beauty, and Inconstancy proves the short Duration of all sublunary Enjoyments, which are lost as soon as attain'd"]; but I fear the young Gentleman never gave himself the Trouble to crack the Nut that he might have the Pleasure of tasting the Kernel.'[26] Opera audiences in Handel's time included their full share of canary-fanciers. No doubt there were also many serious music-lovers who found – as on the whole modern audiences find – that to be moved by the beauty and humanity of the music was enough. But perhaps whether one notices or fails to notice the deeper significances scarcely matters if indeed it is the music that is composing us.

Perhaps the choice of operatic subject might also have been at some level topical: it could involve poet and composer dealing, normally in 'allegorical' mode, with some worldly matter about which people were seriously concerned. *Rinaldo*, addressing itself to an audience variously wearied and excited over the later phases of the War of Spanish Succession, reached its theatrical climax in scenes of clashing religious armies. At the time of the Atterbury plot,[27] *Floridante* presented matters concerning rightful and usurped kingship, and notoriously occasioned a demonstration more flagrant than any other in Handel's career, giving 'great offence … when a very great and unreasonable clapping, in the presence of great ones' occurred at the setting free of the rightful heir and the imprisoning of the usurper.[28] *Tamerlano* fell into step with a well-established London theatre tradition,

[25] Charles Burney, *Memoirs of the Life and Writings of the Abate Metastasio*, 3 vols. (London: Robinson, 1796) (herafter *Memoirs of Metastasio*), vol. III, pp. 316–17.

[26] In Deutsch, pp. 391–2.

[27] In 1721 Francis Atterbury, Bishop of Rochester, was implicated in a Jacobite plot.

[28] Dean and Knapp, *Handel's Operas 1704–1726*, p. 389.

which every autumn saw the staging of a Tamerlaine play by Nicholas Rowe.[29] The theme of *Riccardo primo*, the only Handel opera with its historical subject taken from English history, was linked in a very tangled way with questions of kingship, succession, Englishness and other matters topical in 1727.

Indeed it seems possible, in the light of recent research, that most if not all Handel's operas, certainly during the Royal Academy years, were chosen with such topicalities in mind. While it is, of course, true that with a little wit parallels can be contrived between more or less anything, especially if it concerns politics, Handel's audiences were, in Ruth Smith's words, 'unusually politically aware and opinionated',[30] and they brought their opinions to bear on what they saw in the theatre. Moreover, the more scholarship investigates the circumstances in which the operas were written, the more intriguing and curious become the parallels that can be drawn between the operatic stage and contemporary life.[31] There can be little doubt that, ostensibly at least, such operas offered audiences the same opportunity as the English theatre did to read into them allegorical reflections of the real world. What is difficult to see is how such opportunities can have amounted to anything that was not utterly trivial; or, to put it another way, what conceivable difference such issues might have made to the way opera-goers experienced Handel operas as musico-dramatic events. Did they find a zeal for some dear political cause effervescing within them? Did they find themselves brought up short and needing to reconsider their prejudices? Or did they just smile quietly to themselves as some pleasing and transient suggestion of 'allegory' flickered through their mind. Unlike the English oratorio, the operas, with their telegraphically brief recitatives in a foreign language, and with their preoccupation with the expression of individual feelings in solo arias, could not address the questions to which they may seem to have alluded in an engaging or interesting way; nor, with a few exceptions, did they have the space or the musical means to give rhetorical and emotional weight to these questions.

29 It commemorated both the Gunpowder Plot and the landing at Torbay of William III. See *Documents I*, p. 721. Rowe's interpretation of the story was very different from that in Handel's opera.

30 Ruth Smith, *Handel's Oratorios and Eighteenth-Century Thought* (Cambridge University Press, 1995), p. 10.

31 Space does not allow a full exploration of this matter, but the interested reader may be referred to articles by Fiona McLauchlan on *Ottone* (*ML* 78 (1997)), by Suzanne Aspden on *Arianna* (*MQ* 85 (2001)), by Katie Hawks on *Riccardo primo* (*HIN* 23.1 (2012)) and by Ruth Smith on *Rinaldo* (*HIN* 23.2 (2012)). Thomas McGeary has recently shed an invigorating light on the whole issue in *The Politics of Opera in Handel's Britain* (Cambridge University Press, 2013).

Some Handel librettists

Three Arcadians: Stampiglia – Zeno – Metastasio

Our modern assessments of which were Handel's 'best' librettos – that is to say which librettos helped him compose what we believe to be his finest operas – sometimes diverge sharply from the judgement of his eighteenth-century contemporaries. *Partenope* and *Serse*, librettos in which Silvio Stampiglia, a founder member of Arcadia, had played a crucial part, provide two notable instances.

Many a modern opera-goer has found *Serse*, for its sheer stageability as well as its glorious music, the most endearing of all Handel's operas. But if opera-houses were a little less constrained in their repertories, it might have a close rival in the far less well-known *Partenope*, Handel's 'equivalent of *Twelfth Night*', David Vickers suggests, which Dent thought had 'perhaps the best libretto that Handel ever had to set.'[32] Handel's erstwhile colleague and occasional collaborator Owen Swiney felt very differently. At the time Swiney was in Italy, acting as agent for the Royal Academy, and among other things advising the Academy on new works. In a letter to the Duke of Richmond (August 1726) he described *Partenope* as:

> the very worst book (excepting one) that I ever read in my whole life: Signor Stampiglia (the author of it) endeavours to be humourous and witty, in it: If he succeeded in his attempt, on any stage in Italy, 'twas meerly, from a depravity of Taste in his audience – but I am very sure that 'twill be received with contempt in England … if it is to be done, 'twill bring more scandal & lesse profit, than any opera, that has been, yet, acted to The Hay-Market Theatre.[33]

Nor, in the eighteenth century, was the *Serse* libretto admired by the cognoscenti. Burney, drawing towards the close of his exhaustive and sympathetic survey of Handel's operas, could find nothing civil to say of it: 'I have not been able to discover the author of the words of this drama; but it is one of the worst that Handel ever set to Music: for besides feeble writing, there is a mixture of tragi-comedy and buffoonery in it.'[34] But Burney's words provide the clue. At their stageworthy best, as in *Partenope* and *Serse*, Handel's operas are indeed 'a mixture', because they draw on two very different theatrical traditions: from the world of mid to late seventeenth-century

[32] E. J. Dent, 'The Operas' in G. Abraham (ed.), *Handel: A Symposium* (Oxford University Press, 1954), p. 44. Vickers' appraisal is in *CHE*.

[33] *CHE*, 'Partenope'.

[34] Burney, *A General History of Music*, vol. II, p. 822.

Venetian opera they commonly acquire their elan and variety and the liveliness of their characters; from the world of French classical drama their sense of how a plot can best be organised, where the unifying focus of the drama should be located, how the characters can be explored to give them a three-dimensional emotional wholeness. Over the years of Handel's operatic career, Zeno and Metastasio and some of the lesser Arcadians were using one of these – the French – as a model to help reform the other – not just the Venetian tradition of opera, but the Italian theatre more generally; and in Handel's own operas a dialectic between the two models is more or less continuous. In some – *Almira* or *Ottone* for example – the Venetian plenty is too little constrained by classical French discipline, and the libretto remains scrappy and disorganised; in others, where a 'reformed' Metastasian text is the starting point, the outcome may be – as it is, for example, in *Ezio* – stiff and over-formalised. Handel's librettos are most effective when a Venetian original is rewritten by a librettist sympathetic to its theatrical flair, but who understands how much more deeply a drama can dig with a well-organised plot and a little thoroughness in exploring the psychology of the chief characters. Stampiglia seems to have been such a man.

In 1725, in his obituary of Stampiglia, Zeno spoke as it were sorrowingly of his fellow-Arcadian, as one 'more inventive than learned' and 'having more spirit than study'.[35] But to judge from the evidence of the scores, the Venetian relics of comedy and theatrical animation still found in Stampiglia were what Handel really wanted – notwithstanding Swiney's rudeness about them. His interest in Zeno was negligible. *Faramondo* is Handel's only opera based on his work, though a curiously high proportion of his pasticcio librettos are 'after Zeno'; one presumes he found them serviceable vehicles for some of the modern Italian music he admired.

Of these three Arcadians, Metastasio was, in the wider literary context, incomparably the most important, one of the eighteenth century's most universally admired poets. 'The lovers of Italian poetry as well as vocal Music', declared Burney, 'regard Metastasio as the primary source of their most exquisite delight in the union of those arts.'[36] But Handel set just three of his dramas, necessarily early ones since Metastasio's poetic career began only in the mid 1720s. The three operas – *Siroe*, *Poro*, *Ezio* – are all from the years around 1730, and form, in Strohm's words, the 'most culturally avant-garde' group of Handel's works. His 'take' on Metastasio has been examined carefully and often, by Strohm himself, and by Dean. All that

[35] *CHE*, 'Stampiglia'.

[36] Burney, *Memoirs of Metastasio*, vol. I, p. iii.

need be said here is that the Metastasio–Handel association, while it may have resulted in no operatic masterpiece, nevertheless left a fascinating and fruitful aftermath. For the reforming, classicising, philosophising tendencies of Metastasian-Arcadian opera did not disappear: they were redirected, partly into the series of pasticcios that Handel produced after 1732, all of which have either Zeno or Metastasio texts, and all of which are essentially Handelian arrangements of operas by younger composers, and partly into English oratorios, with which Handel was making a fresh, Racine-inspired start at the same time. As far as his Italian operas were concerned, assuming (what seems almost certain) that work on *Sosarme* was well and truly under way before the ill-fated *Ezio* had been staged, the tendency was quite opposite: the next completely new one was the first, and by a long way the most *furioso*, of his *Orlando furioso*-based operas.

As far as we know there was no personal contact between any of these Arcadians and Handel.[37]

Three courtier-poets: Mauro – Capece – Salvi

Contact there certainly was with other Italian librettists, three of whom – Ortensio Mauro, Carlo Sigismondo Capece and Antonio Salvi – form a conveniently special group. All of them combined their literary accomplishments with professional duties as court servants in courts with which Handel, with varying degrees of closeness or remoteness, was himself associated: Mauro at Hanover, as Secretary to members of the House of Brunswick; Capece, a Doctor of Laws, as secretary to Queen Maria Casimira in Rome; Salvi as physician to the Medici court in Florence.

Handel's relationship with Mauro seems to have been slight. Though they must have known one another during Handel's Hanover years, all that can be said in the way of any direct collaboration is that Mauro perhaps wrote the texts for the chamber duets composed in 1710–12. He was dead when Handel turned to his opera librettos, *Alessandro* (called in Hanover, *La superbia d'Alessandro*) and *Admeto* (in Hanover, *Alceste*). One wonders why Hanoverian memories welled up just then, in 1726–27. Was the choice of these librettos a small unobtrusive token of loyalty to the Hanoverian regime? Was Handel already tactically preparing the ground for his British naturalisation in 1727? He certainly knew, and indeed 'borrowed' from, Steffani's setting of *La superbia d'Alessandro*; we do not know whether he

[37] For further discussion of Metastasian opera, see Chapter 3, particularly the subsection 'The Italian *dramma per musica*'.

had seen or heard anything of Trento's setting of *Alceste*. In some ways his two Mauro-derived operas form a complementary pair. Though they were performed in two different seasons, their casts were virtually identical. While *Alessandro*, adapted for Handel by Rolli, ranks with the more 'classical' operas of the Royal Academy years, *Admeto*, adapted probably by Haym – though the matter is not certain[38] – is the Royal Academy opera that retains best the theatrical verve of seventeenth-century Venice. Noteworthy too is the fact that Handel, rather as he was to do at the end of his career with *The Choice of Hercules* and *Alexander's Feast*, sets an Alexander opera beside a work which is, up to a point, a Hercules opera.[39]

With Capece, Handel's relationship was more direct, for he was the librettist of one of the largest and most brilliant Italian-period works, the oratorio *La Resurrezione*. The librettos of the operas Handel based on Capece, *Tolomeo* and *Orlando*, were both originally written for Domenico Scarlatti, who, like Capece, was in the service of Maria Casimira, and perhaps of all Italian composers was the one with whom Handel enjoyed the warmest personal rapport. The operas were both staged only after Handel had left Italy in 1711, in Maria Casimira's private theatre, but it would be pleasant to think that he might have learned about them from Scarlatti himself. A feature of both librettos as reworked for Handel in London was the broadening out of those episodes that might have been felt to be masque-like: the pastoral note in *Tolomeo*; the supernatural Zoroastrian enchantments in *Orlando*.

Of these courtier-librettists it was Salvi from whom Handel learned most. It seems likely – though proof is at present lacking – that it was he who adapted the *Rodrigo* libretto for Handel's Italian operatic debut. What is certain is that all the librettos Salvi wrote for the Florence theatres during Handel's Italian years were carried off by the young composer for subsequent use, in *Sosarme*, *Ariodante* and *Berenice*. Handel also acquired at least two other Salvi librettos, to be reworked in *Scipione* and *Arminio*, which came from the period before he reached Italy; a further Salvi piece, *Rodelinda*, was staged only after Handel had left.

38 Dean, *Handel's Operas 1726–1741*, pp. 39–40 discusses the question.

39 The linking together of these two heroes, who were, according to some well-established versions of their stories, both sons of Jupiter/Jove, had been a commonplace in Western art and letters since classical times. In fact they are already linked together in *Alessandro* where, in the temple scene of Act One (I.x.), the central elevated statue of Jupiter/Giove Ammone is flanked by statues of Hercules on one side and Alexander on the other. See R. C. Ketterer, 'The Choice of Hercules and Alexander's Feast', *HJb* 54, (2008). Mauro's *Alessandro* libretto is discussed further in Chapter 3, particularly in Excursus 3.2.

Like Stampiglia, Salvi was one of the more open-minded of the early eighteenth-century operatic reformers, both 'more liberal and more theatrical' (Strohm) than Zeno. He earned a remarkable tribute from Alessandro Scarlatti, who wrote of his libretto for *Il gran Tamerlano* that its action was so strong and original and spirited, its recitatives so forceful and eloquent that one did not feel the usual keenness for the arias to begin.[40] What specifically distinguished his work was a close, creative interest in French classical drama. He was apparently – and this was very much in accordance with the wishes of Ferdinando de' Medici himself – the first Italian librettist to adapt these plays as librettos, and in doing so he learned much from Corneille and from French tragic drama more generally. The French were the most admired exponents of a dramatic system acknowledging the ultimate authority of Aristotle, and it was through their work that Aristotle again became a perceptible influence on some Italian theatre poets too. The traces of Salvi's influence on Handel are best seen in a more natural style of dialogue (where this was allowed to survive the scissors of the London adapter) and, most distinctively, in the sensitivity and acumen with which the psychology of the female protagonist is explored. Rodelinda and Ginevra in *Ariodante* are supreme examples.[41]

All the librettists so far mentioned were based in Italy or in Italian-speaking court establishments; their work, before it could be presented to an English audience, required to be abbreviated and often radically rewritten. In England, Handel collaborated with a number of Italian men of letters who did this job for him. The record is far from complete because, after the Royal Academy years, librettos printed in London rarely if ever mention the librettist, a fact which, in itself, seems to imply some belittling of his role in the creation of the opera. But three librettists can be identified: Giacomo Rossi (*Rinaldo*, *Il pastor fido*, *Silla* and probably some at least of the Second Academy operas); Nicola Francesco Haym (*Teseo*, *Ottone*, *Giulio Cesare*, *Tamerlano*, *Rodelinda*, *Siroe*, *Tolomeo*); Paolo Antonio Rolli (*Muzio Scevola*, *Floridante*, *Scipione*, *Alessandro*, *Riccardo primo*, *Deidamia*). Their work will be discussed in the following chapter.

[40] Part of his letter to Ferdinando de' Medici (June 1706) is quoted in F. Giuntini, *I drammi per musica di Antonio Salvi* (Reggio Emilia: Società Editrice il Mulino, 1994), p. 12.

[41] The extent to which Salvi's interest in female psychology is inspired by French models is considered by Giuntini particularly at pp. 32 and 121. For further on these two operas see Chapter 3, subsection 'Recitative and aria', and Chapter 5.

3 | The libretto (2): words for music

The Libretto

The libretto, the 'little book', was provided to help audiences enjoy and understand the opera. In Handel's time such librettos were designed for a particular run of performances in a particular theatre, and because the shape and substance of operas changed so rapidly – according to local conditions, changes of cast, and suchlike matters – they would have been of little or no use at a revival at a later date, or with a different group of singers, or in a different theatre in a different city.

Librettos generally included a dedication, written by the librettist or the impresario or, occasionally, by Handel himself. Being usually addressed to a patron who 'chinks his purse and takes his seat of state' this was predictably sycophantic, in the manner of the period. But sometimes it could be informative too: it is from Heidegger's dedication of *Amadigi* that we learn that Handel composed it in Burlington House; it is from Handel's dedication of *Radamisto* that we learn it had earned King George's 'particular Approbation' before ever being heard in the theatre; the dedication of *Riccardo primo* includes an Italian sonnet by Rolli addressed to the new monarch George II. Only in the special case of *Rinaldo* – proclaiming the dawning of a new era in the musical life of London – did the libretto resemble a modern programme, and contain items written from a variety of perspectives: a dedication to Queen Anne, some remarks from Hill on its artistic ambitions, and some from Rossi on the collaboration between composer and librettist. Other preliminary materials generally included the dramatis personae (including the names of the singers); more rarely it may have included some information about the stage-sets and ballets. There was always an Argument to contextualise the drama; and sometimes – because operas tended to have complicated plots – this reached far back into the pre-history of the story. Occasionally it went on to include a brief summary of what was going to happen in the opera as well, and frequently it gave some indication of what the original literary source was.

The remainder of the libretto – by far its greater part – comprised a complete Italian text of the opera with, in almost all cases (*Silla* was the only exception in London), an English translation on the facing page. These are not translations that could be used for English-language performance, at least not without considerable alteration. While the recitatives were usually translated quite closely, the aria texts were either turned into lyrics paraphrasing the Italian only loosely, or they were replaced by prose summaries.[1] In most librettos an occasional passage of recitative would be found enclosed in inverted commas: such passages were not performed, indeed very likely had never been set to music, because Handel felt the scene was too long. But they are included in the libretto as a mark of respect toward the librettist and as a kind of surety for the coherence of the work he had intended, even though it may have been compromised in the musical setting. This was a custom that, in Italy, went right back to the origins of opera.

Excursus 3.1 – metre in Italian verse

Discussion of Italian verse is not very fruitful without the use of the appropriate technical terms for metre.

The essential point is that these terms depend on the number of syllables in the line of verse: lines with five, six, seven, eight, ten, eleven, twelve syllables are respectively, *quinari, senari, settenari, ottonari, decasillabi, endecasillabi, dodecasillabi.* The syllable count is sometimes lightly disguised by elisions, when a vowel at the end of one word is followed by another at the start of the next, so that – to quote an extreme example – the line 'E al ferire il tempo aspetta' (*Imeneo*, II.ii), with its three elisions, is an example of an *ottonario*. More counter-intuitively the syllable count is also disguised by the fact that most Italian words end on an unaccentuated syllable, as does *aspetta* in the example quoted. If, however, the final weak syllable isn't there, or if it is extended by an additional weak syllable, the fact is ignored in counting the syllables, but acknowledged in a further descriptive term: *tronco* = cut off (very common, particularly in the final line or section of an aria), or *sdrucciolo* = sliding (relatively rare). The following Metastasio text is therefore wholly in *settenari*:

[1] The following example is from *Radamisto* (first version) I.iii, Tiridate's '*Stragi, morti, sangue ed armi*': the English for this aria reads, 'He says, That the Trumpet sounds to Blood, Arms and Destruction: That his Wrath has set a Kingdom on fire, and that he hears the Heavens echo with the fall of the Ruins.'

Tergi le ingiuste lacrime,
Dilegua il tuo martiro
Che s'io per te respiro,
Tu regnerai per me.

(*Ezio*, III. xi)

of which the first is *sdrucciolo* and last *tronco*.

Recitative and aria

The typographical layout of the page – with the recitative running across it from the left margin, and the aria texts indented in strophes, usually between four and eight lines – makes it immediately clear, even to a newcomer to the opera house, and even to someone with a meagre understanding of Italian, that recitative and aria are different things with distinct functions. Action, confrontation, debate, conversation, rumination are the provinces of recitative; and during it time moves relatively realistically. Arias mark a change in the pace; they bring the scene into focus, perhaps stop it in its steps, or distil its mood in some powerful or vivid idea. A convenient generalisation is to say that the aria's principal function is the expression of the passions, that it aims 'to move the affections'. But it is worth discriminating a little more carefully:

(1) There are indeed many arias in which the character is wholly possessed by a passion, becomes a personification of joy or despair, or whatever. This is especially the case where the singer is left alone on stage, free to launch into an impassioned tirade.

(2) But there are also arias where that situation is – we might almost say – inverted. Instead of the singer embodying the passion, losing his personality in the emotion of the moment, the passion characterises the singer, and the aria becomes a character sketch. Dramatically, that can be especially illuminating when an aria is placed at the start of the scene.

(3) In yet other arias there may be a conversational dimension. Certainly the singers are moved by their passions, but they express them in the form of an imagined or internal dialogue. This gives the aria something of an acted quality.

(4) Finally there are the moralising arias and the metaphor arias, of the kind John Gay so enjoyed satirising in *The Beggar's Opera*. Some critics have seen these as being quite different – tedious and absurd perhaps – where

the impassioned aria is admirable. But that would be a false antithesis. All that is happening is that the character is standing back a little from the emotion that moves him, bringing it under control and reflecting on it, as, in the eighteenth century, grown-up people were expected to do. A nice illustration is found in a letter written by Metastasio to Farinelli in 1755, at the time of the catastrophic Lisbon earthquake:

> I have experienced to the bottom of my soul, the most violent affliction for the destruction of unhappy Lisbon. What horror! What a scourge! What misery! Poor humanity! [That might sound like the cue for an aria; but Metastasio gives us a lesson in the aesthetics of the *opera seria* by going a little further.] Yet among all these motives of terror and sorrow, the ample field which Providence has opened to your benevolent sovereign for exercising the great and admirable qualities of his heart, affords me some consolation.[2]

Metastasio and other contemporary poets were eager to insist on parallels between the operatic aria and the chorus of ancient Greek drama, and the moralising style of aria certainly reinforces that claim. But for our purposes it is more helpful to see such arias simply as providing a fourth facet to the idea of impassioned song: to the tirade, the character sketch, the (imagined) conversation, we can add the distancing reflection.

The best way of understanding what consequences all this has for Handelian opera is to examine one relatively extended passage contained within the confines of a single set or tableau. I take the garden scene from Act I of *Ariodante*, one of the supreme love scenes in all opera. The passion of love between the princely pair, and the accompanying sense of general well-being (for this is a social episode as well as a private one), fills a scene of twenty minutes or so – and quite without tedium, because of the exquisitely judged shifting of perspective embodied in the arias, and the variety of musical opportunities that this offers.

'Qui d'amor' (aria)[3]

Ariodante is alone in the garden: in part this is a character portrait, because smiling Nature in pathetic-fallacy mode holds up a mirror to his tender emotions, his '*core innamorato*'. But in order to bring Nature into the music, the aria must also serve as a descriptive sinfonia.

[2] Letter of 5 December 1755; in Burney, *Memoirs of Metastasio*, vol. II, p. 145.

[3] The aria is of a type that is sometimes described as an 'arioso' or 'cavatina'; which is to say that it is short, and has neither Middle Section nor da capo.

'Prendi da questo mano' (duet)

An intimate, conversational expression of the passions.

'Volate, amori' (aria)

Ginevra's ecstasy of happiness explodes in pure feeling; she also sets the Cupids flying; the language begins to be figurative.

'Voli colla sua tromba' (aria)

The King's paternal and royal joy is projected out into the wider world by the trumpets of Fame. The passion is becoming more clearly metaphorical in expression, with more obvious consequences for Handel's compositional choices.

'Con l'ali di costanza' (aria)

Finally, in the first of the series of stupendous da capo arias which Handel composed for Carestini, Ariodante's joy is expressed in reflective fullness; we sense the wise and thoughtful man (the moraliser, if one will) inhabiting the lover.

Italian recitative verse is arranged flexibly in *endecasillabi* and *settenari*, rhyming only occasionally except at the end of a speech or scene, when rhyme is normal. (A parallel suggests itself with Shakespeare's use of rhyming couplets placed at similar strategic junctures.) In the hands of a good writer it has all the variety of pace and articulation that we would expect in English from a good writer of blank verse.

Massimo:	*Io non so figurarmi*	7
	In Ezio un traditor; ma pur l'amore –	11
	L' ambizion, la lode, e l'assoluto	11
	Commando delle schiere –	7
	Chi sa? – potria scordarsi il suo dover.	11

Maximus: I can't in Aetius yet perceive the Traitor,
And yet the Power of all prevailing Love,
Ambition, loud Applause, and the Command
Of all your Host – Who knows? – they may deface
Each Trace of Duty in his dazzled Soul.

('Done into English by Mr Humphreys'; from the 1732 libretto of *Ezio*, II.ii)

In arias a wider range of metres is employed. *Ottonari* and *settenari* are the most common, but almost always librettists provide at least a few both in shorter and in longer lines: *quinari*, *senari*, *decasillabi*, even *dodecasillabi*. In the da capo layout, the aria text needs to be effective when the words of the first part of the aria are repeated after the words of the second;[4] and it needs to be easy for the composer to break the lines into smaller units, to single out individual words or groups of words for expressive emphasis, to repeat or linger over them, because that is what the musical style of the period demanded. Of Handel's librettists Rolli was something of a master in this respect.

In recitative, composers were happy to take second place to poets; it was after all, as John Hughes put it, only 'a kind of improved elocution'.[5] There were established musical routines for dealing with every kind of phrase likely to occur in recitative verses, and only in a small number of accompanied recitatives was much musical invention called for. If a composer didn't have time to finish composing the recitative, singers could have made it up themselves, and sometimes, in Italy at any rate, they did. It is unlikely that this ever happened with Handel, but he too left the composition of the recitative until the last minute, simply writing out the words, suitably spread out in his manuscript to show how much page space was required between one musical number and another, and returning to set them only when the serious task of composition was finished.[6]

Whether as performer or as spectator-listener, one needed to be comfortable with this two-fold articulation of the opera into recitative and aria. It was an artistic principle which claimed its distant historical authentication in classical Greek tragedy, but as far as opera was concerned it really achieved a focussed and masterly form only in Handel's youth – not in England of course, but in Italy itself. A brief digression is called for.

The Italian *dramma per musica*

As the seventeenth century drew to a close, many leading men in Italian cultural life – if their theoretical and critical writings on literature and

[4] This is not necessarily the same as being syntactically watertight. For instance, in a simile or metaphor aria the important thing is that the picture is held in view, not that the thought linking this picture with the action is logically complete.

[5] Quoted in H. M. Schueller, 'Correspondences between Music and the Sister Arts according to 18th-century Aesthetic Theory', *Journal of Aesthetics and Art Criticism* 11 (1953), 352.

[6] What the relation between verse and music was when, in the arias, music had the primacy will be discussed in Chapter 5.

music are to be believed – looked about them in near despair. What they witnessed was a profound cultural decadence; and what they most specifically deplored was the lack of a great theatrical tradition to set beside the achievements of Corneille, Racine and Molière in France. Of course there were lively theatrical traditions in Italy: *commedia dell'arte* and opera. But these were not practices much in tune with the aspirations of the leaders of intellectual and artistic life, not ones to serve as a school for national regeneration. Nevertheless, it seemed probable that, if the theatre was going to play a part in overcoming the 'crisis of decadence' and setting in train 'the beginning of a national renewal',[7] it would be through opera rather than through the spoken theatre – for which at the time there was little appetite in Italy – that change might come.

So thought Apostolo Zeno, a Venetian scholar and playwright, an Arcadian, and later Metastasio's predecessor as Imperial Poet in Vienna. Though he cared rather little for music and would much rather have spent his time writing 'proper' drama, he reluctantly recognised the '*necessità della musica*'; and resolved to bring enlightenment to the Italian theatre by reforming opera. He would eliminate filthiness and buffoonery, the childish magical spectacle, the preposterous fustian and bombast of the language; he would focus on historical themes: real men and women facing real human crises and speaking in clear, rational Italian, albeit a clear Italian oozing with high-minded sententiousness. Stefano Arteaga, one of the most important eighteenth-century writers on opera, was to describe Zeno as 'the Pierre Corneille of the lyric theatre', and explained his tribute thus:

> Wherever he found in the vast field of history, in which he was so deeply versed, luminous examples of patriotism, or of a virtuous desire for glory, or of a generous constancy in friendship, or of nobleness and fidelity in love, or of compassion towards one's fellow men, or of grandeur of soul in adversity, or of prudence, or of fortitude, or of any other virtues, he took them up in order to adorn the theatre with them.[8]

If history was to be the subject of opera, its form was to be sought elsewhere. Greek tragedy had been one of the inspirations for the invention of opera in the first place; a hundred years on it was clearly time for a reminder of what that inheritance might mean. Zeno's Greek scholarship was part of his prestige: 'Zeno found the opera quite rude and imperfect,

[7] The phrases are Croce's: Benedetto Croce, *Letteratura italiana del settecento* (Bari: Laterza, 1949), p. 5.

[8] S. Arteaga, *Le rivoluzioni del teatro musicale italiano dalla sua origine fino al presente*, 2nd edn, 2 vols. (Venice: Palese, 1785), vol. I, p. 326.

and he brought it within the jurisdiction of the Aristotelian precepts. As he was a great master of Greek, he endeavoured to give it a Greek cast … imitating as much as he could the strophe, antistrophe and epode of the ancient Greek tragedies.'[9] Joseph Baretti's tribute will probably strike us as a curious analysis of early eighteenth-century opera. But Metastasio (who wrote a commentary on Aristotle's *Poetics*) helps make a little clearer what these critics were getting at, for he too draws quite explicit parallels between ancient Greek tragedy and contemporary Italian opera: the recitative performs the same function as scenes of action in Greek drama, and as for the arias – 'What else are the ARIAS of our musical dramas, but the ancient strophes? And why such an out-cry against these visible relics of the Greek theatre?'[10]

The principle, therefore, was this (and we have already seen it in the physical layout of the libretto): the unfolding of the dramatic action, the creation of dramatic atmosphere, the eloquence and individuality of voice of the principal figures – all this was the work of the poet, to be set by the composer in simple or *secco* recitative. At the end of each scene came a lyric verse to be set to 'full music', almost invariably in the form of a solo aria and sung by a character who then leaves the stage. Here was where the composer showed his power: 'fine language [or music]', as Aristotle had remarked, 'should be kept for moments in the work where action, character and argument are not presented.'[11]

This was the form of opera Metastasio inherited and perfected, and more than once he expressed his appreciation of Zeno's achievement in demonstrating that 'our melodrama is not incompatible with reason',[12] that it was perfectly possible for opera to be an object of interest and enjoyment for reasonable, modern, Enlightened Man. Indeed, for many music lovers it soon came to seem as if they were living through a Golden Age of opera. Burney may be their spokesman.

> Between the years 1725 and 1740, the musical drama in Italy seems to have attained a degree of perfection and public favour, which perhaps has never since been surpassed. The opera stage from that period being in possession of the poetry of

[9] J. Baretti, *An Account of the Manners and Customs of Italy: with Observations on the Mistakes of Some Travellers, with Regard to that Country*, 2nd edn with notes and an appendix added, in answer to Samuel Sharp, Esq., 2 vols. (London: Davis & Davis, 1769), vol. I, p. 175.

[10] Burney, *Memoirs of Metastasio*, vol. III, p. 374. Cf. the comments of Shaftesbury quoted in Chapter 1, at p. 20.

[11] *Poetics*, XXIV, cited in K. McLeish, *Aristotle (The Great Philosophers)*, (London: Phoenix, 1998), p. 53.

[12] For example in a letter to Abbate Fabroni written on 7 December 1767; in Burney, *Memoirs of Metastasio*, Vol. 3 p. 19.

> Apostolo Zeno and Metastasio; the compositions of Leo, Vinci, Hasse, Porpora, and Pergolesi; the performances of Farinelli, Carestini, Caffarelli etc etc.[13]

At exactly the time of Handel's career in the theatre, opera had been recruited to serve Enlightenment aspirations.

But to accept Metastasio's parallels (parallels of form) between the chorus of Greek tragedy and the arias of *opera seria* is one thing. On the other hand, it is certain that parallels in substance are all but non-existent, for interesting reasons. Aristotle, we recall, explained that a primary aim of tragedy was to move us to pity and terror, and so to purge those emotions from our souls. Many of the greatest classical tragedies (French as well as Greek) do indeed culminate in harrowing and fearsome catastrophes. Such catastrophes depend, however, on the world-view of the author, and rarely are they to be found in Zeno's reformed *dramma per musica*, still less in the smiling, enlightened, optimistic world of Metastasio's art. There will be some suspense (*sospensione*) in the unfolding of the tale, obstacles, and vexations and temptations to be overcome in the practice of virtue. But almost always the final aim and objective of his dramas is the *lieto fine*, the happy ending – what Gluck's librettist Calzabigi wittily dubbed the *catastrofe matrimoniale*.

So Metastasio, blithely, unblushingly, steered his way around the central function of tragedy and aimed for a quite different one:

> All the just respect which I feel for the great philosophers is not sufficient to convince me that tragedy, in its operations, can avail itself of no other instruments than Terror and Compassion. It appears to me that the admiration of virtue, under a thousand different aspects: as friendship, gratitude, patriotism, fortitude, generosity to foes, and innumerable other modifications; as well as the abhorrence of the vices of the human heart, which often impede and oppose those virtues; all these, I say, appear to me efficacious, and fair means of affording delight and instruction, without eternally condemning the spectator to tremble with horror, or weep with affliction.[14]

As Burney wrily comments after translating this passage: 'it is manifest that Metastasio was no terrorist': purging the soul of pity and terror has been replaced by 'affording delight and instruction'.

Opera seria in London

The composers named by Burney to testify to the 'perfection and public favour' enjoyed by opera in the years between 1725 and 1740 did not

[13] Burney, *A General History of Music*, vol. IV, p. 561.

[14] Burney, *Memoirs of Metastasio*, vol. III, pp. 376–7.

include Handel. True, Burney was writing about 'the musical drama in Italy', but it is questionable, even if he had cast his net wider, and despite his great love of Handel's music, whether he would have added him to his list. Handel did set Metastasio dramas; but they occupied him only for a short period (1727–32) in a long career, and neither in Handel's day nor in ours have the three operas in question – *Siroe*, *Poro*, *Ezio* – ranked among the more popular or the more admired. The geniuses of the two men were not compatible, for reasons that become apparent the moment one reads what Metastasio had to say about his composer colleagues.

He was, unlike Zeno, a great lover of music – he sang, played and improvised himself, apparently as an aid to poetic composition. But when it came to opera he had very clear ideas of the relative roles of poet, composer and singers, and the essential tenet of his creed was that musicians were servants of the poet. In the *Gesamtkunstwerk* that was musical drama, his was the controlling intelligence: 'If in this lyric theatre, an action is represented, if a fable is interwoven and unravelled, if there are personages and characters to be supported, music is in the house of another, and cannot be called the mistress.'[15] The function of a composer was 'to imitate the speech of men, with numbers and harmony'[16] and Metastasio mistrusted those who got carried away with the resources of their own art. Galuppi he thought 'a good composer for violins, cellos and for singers: but a very bad workman for poets';[17] Gluck 'has surprising fire, but is mad'.[18] It is unlikely that he would have thought differently of Handel's settings. For Handel was the last person to satisfy himself simply with 'imitating the speech of men, with numbers and harmony', though he would do that as well, or as a starting point. But he would go on to lavish on the poetry all the resources of his art – contrapuntal, harmonic, rhythmic, colourful, rich and sometimes complex beyond the imagining of a Galuppi or even of a Gluck.

That was surely not due to any inappropriate vaingloriousness on Handel's part. It was because in England the composer did have to assume a far heavier share of the dramatic responsibility – a state of affairs that applied of course not only to Metastasio's dramas, but also to those that Handel had set before he discovered Metastasio: those by Stampiglia and Salvi, and any other of the Italian authors who wrote librettos for operas in some measure under the aegis of Zeno's Franco-Greek 'reform'. If we were

15 Letter of January 1766, to the Chevalier de Chastellux; in Burney, *Memoirs of Metastasio*, vol. II, p. 325.

16 Letter of August 1755, to a Roman friend; in Burney *Memoirs of Metastasio*, vol. II, p. 135.

17 Letter of December 1727, to Farinelli; in Burney *Memoirs of Metastasio*, vol. I, p. 297.

18 Letter of November 1751, to Farinelli; in Burney *Memoirs of Metastasio*, vol. I, p. 402.

to take the Italian *Rodrigo* as our starting point rather than the German *Almira*, we might almost say that Handel's operatic career mirrors Zeno's, but in reverse. Whereas Zeno aimed to keep music in its place, gradually – as he saw it – rescuing from its tentacles as much of the action and the poetry as possible, and confining 'full music' to a few minutes at the end of the scene, Handel's strategy was quite opposite, and became more and more opposite as the years passed.[19]

The primacy of the poet could only be an ideal, if it was indeed an ideal, in an environment where audiences were completely at home with the poet's own (Italian) language; that did not include London, though doubtless a small number in the London audience will have been tolerably well read in Italian. But here the music – and on good evenings the spectacle and the acting too – were the primary means for dramatic expression. And if, in performing its dramatic function, simple recitative could not give satisfaction, it had to be shortened quite ruthlessly; and as the recitative shrank, the aria came to occupy a correspondingly dominant place. Giuseppe Riva, the Modenese diplomatic representative in London explained that

> operas that come from Italy cannot be of service in this theatre [i.e. in London]. It is necessary to revise or rather deform them in order to render them acceptable. Few verses of recitative and many arias is what they want over here, and that is the reason why it has never been possible to perform some of Signor Apostolo's [Zeno's] best operas and why Metastasio's two finest operas, that is to say his *Dido* and his *Siroe* have met the same fate.[20]

But symptomatic of Handel's rethinking of Italian *opera seria* for his London audiences is the fact that, in many scenes, the adaptation entails not just shortened recitatives and proportionally more arias. Often the function of these arias, vis-à-vis their Italian models, has been rethought. While many aria texts are indeed retained, they are often revised; they may be given a quite different expressive or dramatic thrust; they may even be allocated to different characters.[21]

Changes of this kind are one of the most helpful clues towards understanding how Handel conceived or interpreted the dramatic theme. While he could perfectly well have done the job of shortening the recitatives himself, and no doubt had his own very clear ideas about such reorganisations

19 See Chapter 5, particularly the subsection 'The shape of an opera: frames and points of articulation'.

20 Letter to Ludovico Antonio Muratori, one of the high priests of literary taste in Italy in the first half of the eighteenth century, 3 October 1726; in Deutsch, p. 197.

21 The fullest discussion of this matter is to be found in Dean and Knapp, *Handel's Operas 1704–1726* and Dean, *Handel's Operas 1726–1741*, in the chapters on the individual operas.

of plot as may have been necessary, he did need collaborators for the finer or more literary details of such rewriting.

Librettist colleagues in London

Three of the Italian men of letters resident in London – Rossi, Haym and Rolli – were particularly active in this collaboration with Handel.

It was Rossi who had the privilege of helping introduce Handel to the opera-going public in London, and his wide-eyed stupefaction over the experience of working with 'the *Orpheus* of our century' on *Rinaldo* is the best remembered thing about him. Such was the speed at which Handel composed, declared Rossi, that he 'scarcely gave me the time to write, and to my great wonder I saw an entire Opera put to music by that surprising genius, with the greatest degree of perfection, in only two weeks'.[22] No doubt this was in part a conventional puff for a new artistic venture. But the tone of the preface, and the fact that there are in both *Rinaldo* and *Il pastor fido* several aria texts that must have been inserted on Handel's instruction, since they come either from earlier works written by Handel himself, or from the librettos of operas he had seen and admired in Venice,[23] leaves little room for doubt that Handel had much the upper hand in this collaboration. After *Silla*, Rossi seems to disappear from the ranks until Haym's death in 1729.

What exactly he did thereafter for the Second Academy is uncertain, but one of Rolli's letters to Riva mentions him mockingly as 'the famous Rossi … Handel's accredited bard'.[24] This was when Handel was just starting work on *Lotario*. A few years later Rossi is honoured by the same pen with a satirical epigram, which describes him as 'one of the two friars emigrated from Italy, who exercise their poetic talent where the German harpsichord has banished good sense'.[25] It is unlikely that he would have been accorded even this modest expenditure of Rolli's wit had he not had some significant role in helping prepare the repertory of works for the Second Academy.

Haym's work with Handel is better documented. Their collaboration began as early as *Teseo* in 1713 and continued until Haym's death in 1729, and since it includes the great central group of Royal Academy masterpieces – *Giulio Cesare, Tamerlano, Rodelinda* – he enjoys the reputation of being the

22 In Deutsch, p. 33. All the prefatory material from the *Rinaldo* libretto is given in *Documents I*, pp. 199–203.

23 Full details are given in W. Dean, 'Handel's Relations with the Librettists of his Operas', in *Baselt Gedenkschrift*, p. 102.

24 Letter of 3 September 1729; in Deutsch, p. 245.

25 *CHE*, 'Rossi'.

most admirable of Handel's collaborators, the one who best understood what Handel needed from a libretto, the one with whom he is likely to have worked most happily. He was also a man who had given some thought to the needs of an English audience; indeed, in the early years of the Haymarket Theatre he had been one of the advocates of singing Italian-style opera in English.[26] He took over as Secretary of the Royal Academy after Rolli fell into temporary disgrace in 1722, and retained that position until his death.

As far as his Italian librettos for Handel were concerned, Dean has sufficiently demonstrated how judicious Haym usually was in eliminating the extraneous, abbreviating the long-winded, focussing attention on the important characters in their most dramatically vital crises. However, the very qualities that must have endeared him to Handel, and to those who wished to see Italian *opera seria* effectively tailored to English taste and circumstance, helped alienate him from those in the Italian faction who favoured a different policy. Rolli and his supporters believed, probably correctly, that it was they who best understood the reform of opera progressing in Italy and Vienna under the aegis of Zeno and the Arcadians, and that this reform was too urgent a matter to be trifled with. As a matter of fact, it is debatable whether Rolli's librettos for Handel came so much closer to any reform ideal, or whether the Rolli clique's contempt for Haym had any other basis than professional jealousy.[27] But in any case, whatever his shortcomings as a poet, as a librettist Haym served Handel well, as the opening scene of *Rodelinda* famously demonstrates.

Ultimately *Rodelinda* goes back to the *Gesta Langobardorum*, a chronicle by the eighth-century courtier, monk, poet and historian Paul the Deacon (Paulus Diaconus). On one episode from this history Pierre Corneille had based his tragedy *Pertharite, roi des Lombards* (1651), which, despite the pride its author took in 'the artistry of the plotting, the skill of the verse, and the liveliness of the passions depicted', failed dismally when exhibited in a theatre. Confident that it could enjoy better success at the Pratolino Theatre in 1710, Salvi took up Corneille's drama in an opera libretto for Perti, which he called *Rodelinda, regina de' Longobardi*. He preserved most of Corneille's characters and their attributes, but felt free, he declared, to depart from the organisation of the plot and the details of its staging. Haym, presumably at Handel's prompting, turned to *Rodelinda* again fifteen years later. Rather disingenuously, he quotes Salvi's Argument verbatim, including the words

[26] See the letters (to the *Spectator*) of which he was a signatory, 20 December 1711, and 18 January 1712; in *Documents I*, pp. 234–6.

[27] Haym was 'a complete idiot as far as Letters are concerned', wrote Riva to Muratori, 7 September 1725; in Deutsch, p. 186.

'All this is from the history of Paul the Deacon … the rest is invented'; but neither Salvi nor Corneille, who had done the inventing, is mentioned.

Corneille's opening scene recapitulates and reinforces the dynastic and political matters outlined in the Argument, and shows Rodelinda, the Lombard queen, indignantly repulsing a claim of marriage brought to her from the usurping Grimoald. Unulphe/Unulfo, the court counsellor who bears Grimoald's message,[28] is transformed in Salvi's libretto from a loyal spokesman for Grimoald into an ally and friend (albeit secretly) of Rodelinda and her exiled husband; the conversation between Rodelinda and Unulfo is therefore more warm-hearted and encouraging on the courtier's part, and it is he who first leaves the scene, with an aria ('Vivi a te'). In Haym's adaptation – and it is a masterly stroke – this opening scene of Salvi's is simply omitted, or rather it is replaced with an aria, 'Ho perduto il caro sposo', which presents 'the emotional nucleus of the opera in the first five words.'[29] Then (scene ii) Grimoaldo enters to do his own wooing: this proceeds entirely in Salvi's words, abbreviated by about a third, and closes with an aria for Rodelinda which Haym has deftly rewritten. It says next to nothing which is not already in the earlier libretto; but shrugging off the slightly precious literary inversions of the Florentine text, Haym turns his into a straightforward chain of vivid ideas:

> SALVI: Misera, sì, non vile, / della sorte mi fé l'empio rigore.
> Può ben laccio servile / incatenarmi il piè ma non il core.[30]
> HAYM: L' empio rigor del fato / vile non potrà farmi, / se misera mi fé.
> E tu, crudo, spietato, / invan tenti placarmi, / se m'hai legato il piè.[31]

The whole scene has been brilliantly reimagined in operatic terms. Salvi, hardly less than Corneille, had felt it necessary to set the drama in motion with explanations, with the carefully argued exposition of various points of view. Thanks to Haym, Handel's opening scene expounds character, dilemma and the first stirrings of plot overwhelmingly in music; and its two framing arias, introspective and heroic respectively, make it clear that this is the woman who is to be the protagonist in their version of the story.

28 Voltaire was to complain of this play that the very names of the characters were repellent.

29 Dean and Knapp, *Handel's Operas 1704–1726*, p. 576.

30 Translated literally to clarify the argument:

> Wretched, yes, but not ignoble, / made me Fate's pitiless harshness.
> Servile shackle may be able / to chain my foot but not my heart.

31 Also translated literally:

> The pitiless harshness of Fate / will not be able make me ignoble / though it made me wretched.
> And you, cruel, ruthless one, / in vain attempt to appease me, / though you have shackled my foot.

What gives the whole episode a particular fascination is the very strong probability that all Haym's rewritings were made under firm instruction from Handel himself.[32]

Next to Haym, Rolli was the most productive of Handel's librettist collaborators. But he was a man of decidedly higher standing in Italian cultural life; like his younger contemporary Metastasio, he had been a pupil of the redoubtable Gian Vincenzo Gravina, from whom he received a rigorous classical education, and a lofty conception of the civil responsibilities of a dramatist or poet. At an early age he became an Arcadian, and enjoyed a brilliant reputation as an *improvvisatore* whose effusions were still remembered with respect by the elderly Metastasio. His reputation as a lyric poet survives, authoritative critics declaring, as they did in his own day, that his canzonette are 'with Metastasio's lyrics, the cream of Settecento poetry'.[33] He was an obvious first choice for the position of Italian Secretary to the Royal Academy, and fulfilled this role for the Academy's first three seasons. His translation of Milton's *Paradise Lost*, made at a time when Italian was a language more widely read among educated Europeans than English, earned him a European reputation; he was elected to a Fellowship of the Royal Society in 1729, and became Italian tutor to the royal family, in which post his didactic methods aimed to bring his distinguished pupils at the earliest possible stage to appreciate the best in Italian literature. In England he was in effect the 'cultural ambassador of all things Italian'[34] – a man, then, of some considerable distinction.

Rolli had arrived in London in 1715 or 1716, but he never became anglicised, as Haym did; he had a propensity for getting involved with Italian cliques, and was therefore at the heart of any grumblings about Handel and his ways of doing things. Besides, canzonettas, however delicious, do not necessarily make an effective opera libretto; and Rolli's conviction that his task in London was to keep the better class of people there in tune with contemporary cultural life in Italy, while congenial to a Bononcini, may have made him a less willing and less effective supporter for Handel's shrewd pragmatism. Dean has been scathing about Rolli's lame organisation of plot, his inconsistent characterisation, and his platitudinous philosophising, and I see no reason to dissent from that view, except perhaps in the matter of platitudinous philosophising, which opera could ill spare.

32 This matter has been discussed fully and persuasively in A. V. Jones, 'The Composer as Dramatist: Handel's Contribution to the Libretto of *Rodelinda*', *ML* 88 (2007), especially 54–7.

33 Franco Fido, 'The Settecento', in *CHIL*, p. 351

34 Dorris, *Paolo Rolli*, p. 145.

But that is not the whole story. If one may judge from the number of performances given – comparing, let us say, the Haym and Handel *Flavio*, *Tamerlano* and *Rodelinda* with the Rolli and Handel *Floridante*, *Scipione* and *Alessandro* – it is clear that modern views of what makes a Handelian operatic masterpiece do not always coincide with the views of his contemporaries. The question of what Rolli did and what he failed to do in his capacity as Handel's librettist is worth re-examining. Apart from anything else, he was a real poet; a poet moreover who – being himself, like Metastasio, something of a singer – understood the relationship between poetry and music. That is clearest in his aria texts. One can read through the whole libretto of, for example, *Riccardo primo* and will find that in every aria the sense emerges in clear, natural sequence in flowing harmonious words; each line of text, and therefore every constituent part of the verse, and therefore potentially every musical phrase, is transparent in meaning, expressive and often vivid. Of course there are caesuras and enjambements – the verses would be intolerable without them – but what these niceties tend to do is not complicate the issue, but provide now shorter, now longer elements of verse in which the same naturalness, expressiveness and vividness are found. Syntactically more ambitious flights of verse almost always come at the end of the principal A section, precisely where the composer would be looking to write grander, clinching phrases; or they occupy the whole or much of the B section, where a more *parlando* style of setting is likely to be felt appropriate.

For a more rounded picture of Rolli's vices and virtues, *Alessandro* provides a fascinating test-case. Through the original librettist Mauro, it has, of all Handel's operas, the closest links with his Hanover years, and therefore with the loyalties of his most important patron, King George; and because it was the first opera to be written for the 'rival queens', Cuzzoni and Faustina, it also put Rolli on his mettle, presenting him with a very constraining logistical challenge. The shortcomings of the libretto have been sufficiently proclaimed by Dean: in particular the poet's treatment of the anti-Alexander conspiracy, its climactic *coup de théâtre* and the consequences.[35] To deem this 'ludicrous' is, if anything, too polite; it is staggeringly silly, and if this strand of the opera mattered much to Rolli, he was a bungler of the first water.

But while in simplifying for a smaller cast the ramifications of a shilly-shallying sort of plot Rolli, it must be granted, managed feebly, what emerged from his reworking in other respects was far from feeble, and it is these things we should perhaps recognise as his priorities: a series (a gallery's-worth, one might almost say) of emotionally strong stage pictures;

35 Dean, *Handel's Operas 1726–1741*, p. 13.

a more dignified and plausible psychology for the principal character, Alexander himself, and in some measure for the other important characters too – Rossane, Lisaura, Tassile; a rhetorically effective use of language in the (usually shortened) recitatives, freer in syntax and more direct than Mauro's, and communicating the sense of the action more immediately; a polishing and perhaps a modernising of the more elevated language in the arias, which makes almost every one of them clear in sense and vivid in expression – in short, more *musicabile*. All this goes a long way to explain Rolli's reputation as a poet; does it not even offer a legitimate alternative model of opera?

Mauro has been given credit, and rightly so, for the effectiveness of two of the finest stretches of Handel's *Alessandro*: Act I scenes i–iv and Act II scenes i–ii, where Rolli has used Mauro's text 'almost without change'; they are 'virtually the same'.[36] Indeed they are, but quite a lot of poetic craftsmanship went into earning that 'almost' and 'virtually'. In fact, every scene which Rolli modelled closely on Mauro proves, on examination, to have improved its model formally or structurally (in terms of the individual scene, not of the overall plot), psychologically and linguistically. For the reader who cares to examine the matter, Excursus 3.2 provides a few illustrations.

Excursus 3.2 – Ortensio Mauro and Pietro Rolli: some passages compared

(Rolli I.i–ii; Mauro I.i)

This is one of the scenes much expanded when Mauro revised his libretto for a 1691 revival: the chief novelty was the addition of a substantial recitative and aria for Leonato, cued in towards the end of the stage directions (which are largely a description of the spectacular action which follows 'Son prole del Tonante, e tanto basti'). Given the tumultuous context, the recitative seems overlong – eighteen lines – and the aria, urging Alessandro to 'temper his ardour', seriously misjudged. Rolli omits the latter and rewrites the former comprehensively. It comes closest to Mauro at the close: 'What would the conquest of Oxidraca, indeed of all Persia and India avail if Alessandro himself were to be lost?' In the first part of the recitative Rolli reduces Mauro's text by more than half: he takes over one or two expressions ('grand'alma' – 'pubblica salvezza' ['salute' in Mauro]) but otherwise does it afresh, and surely rather well. It

[36] Dean, *Handel's Operas 1726–1741*, p. 12.

is a distinct improvement to start so frantic a scene not, like Mauro, with a long, persuasively argued sentence laden with inversions and subordinate clauses ('Sire, so che la gloria / Di magnanimo Eroe stimolo e meta / T'agita e t'inquieta, / E ch'ardor generoso invan si frena: / Ma tu sai com' é unita / La publica salute a la tua vita' etc), but with a heartfelt exclamation – 'Grazie all'eterno Giove, Sire, sei salvo'.[37]

The rest of the scene is handled well too. Rolli's two additional recitatives – Alessandro's opening words and Clito's [?or Leonato's] 'Oh smisurato ardir', both introduce instrumental movements and helpfully highlight the exact nature of what is going on amid all the racket of the battle. The recitative he does take from Mauro – the *accompagnato* following the first instalment of the Sinfonia – is rhetorically more effective too, with the challenge 'Ossidraca superba', ringing out at the start, instead of being embedded in the middle of an inverted phrase, 'Contro l'ira del Cielo / Sidraca in van contrasti'.[38] Rolli's uses Alessandro's aria text 'Fra le stragi' unchanged.

(Rolli I.iv; Mauro I.iii, I.v, I.vii)

Often more careful than Mauro in how he brings in a character, Rolli here adds a couple of lines of recitative to introduce Tassile (which is helpful for clarity) and then gradually begins juggling the action to provide a sequence of three recitatives and arias, each of which is, despite the bystanders, in effect a soliloquy: Lisaura, Rossane, Tassile – all of them nicely given their prevailing notes – the love/jealousy complexity that Lisaura has to live with, Rossane's confident delight in her own charms, Tassile's rather passive, dog-like loyalty as soldier and lover. The three texts do credit to Rolli's poetic judgement:

'Quanto dolce amor saria / se non fosse gelosia / col gelato suo velen!' – *ottonari*; every word tells and plays its part in bringing to life the prevailing idea; the text unfurls syntactically in a way which is very easy for an audience to follow.

'Lusinghe più care, d'Amor veri dardi' – *dodecasillabi* or *senari doppi* – the metre dances to reinforce the exuberance of Rossane's high spirits. If one scans it in *senari*, every group of three words is vivid, nothing is padding; it is the final pair of *senari* in each half that gain most from being linked together as

[37] Mauro: 'Sire, I know that glory, / of a magnanimous hero the stimulus and the goal, / stirs you and makes you restless, / and that generous ardour restrains itself in vain: / but you know how inseparable are / the public weal and your life'; Rolli: 'Thanks to the immortal Jove, Sire, you are safe.'

[38] Mauro: 'Against the wrath of heaven / Sidraca, in vain you stand opposed'; Rolli: 'Proud Ossidraca'.

dodecasillabi (in the B section they have to be), which helps Handel give the music a breadth of phrase at the close of each main section of his aria.

'Vibra, cortese Amor' – *endecasillabi* and *settenari* mixed (very dignified and thoughtful); the aria text is one of some formal sophistication, in which internal rhymes break up the long lines into shorter groups of words. Though sufficiently transparent, the sense of the words is rather more complex than in the women's arias, and the more elaborate syntax in which they are expressed stimulates that 'tendency for the phrase to extend beyond what the ear expects', which Dean admires in this piece.[39]

(Rolli I.ix; Mauro I.xix)

As well as I.xix, Rolli tucks into his scene material based on Mauro's I.xvii and I.xviii; in the remarks that follow, I focus simply on matters relating to the temple of Jupiter Ammon, which forms the central feature of the stage set.

In Mauro the temple provided a backcloth for the first weavings of the conspiracy against Alessandro. Rolli, for logistical reasons to do with casting and probably for reasons of artistic priority too, decided to do without a proper conspiracy and, very feebly and with no proper follow-up, merely suggests, in the inconsequential scene I.viii between Cleone, Clito and Leonato, a mounting resentment among some of the leaders of the Greek army. In his recasting of the scene (and there seems no reason to doubt that he would have had Handel's encouragement in doing this) the temple does not just stand around on the stage until the action slowly closes in on it; it is revealed of a sudden, as a superb tableau, instantly the focus of a musically saturated spectacle. The outcome is a grand sequence of Sinfonia (as it were the first movement of an overture), a recitative of acclamation, a polyphonic Allegro (beginning as if it might be the second movement of an overture), and an *accompagnato*, a prayer offered by Alessandro: a magnificent climax to a magnificent act. This is one of several changes in the libretto which Rolli makes in the interest of turning Alessandro into a more sympathetic figure. In Mauro's original libretto he had said nothing at all until the time came to stride forward, throw Leonato to the ground and demand that he prostrate himself (*proskynesis*).

The solo scene with which Rolli ends the act also depicts a more congenial Alessandro. He takes up some of the thoughts expressed by the gods in the Prologue of Mauro's libretto: love is a legitimate refreshment and reward for heroes just as it is for the gods, not a deplorable distraction, as Mauro's unlovely hero seems to think.

[39] Dean, *Handel's Operas 1726–1741*, p. 22.

4 | The music (1): mastering the medium

Preliminary Note: Where an opera has already appeared in *HHA* the numbering of the individual movements follows that source; where there is not yet an *HHA* edition, Baselt's catalogue is used (*HHB I*).

German origins: *Almira*

Hamburg was a good place to launch a career in opera. The great commercial city, independent and cosmopolitan, knew little of the fears and favours and particularities of taste which affected the court theatres of central and southern Germany; and the musicians and patrons of music who guided the Theater am Gänsemarkt through its first quarter century followed their own judgement in creating an indigenous opera. They drew deeply on the great operatic traditions of both Italy and France, and fused what they discovered there with the achievements of their own North German music, ecclesiastical and domestic. The Hamburg opera may have lacked the elevated aesthetic purpose and the purity of style of the best Italian and French operas, but for the purpose of initiating a young composer into the ways of what Mattheson called a 'university of the fine arts', it had no equal.[1] *Almira* therefore merits rather fuller consideration than its purely artistic merit might suggest: in it are to be found the seeds of all Handel's achievements in the field of opera.

To compose for the Hamburg opera in the early years of the eighteenth century demanded versatility, fluency and energy. An opera consumed huge quantities of music. There are more than seventy musical numbers in both *Almira* and the lost *Nero*, the two operas which the twenty-year-old Handel staged in Hamburg within a few weeks of each other in January and February 1705; that is nearly twice the number found in his mature operas

[1] 'A university of the fine arts' – Mattheson used a number of similar phrases in a number of different contexts, most clearly perhaps in *Der musicalische Patriot* (Hamburg, 1728), p. 176, and *Ehrenpforte*, p. 189. For the latter, see the discussion in Beekman C. Cannon, *Johann Mattheson. Spectator in Music* (New Haven: Yale University Press, 1968), pp. 20–1.

from the 1720s and 1730s. One can perhaps best steer a path through this abundance by considering the use he makes of his orchestra.

When arias (and a few ensembles) are required in this profusion, they clearly cannot always have the vital dramaturgical role which they come to perform in Handel's later operas; nor, though almost all of them contain some point of imaginative or craftsmanly interest, can they always be worked up into substantial, autonomous works of art. Many of the arias in *Almira* are tiny: they are songs sung almost in passing, perhaps in a fleeting moment of introspection, perhaps even 'aside', as Almira herself sings 'Vollkommene Hände' aside (No. 14), without the other character on stage so much as noticing her. In fact, the largest group of arias, close on half of them, have no real role for the orchestra at all. Like movements from an Italian chamber cantata or a set of German continuo songs, they are accompanied by simply the continuo group of instruments.

Handel had a number of distinctive ways of managing these. Three of them are comic or satirical and, as it were, popular songs for Tabarco, the servant, Hamburg's indispensable 'lustige Person'. And others besides Tabarco sing numbers that merit no grander description than continuo song, though Osman, in 'Ich will euch verdammen' (No. 20) and Consalvo in 'Unartige Schöne' (No. 59) fire off little flourishes of pictorial coloratura more self-important than anything attempted by Tabarco. Several continuo arias, most obviously Fernando's 'So ben che regnante' (No. 6), entwine voice and bass contrapuntally;[2] while others again – 'Werter Brief' (No. 66) is a good example – spin out ingratiating cantilenas over a 'walking' bass. Any of these types may shade over into any other. In what is certainly the most distinctive of the *Almira* continuo-song types, the 'walking' bass, instead of simply walking, limps or hops or leaps, as a result of absorbing some idiosyncratic instrumental figure which perhaps provides a symbolic equivalent for an idea in the text: the quiverings of rage in 'Svenerò' (No. 42); the tears in 'Quillt, ihr überhäuften Zähren' (No. 55) (see Example 4.1). In a few of the more finely worked chamber cantata-like pieces, obbligato instruments are added to the continuo without detriment to the chamber music-like intimacy.

A startling contrast with this group of arias is provided by those accompanied by the full orchestra in four parts. For these the model is the modern concerto, and the brilliant flights of the singing voice are marked off by

[2] The reader will notice the Italian text. Beginning with Keiser's *Claudius*, staged in 1703, Hamburg operas had commonly included a number of Italian-language arias. In the case of *Almira*, 'So ben che regnante' is one of fifteen (out of some sixty) vocal movements with Italian text.

Example 4.1

recurrences of an orchestral ritornello. What Dean and Knapp describe as the 'crude, animal impact'[3] of these half dozen or so pieces is owed to a style in which the most basic diatonic harmonies are defined in fanfares, scales and arpeggios, and clinched at the cadences with hammering chord repetitions. Vocal and instrumental forces engage in only the most rudimentary interplay, and in several numbers (No. 43, 'Ob dein Mund', for example) Handel's architectural ambitions are so limited that the principal section of the aria fails even to escape from the tonic key. The vocal writing is surprisingly unlovely: once the thematic material has been presented, its continuation is likely to veer between mechanical melismatic writing of fearsome difficulty and mouth-foaming outpourings of syllables. Though the style is crudely overdrawn, it serves a clear dramatic purpose. For every one of these arias is a tirade launched by a principal singer (Almira, Edilia, Fernando) in a mood of vindictive rage. Feustking's libretto does not help Handel place them very effectively, and several come close to tautology: three of Almira's arias in this manner ('Ingrato, spietato', No. 28;[4] 'Vedrai, s'a tuo dispetto', No. 62; 'Kochet, ihr Adern', No. 65) are enraged denunciations of Fernando.

[3] Dean and Knapp, *Handel's Operas 1704–1726*, p. 60.

[4] This aria is not in the *HHA* edition of *Almira*, but see R.-S. Pegah 'Neues zur Oper *Almira*', *GHB* 10 (2004), 44–6.

Less extraordinary than these, but musically rather more rewarding, are the arias with accompaniment for *tutti unisoni* (or *violini unisoni*) and continuo. This was to remain one of Handel's favourite orchestral distributions for the rest of his career, in opera and oratorio alike, and already in *Almira* it proves admirably versatile. Several of these arias, too, are concerto-like, with vivid orchestral ritornellos standing out in high relief: the opening aria, Consalvo's 'Almira regiere' (see Example 4.2) is an excellent example. At other times, without the ritornello function necessarily being lost, the violins duet with the voice like an obbligato instrument in a chamber cantata. And with both these options admitted, the scope for combining them, or moving to and fro between them, is potentially infinite.

Excursus 4.1: 'Almire regiere' – a *Devisenarie*

It will be worth pausing a moment over 'Almira regiere', which is an excellent example of a type of '*Devisenarie*' which in these early years Handel made uniquely his own. The form has been discussed very fully by Gerhard Poppe;[5] in the present context it will be sufficient to highlight just three features.

First, an opening, introductory ritornello which provides a very clear prototype of what was to become a frequent proceeding of Handel's: a pattern of Incipit, Continuation, Cadence. The Incipit is that phrase or motif which the voice will shortly take up in combination with the opening words of the aria (bars 1–3); the freer and more florid Continuation is often sequential in character (bars 3–5), and will often provide material for those patches of three-part writing (still rare in the *tutti/violini unisoni* arias of *Almira*) where the singing voice is projected against, or sings in dialogue with the instruments (see bars 17–19); the Cadence rounds off the design in emphatic and distinctive style (bars 5–7). (Anyone doubtful about how the harmony should be realised in bars 5–6 will find a comparable progression fully harmonised in the Ouverture, bars 12–14.)

Second, this ritornello returns with strict exactitude at the principal cadence points during the course of the aria (which is in free ternary form): bars 8–12 (Continuation and Cadence, tonic key); bars 21–25 (Continuation and Cadence, dominant key); bars 31–35 (Continuation and Cadence, tonic key); bars 51–57 (Complete Ritornello, tonic key); additionally, a compressed variation of the ritornello (Continuation and Cadence) is heard at bars 40–43 in the submediant minor key.[6]

[5] G. Poppe, 'Geniestreich oder Werk eines unerfahrenen "Pedanten"? – zur Musik von Händel's Oper, Almira, Königin von Kastilien', *HJb* 52 (2006), 285–301.

[6] Strict exactitude is, with Handel, always a relative term: cf., for example, the bass in bar 2 with that in bar 52.

Incipit
Continuation
Oboe I, II
Violin I, II
CONSALVO
Bassi
Cadence
Devise
Al-mi-re re-gie-re,
senza Ob.
Al-mi-re re-gie-re und füh - - re be-glük-ket den
con Ob.
Zep-ter, groß-mü-tig die Kron', be-glük-ket den Zep - - - - - - - - - - - - -

Example 4.2

Example 4.2 *(cont.)*

Example 4.2 (*cont.*)

Third, the '*Devise*' itself – the 'motto' or 'device', in the heraldic sense – which proclaims the purport of the aria in a short resounding motif, or call-to-attention; it is sung unaccompanied at the end of the opening ritornello, and is cut short by the next ritornello's immediate return.

Dance music plays a prominent part in *Almira*; there were few Hamburg operas of the period in which it didn't. For dance – usually directed by French ballet masters, members of the Académie de Musique et de Danse in Paris – was still, in the early eighteenth century, the most obvious legacy from the francophile days of the foundation of the Gänsemarkt opera.[7] Instrumental dances adorn the coronation scene at the start of the opera, and a suite of five dances forms a ball scene towards the close of the act (I.xi). More dances are heard (and seen) in the Masque of Continents (III.i–iv), and very colourful they are. Each of the principal masquers is attended by a retinue of distinct 'continental' types, and each of these groups dances to what was clearly felt to be an aptly characterising ensemble of instruments: for Fernando, Europeans dance to a band of oboes; for Osman, Africans dance to a band of trumpets and kettledrums; for Consalvo, Asians dance to a band of cymbals, drums and fifes; for Tabarco, charlatans dance to hurdy-gurdy and bagpipes. This scene is the only echo we have in Handelian opera of the consort-based 'audio-visual' instrumentation that was still a trait of Keiser's early scores.[8] Moreover, several of the arias are essentially dances. Tabarco's three continuo songs (Nos. 18, 31, 46) are all dance-like, and are transformed into real instrumental dances (described as 'ritornellos') when he has finished singing. His fourth dance song, 'Kommt, vermehrt der Thorheit Ruhm' (No. 53), forms part of the Masque. A gavotte in Lullian vein, it has the voice doubling the continuo throughout, while melody and harmony are provided by two oboes. Of the more subtle dance arias, 'Ich brenne zwar' (No. 71) adopts the binary form normal for dances at this period; after each half has been sung with continuo accompaniment, it is repeated by full orchestra. The supreme example of a dance-inspired aria in *Almira* is 'Move i passi' (No. 41), a large da capo (or rather dal segno) aria in the manner of a chaconne, which retains the traditional French scoring for strings in five parts. Both 'Ich brenne zwar' and 'Move i passi' are

7 M. Brauneck, C. Müller, B. Müller-Wesemann (eds.), *Theaterstadt Hamburg* (Reinbek: Rowohlt, 1989), p. 30.

8 Andrew D. McCredie, *Instrumentarium and Instrumentation in the North German Baroque Opera* (University of Hamburg *Habilitationsschrift*, 1964), p. 321.

love songs, as most dance-inspired arias were to be for the rest of Handel's operatic career.

Four times in *Almira* Handel composes the recitative in the *accompagnato* style, that is to say with accompaniment for four-part string orchestra rather than simple continuo; three of the four come in Act III.[9] By enhancing the expressive weight of the recitative and drawing it into the sound-world of the aria, this makes possible a more gripping interrelationship between recitative and aria, potentially transforming it into what may be described as a dramatic *scena* – an operatic equivalent of the great self-communing monologues of poetic drama. The outstanding example in *Almira* is the prison scene (No. 69). Here, after a lengthy *recitativo accompagnato*, Fernando begins to sing an *arioso*, which is interrupted at cadence points, not by instrumental ritornellos, but by simple phrases of recitative, whispered by Almira from her hiding place in the shadows, and audible only to the audience. Less obviously theatrical, but no less finely imagined, is the fusion of cantabile and recitative elements in 'Geloso tormento' (No. 15). The voice, led by and then emulated by the solo oboe, sings in a manner where cantabile seems always on the point of dissolving into recitative; meanwhile the string accompaniment, from first bar to last, is built on the stock juxtapositions of *accompagnato* recitative: repeated quaver chords, *piano* and *legato*, alternate with repeated semiquaver chords, *forte* and *furioso*.

In Hamburg, as in French opera, verses for recitative were fully rhymed. This seems to invite the composer to provide a more *arioso*-like setting for it, but that does not really happen in *Almira*. Except in the dramatic *scena* there is always a very obvious contrast of musical style between recitative and even the simplest of continuo songs.

An aria may then adopt the manner of chamber music, or of the virtuoso concerto, or of dance music, or of the dramatic *scena*. With these resources Handel already commanded an inexhaustibly flexible musical language; there were few emotions, few states of mind, few secret corners of personality to which he could not give voice. But there is something else in *Almira* that we should not overlook; indeed, it is more obvious in *Almira* than in many later operas. The composer of an opera is not simply setting dramatic poetry to music; he is setting to music a staged spectacle too, and if he is ever to become a real master of his craft, he will need the faculty of seeing that spectacle in his mind's eye as he writes.[10]

[9] This compares with five *accompagnati* in Keiser's contemporary *Octavia*; he too, rather more tellingly than Handel in fact, concentrates them as the drama moves to its climax.

[10] See Mattheson's remarks on this matter cited in Chapter 6 at p.164.

Apart from the dances, the most obvious evidence for this is the series of 'ritornellos', tiny movements reworking in instrumental form ideas from the aria or duet that preceded them. As well as the three antimasque-like dances that follow Tabarco's arias, the remaining ritornellos (see Nos. 8, 17, 21, 28, 37, 43, 62 and 70) are also related to stage action; each of them rounds off a tableau before a change of scene, and accompanies the exit from the stage of the last character to have sung. In the Act I garden scene (I.iv–vii) Handel even provided one of these exit ritornellos after No. 12 to cover the break in 'liaison' at the exit of Osman and before the entry of Fernando. Though in almost every case the ritornellos draw on the aria for their thematic material, several of them besides Tabarco's are dance-like in their symmetry and regularity of phrase. Very strikingly, the ritornello that follows No. 70, the duet 'Spielet, ihr blitzenden Augen', is a genuine celebratory dance, a minuet with no obvious thematic link to the duet at all.

And Handel likes to usher characters on to the stage with music as well as to see them off: the overture-like *Entrée* that introduces the grand spectacle at the start of Act III is an obvious case. Under certain circumstances the same tendency appears in arias, as it does in the Act I garden scene. Both 'Schönste Rosen' (No. 9), for Edilia, and 'Liebliche Wälder' (No. 13), for Fernando, take the form of self-characterising soliloquies in which the singers, coming on to the empty stage, find their moods reflected in the beauty of the scene. It is part of the role of the orchestra to make that experience vivid for the theatre audience too: the ritornellos and interludes become episodes of tone-painting – hence, in these particular pieces, the 'pastoral' recorders. Such arias as these, almost always placed at the start of a new tableau (so we may call them entrée-arias or, better, sinfonia-arias), were to remain a constant feature of Handelian opera.

Each of the aria types I have described has its own distinctive scoring or orchestral manner. The arias with *violini unisoni* or *tutti unisoni*, popping up here and there in all these categories, do, however, provide a useful reminder that Handel's art does not lend itself well to classifications which attempt to be too systematic. The aria types borrow from each other, blend into each other, undergo transformation as they proceed. And it is in the arias that most defy classification that one is most likely to find evidence that, from the start, Handel's inner eye did not always limit itself to such obvious elements of spectacle as dances and entrances and exits; it affected the vocal music too. An aria was indeed the expression of a mood or passion or reflection, but the expression might go beyond the generalised or the allegorical and take the form of a kind of interior dialogue played out in the mind of that particular singer on the stage in front of us, and embodied in the intercourse of voice and instruments. In 'Mi da speranza' (No. 38), at bars 22–28 there is a passage where Raymondo, having fallen silent for a ritornello, joins in again towards the end of it with his last few words, as if the *tutti unisoni* music of the ritornello had been sounding in his mind all the time, and he must suddenly let out what it means to him. It is no more than a tiny detail, but it hints at a theatrical and psychological insight which in the long run will prove as important as Handel's superlative compositional skills.

Adapting to new audiences: from *Almira* to *Rodrigo*

After Hamburg, each of Handel's next three operas was composed for an audience that did not know him or knew him only from reputation. *Rodrigo* was first staged, almost certainly, at the Teatro del Cocomero in Florence in Autumn 1707; *Agrippina* at the Teatro San Giovanni Grisostomo in Venice during the Carnival Season 1709–10; and *Rinaldo* at the Queen's Theatre in the Haymarket, London, from February to May 1711. For new audiences in new cities it was part of Handel's strategy to introduce himself properly: to demonstrate what he could do, where he had come from, what the theatrical and musical experiences he had hitherto enjoyed now added up to. Handel being Handel, this circumstance gives us the opportunity to reflect a little on one of the perennial themes of Handelian scholarship: the manner in which, in virtually every new piece, he adapted and reworked earlier compositions. It is a tantalising theme which threatens to become illimitable, but which in this small group of operas can perhaps be viewed in a usefully circumscribed way. My aim is not to hope to understand 'how Handel composed', nor to pass any kind of moral judgement on what he was doing. I am simply choosing one particular way of paying close attention to the notes (something of a neglected field in operatic scholarship), in the belief that this will help to make us more aware of certain features of Handel's art we might otherwise miss.

The opening eight bars of the *Rodrigo* Overture paraphrase the opening eight bars of the *Almira* Overture. This is only the first of an extensive series of recompositions of *Almira* found in the new opera, and the manner of the reworking is typical of what Handel achieves in most of them.[11] In *Almira*

[11] Because what happens is typical, I have availed myself of the traditional association of this overture with this opera, and it is in *HHA* II. 2. *Rodrigo* (2007) that the most reliable edition of it is to be found. In point of fact, although the overture is certainly from the right period, its link with the opera is a tenuous one. See Excursus 5.1 in Chapter 5.

the harmonies had moved slowly and blockishly in two-bar chunks, animated by the 'French' rhythms and by streaking scale passages in treble and bass. Reworked for *Rodrigo*, the music is less beholden to elemental mannerism. The opening melodic figure is not simply played once and forgotten; it recurs in free variation at the start of the answering phrase, bar 5 and it is freely imitated in the bass in bars 2 and 4, binding together the two-bar blocks, and setting off consistently bolder movement in the bass. The inner voices, too, have more linear and harmonic life; they are not mere inert sonorities carried on the rhythms of treble and bass. In short, the *Rodrigo* paraphrase integrates the melodic, harmonic and rhythmic substance more completely. Similar qualities – balance, integration, fluidity, proportion – are the hallmarks of most of the reworkings of *Almira* material found in this opera.

'Sommi Dei' (No. 11) (see Example 4.3) takes up from 'Quillt, ihr überhäuften Zähren' (see Example 4.1) one of those perhaps over-intrusive quasi-ostinato basses that are such a feature of *Almira*. What first arrests the attention in the *Rodrigo* aria is the extraordinary harmony and the tormented melodic line that writhes through it. But these can only stand out so vividly because Handel now treats the bass more flexibly, dissolving

Example 4.3

the dotted rhythms from time to time in a varied series of continuations which sustain the momentum of the aria without the abrupt starts and stops of its German prototype. It will be noted that it was the instrumental bass that Handel wanted to reuse, not the vocal part; and this is true of most of these reworkings. In the teeming and occasionally ill-groomed Hamburg score he had coined a profusion of striking instrumental ideas, many of which he evidently felt had not been put to such effective use as they might be. He now went back to them, often in quite different contexts, in arias for a different voice type, or with a text in a different metre bearing a different expressive burden; and now, usually, the instrumental brainwave is matched with comparable flair in other dimensions of the music.

Understandably pleased with the ritornello of 'Almira regiere' (see Example 4.2), Handel decided to parade it again in 'Vanne in campo' (*Rodrigo*, No. 12); but here instead of simply framing and punctuating the song, the ritornello's florid Continuation is the source of all Rodrigo's vigorous coloratura. The vocal–instrumental integration is clinched in the entwined violin–voice imitation starting at bar 30. The effect of the *Devise* is transformed too. Omitting any introductory ritornello, Handel brings the initial exclamation, 'Vanne in campo', directly into the dramatic action, launching the aria with urgent theatrical rhetoric; he does not wait to present it within the stylised space set apart from the action by the orchestra.[12]

In undertaking this kind of recomposition Handel did not hesitate to discard what had seemed particularly pleasing features of the original music. In 'Eroica fortezza' (No. 8), recomposed from the substance of 'Zürne was hin' (*Almira*, No. 12), neither the most skilfully wrought passage of composition (the ritornello-postlude) nor the witty effect of making the final cadence phrase a spaced-out restatement of the *Devise* is retained. It was the busily seething *unisoni* figure that Handel wanted to reuse, but now in a more spacious context. 'Eroica fortezza' deftly produces an opening vocal phrase out of a paraphrase of the ritornello Incipit, and in the B section shows that, once the upper octave doubling has been dropped, the semiquaver figuration can be effectively employed as bass to a more lyrical type of theme too (see Examples 4.4a and 4.4b).

[12] Poppe, in 'Geniestreich oder Werk eines unerfahrenen "Pedanten"?', points out that this happens in all the *Rodrigo* arias that make use of the *Devise*.

Example 4.4a

As a last example of these *Almira* recompositions for *Rodrigo* we may take 'Pugneran con noi' (No. 2), a reworking of 'Ob dein Mund' (*Almira*, No. 43). Curiously, the aria still does not modulate in the principal section, nor does it altogether cast off the stiffness of the earlier aria; but the opening ritornello has been laid out on a more generous scale, to match the energy of the whole scene. And, working with a better focussed text than Feustking's, Handel can address all the coloratura to the idea of vengeance

Example 4.4b

and the metaphorical arrow which is its instrument; he is not tempted to replicate the awkward change of gear found in *Almira* between two types of coloratura, one for 'Pluto's maw', the other for mocking laughter. Notable, too, in the Italian aria is an altogether greater variety of phrase-length.

In both 'Vanne in campo' and 'Eroica fortezza' free aria forms are refashioned into da capo arias. And since, from this stage in Handel's operatic career, the so-called da capo form is ubiquitous, this seems an opportune moment to define the type, and to introduce the terminology I propose to use throughout this chapter and the next.

Excursus 4.2 – The da capo aria

The da capo aria is a setting of a stanza of verse in two equal or nearly equal parts, of which the first is repeated after the second; the repetition is not written out but indicated by the words 'da capo' (from the beginning). In some arias the repetition is shortened in some way and the indication is then 'dal segno' (from the sign).

The Principal Section (A) generally falls into at least two major subdivisions, each a setting of the complete text of A: the first modulates to the dominant or some other closely related key (A1); the second returns to the tonic (or is entirely in the tonic) (A2). Often, after this apparently conclusive section, there is a further Coda-like setting, partial or complete, of the words of A.

These vocal parts of the Principal Section are normally framed in orchestral ritornellos. The Opening Ritornello and the Closing Ritornello are both in the tonic key; an Intermediate Ritornello is commonly found reinforcing the cadence at the end of A1. This Intermediate Ritornello is almost always much slighter than the Opening and Closing Ritornellos; it commonly confirms the new key reached towards the end of A1, but Intermediate Ritornellos that re-establish the tonic key are by no means exceptional.

Normally the Opening Ritornello is the source of all the thematic material. Commonly it falls into three distinguishable phases: Incipit – Continuation – Cadence (see Excursus 4.1 and Example 4.2).

The Middle Section (B) of the da capo aria is generally less structurally elaborate. Almost all the features of the A section are occasionally to be found, but usually it simply falls into two halves (B1, B2). Each is a setting of the full text of B, and each cadences on a different related key; in major-key arias the final cadence in B2 is most often on the mediant minor.

Agrippina: 'borrowings' and reworkings – Handel and Keiser

Like *Rodrigo*, *Agrippina* is full of music which Handel had reworked from earlier compositions. In quite a number of cases those earlier compositions were not his own; in fact they offer a perfect opportunity to examine the relationship between Handel's music and that of his senior colleague in Hamburg, Reinhard Keiser, from whose *Octavia* the majority of the 'borrowings' come. The complexity of the whole topic begins to be clearer too. The *Rodrigo* reworkings showed the fast-maturing Handel deliberately recomposing material to put it in a more modern and polished form. That practice of course continues in *Agrippina*, but sometimes the changes are scarcely more than nuances of expression or emphasis, and often it is difficult to know what impulse they stem from: what part deliberate choice plays, what part subconscious memory.

Though I put inverted commas around it, it is too late to object to the use of the word 'borrowing'. I think 'concordance' would be generally a more judicious term: but 'borrowing' has established itself and, as a metaphor with something of the smack of mercantile capitalism, it has a fine period ring. It was the term already adopted by Mattheson, who remarked: 'Borrowing is permissible; but one must return the thing borrowed with interest, [so that your music] is prettier and better than the pieces from which it is derived.'[13] In a contemporary literary context, Alexander Pope also used the mercantile metaphor: 'A mutual commerce makes poetry flourish', he wrote, 'but then Poets, like Merchants, shou'd repay with something of their own what they take from others; not like Pyrates, make prize of all they meet.'[14]

Handel worked in an age when to imitate, to 'borrow', was an integral part of all high art; but thanks to the researches of Handel scholars we have learned that in much of Handel's music, and perhaps especially in his second Italian opera *Agrippina*, this feature is no occasional flourish: there are dozens, if not hundreds of 'borrowings'. But what kind of 'borrowings' are they? Was Handel a 'pyrate' or an honest Hanseatic merchant? What musical interest do they have? What do they tell us about Handel as a composer of opera?[15]

Before that can be answered, it might be helpful to reflect briefly on the nature of Handel's genius:

First, obviously, he was a colossal musical personality, whose composing and performing skills together took the breath away, and overcame – not gradually, but instantaneously – all barriers of rank, religion and language. The 'together' is important; every time we speak of Handel the composer, we mean Handel the performer too.

Second: Handel the composer-performer made this sensational impact in an age when no particular weight attached to originality. In Rome, for example, he did not need to reinvent the chamber cantata every Sunday. His task was to say what needed to be said in a way that was apt to the occasion and intelligible to the audience; to say it eloquently and well, with irresistible rhetorical weight or beguiling charm or whatever was appropriate – so that it had the effect not of something unheard of before, but rather of Truth to Nature.

> Nature to advantage dress'd, [of course]
> What oft was thought, but ne'er so well expressed;
> Something whose truth convinc'd at sight we find,
> That gives us back the image of our mind.

13 Johann Mattheson, *Der vollkommene Capellmeister 1739*, facsimile edition, Margarete Reimann (ed.), *Documenta Musicologica V* (Kassel and Basel: Bärenreiter, 1954), p. 131, para. 81.

14 Letter to William Walsh, 2 July 1706, quoted in J. T. Winemiller, 'Recontexturalizing Handel's Borrowings, *JM* 15 (1997), 448.

15 A huge contribution to this topic has been made by John H. Roberts. My bibliographical references mention several, but by no means all of the publications by means of which Roberts has extended our knowledge – and, one sometimes feels, our perplexity – when we attempt to address the matter of Handel's 'borrowings'.

Third: in the eighteenth century, a meeting point of composing and performing was improvisation, and this formidable musician was really a composer-performer-improviser. From the time the young Handel arrived in Hamburg and bewitched Mattheson with his improvised fugues to the time of those late organ concerto performances when the blind Handel improvised within a framework of written-out orchestral ritornellos, he was admired as one of the supreme improvisers in an age when every educated composer was able to improvise at least competently. He could not have enjoyed this reputation unless he had had a superabundance of musical ideas always and instantly at his command. The gift demanded exceptional facility both of hand and mind – sometimes a facility freely exercised (though that freedom may have taken as its starting point one or other of the traditional ground basses like the *romanesca* or the *folia*), sometimes controlled by a (figured) bass. To judge from a remark in the dedication of his 1717 *Orchestre*, Mattheson felt that when it came to improvising over a figured bass, Handel was in a different league from every other player he had heard.[16]

To be able to do all these things so unhesitatingly in so many different contexts – German, Italian, English – Handel must have been a fast learner, whether it was Telemann and Keiser, or Corelli and Scarlatti, or Purcell and Arne he was learning from. He must have been a good listener; good at observing exactly how things were done and why, at trying them out for himself (imitating and borrowing), at storing them in his memory (by which I mean not just his mind but his fingers too). He obviously had 'the ability and the inclination to see and to hear, to discriminate and to choose, to animate what [he] had seen and heard with some spirit, and create it afresh with some skill'. The quotation is from Goethe, speaking about himself just a few weeks before his death.[17]

I select a group of arias which originate in material 'borrowed' from Hamburg, mostly from Keiser, but which also reflect the influence on Handel's work of Corelli (often a colleague of Handel's in the years preceding the premiere of *Agrippina*) and of Corelli's imitators and epigones. These particular 'borrowings' show Handel reworking music that originated in a lively, but provincial musical centre (Hamburg), to make it presentable for such cities as Rome, Florence and Venice (Rome in particular), which during the previous twenty years had come to regard the Corelli sonatas as a kind of encyclopedia of musical etiquette. For Corelli had distilled out of the somewhat ramshackle musical language of the middle decades of

[16] See *Documents I*, pp. 277 and 377.

[17] J. P. Eckermann, *Gespräche mit Goethe*, Friday, 17 February 1832. See further, p. 121.

the seventeenth century a repertory of musical procedures – contrapuntal gambits, harmonic sequences, cadence patterns, etc. – by means of which he spread a humane and civilised order over the whole tonal system. His younger contemporaries rejoiced in this new musical world, and disported themselves in it zestfully for decades. Handel was no exception.

One is tempted to describe 'Vaghe fonti' (*Agrippina* No. 29) as one of Handel's more shameless appropriations. Keiser's aria 'Ruhig sein' (from *Octavia*) is a moralising one, in which Seneca instructs an unappreciative Nero in the beauty of Stoic inner calm. ('Clear off with your calm,' Nero retorts, 'and mind your own business') (see Example 4.5a). The ritornello Incipit, the essential motif of the *Agrippina* aria, is there in every detail (except that the scoring in Keiser is vague, and Handel's 'borrowing' begins only at bar 3) (see Example 4.5b); the style of the song is the same too, gently flowing over a walking crotchet bass. That opening vocal phrase, as was common practice, is distilled from the preliminary bars at the start of Keiser's ritornello – the bars unused by Handel (see Example 4.5c).

Keiser, *Octavia*, 'Ruhig sein', bars 1-4

Example 4.5a

Handel, *Agrippina*, 'Vaghe fonti', bars 1-4

Example 4.5b

Keiser, *Octavia*, 'Ruhig sein' continued, bars 8-11

Example 4.5c

Handel, *Trionfo*, 'Crede l'uom', bars 6-9

Example 4.5d

Handel first appropriated this material in *Il Trionfo del Tempo e del Disinganno*, in No. 13, 'Crede l'uom', an aria sung by Disinganno as a warning against self-deception: amid the joys of life we may imagine that Time sleeps; but though all may seem calm, Time's ravaging work continues remorselessly. There is a nice little detail to be noted right at the start: since Handel has not used the opening two bars of Keiser's ritornello, he cannot properly simply 'borrow' the opening of Seneca's phrase either; it has to be rewritten on the basis of that part of the ritornello he has kept (see Example 4.5d).

In *Il trionfo* the aria does not express a state of mind to be aspired to and achieved by philosophy, but a deception to be resisted; perhaps that is the reason for the exaggeratedly somnolent quality of the coloratura. Handel's aria is more expansive than Keiser's (sixty-one bars to forty-five) and introduces some new material, notably rocking passages over dominant pedal points at bars 25–27 and 42–47, and florid melismas. Recorders are added to the four-part string scoring, turning it more clearly into drowsy descriptive music.

All this material is taken up again and finds its perfect home in *Agrippina*. The scene is set in a garden; through it winds a stream, flowing from a fountain beside which Poppea pretends to sleep. With the aid of this stage-set the aria ritornello is transformed into a descriptive sinfonia; the murmuring of the fountain and the winding course of the water through the grass provides an ideal pretext for the gentle coloratura already tried out in *Il Trionfo*. In the interest of theatrical functionality the whole aria is concentrated into thirty-six bars. And one detail shows Handel with, I suggest, the stage picture in his eye. Ottone's opening phrase is not, like Seneca's or Disinganno's, thematically derived from the ritornello, nor does it have their steadily moving bass. For the sinfonia-ritornello describes the scene, not Ottone: he comes into the garden, as it were by chance, and stops, spellbound, in what I take to be a tiny, rhythmically free apostrophe-cum-cadenza (see Example 4.5e).

Handel, *Agrippina*, 'Vaghe fonti' continued, bars 4-7

Example 4.5e

Another thought-provoking link connects *Agrippina* with Handel's own *Almira*. Why, in 'Io di Roma il Giove sono' (*Agrippina*, No. 43), when the Emperor Claudius is proclaiming himself to be the Jupiter of Rome, whose authority is to be shared with no one, does Handel choose to rework 'Move i passi' (*Almira*, No. 41), an aria in which Almira had declared that anyone allowing his footsteps to be guided by the blind God Cupid is heading for ruin? The very close resemblance between the arias is unmistakable – that the one is the starting point for the other unquestionable. The basic thematic material is the same; the orchestral fabric is relentlessly full throughout (in five or six parts in *Almira*, in four parts in *Agrippina*); both make identical use of a *Devise* opening; in both the crotchet tread of the harmony is unceasing, even to the extent that, by means of a modulation back to the dominant at the end of the B section, the music flows over into the da capo almost without its being noticed. So it is a concordance on a grand scale. Might it be an instance of the irony that John Sawyer has claimed in so many *Agrippina* borrowings, where the source of the borrowing seems to suggest a kind of sceptical subplot to what the character is ostensibly singing about?[18]

Maybe; maybe not. The question of what triggers a Handelian reworking or 'borrowing' is a fascinating one, so fascinating that it is difficult to avoid hallucinating. Here there are two points which might conceivably have stirred memories of his *Almira* aria in addition to Sawyer's irony. (And, incidentally and punningly, what sort of irony is it that here, of all places, in this most imperial of arias, Claudio 'borrows' not music by Keiser but Handel's own?) One is that a *Devise*-style opening is almost demanded by the opening line, 'Io di Roma il Giove sono', and the chaconne-like rhythm,

[18] J. Sawyer, 'Irony and Borrowing in Handel's *Agrippina*', *ML* 80 (1999), 531–59.

with its tendency to hemiola, provides the perfect rhetorical highlighting for the two crucial words 'Roma' and 'Giove'. The other is that appearing in the B section is the word 'ramminghi' – wandering, fugitive. Claudio uses it to describe other people, not himself, but the word is a perfect description for Almira's self-analysis too.

In any case, once Handel's memory had been jogged, the music was transformed. We are surely not deluding ourselves if we imagine Almira's aria as an expression of helpless, pathless wandering, while Claudio's seems to tramp as purposefully as a Roman legion. For what we are registering is the large-scale control of modulation – of tonal architecture – which Handel had by now acquired. In the *Almira* aria modulations ramble as directionless as Keiser's often do; in *Agrippina* they eye the final goal over magnificently broad vistas. At least, that is what happens in the A section, which modulates broadly from E minor to G and back again, using passing patches of chromaticism immediately before the clinching cadence phrases. In the B section, however (and this is why 'ramminghi' was worth highlighting), the music modulates G, B minor, A minor, G, half cadence on B, each new key centre hovering around the tonic like suppliants before the imperial audience chamber.

Memories took Handel back to Hamburg again in Pallante's 'Col raggio placido' (No. 37), another Keiser 'borrowing'. In the *Octavia* aria 'Costante ognor', Livia rejects the love of Tiridates, declaring that she will be 'constant in saying no'. It is an inscrutable aria, in which the bass that supports her song is doubled at the upper octave, even during the *Devise*, perhaps to give the music a kind of unadorned bluntness. The accompaniment of bars 16–21 is used as an Opening Ritornello (see Example 4.6a).

Handel saw that the Incipit of this ritornello (with the relatively unusual feature of the immediate upward sequential movement) had the potential for more energetic characterisation than Keiser had given it, and in his second Roman oratorio, *La Resurrezione*, turned it into a bass aria, in 3/8 rather than 6/8 metre: 'O voi dall'Erebo' (No. 6) for Lucifero's invocation of the powers of Hell. Handel 'borrowed' the first two bars of Keiser's aria (making four bars of his own aria); rewrote completely the answering phrase; removed the next, tonally dithering bars completely; transformed the diminished seventh of bar 9 into a sensational melodramatic frisson; and cadenced, again without reference to Keiser (see Example 4.6b). For much of the rest of the aria he used those sensational scales from the opening ritornello as the accoutrements of Lucifero whenever he was urging the infernal hosts to do battle.

Example 4.6a Keiser, *Octavia*, 'Constante ognor', bars 1–21

Example 4.6b *La Resurrezione*, No. 6, 'O voi dall'Erebo'

In *Agrippina* Handel again takes up the Keiser Incipit, together with the answering phrase he had written for Lucifero, and draws it out into a tour de force of compositional resourcefulness in the rather unpromising (and mercilessly revealing) *tutti unisoni* style, sustaining it from first bar to last (160 bars with da capo) with total tonal control and perfectly judged episodes of stasis and movement. The leaping coloratura at bar 28 is adapted from *La Resurrezione*; otherwise this is a completely new composition (see Example 4.6c).

Example 4.6c *Agrippina*, 'Col raggio placido', bars 1-16

Here too there is no very clear verbal or associative prompting to set Handel off. Sawyer's observation that there is 'striking discrepancy between words and music' may be accepted, but one might also underline the fact that this discrepancy has been composed specifically for the occasion; it has not just happened as the result of a supposedly labour-saving 'borrowing'. The ardent words are composed with tight-lipped dourness, without the faintest trace of tenderness or sensuality. That, as it happens, is a perfectly valid musical interpretation of the situation.

In all these cases the source of the 'borrowing' is clear enough, however mysterious the process may have been by which the 'borrowing' was transmuted into the Handelian aria. In many cases, however – Poppea's first aria, 'Vaghe perle' (No. 10) provides an excellent example – the music seems to be dipping into something fresh every few bars. To keep my comments to a manageable scale I shall identify just a few of its sources, starting with four self-borrowings, which I shall call the Winter, Spring, Summer and Autumn arias, the year being 1707.

In January 1707 in Rome Handel composed the cantata *Da quel giorno fatal*. The aria '*Lascia omai*', No. 3, imagines a mistress crossing the rivers of Hades in search of her dead beloved. It introduces a watery figuration – or is it a breezy one? – at any event something of a commonplace, one might think (see Example 4.7a).

Material from this winter cantata was reworked in the spring cantata *Clori, Tirsi e Fileno*, where, after a different Incipit, the watery semiquavers were transformed into birdsong, for in this aria, 'Va col canto lusingando', No. 3, Clori is reflecting how the nightingale beguiles his beloved with its song. The aria also adds a deliciously intertwining cadence phrase, and

Example 4.7a *Da quell giorno fatal*, No. 3, 'Lascia omai', bars 13–22

makes use of coloratura supported on 5/3–6/3 harmonic sequences (see Example 4.7b).

Example 4.7b *Clori, Tirsi e Fileno*, No. 3, 'Va col canto lusingando', bars 49–51, 58–60

In the autumn aria (we are now in Florence for *Rodrigo*) the Incipit and Continuation of the winter cantata ritornello and the intertwining cadence and touches of coloratura of the spring cantata are conjoined to provide much of the substance of Evanco's joyful love-song 'Il dolce foco mio' (*Rodrigo*, No. 35).

But meanwhile, in the summer, down in Naples now, Galatea has been singing about a mariner tossed on the ocean and guided to harbour by the stars ('S'agita in mezzo all'onde', *Aci, Galatea e Polifemo*, No. 10). It is no surprise to find that the watery figurations are back, but now thrown into higher relief, treated as the main substance of the aria, with the harmonies moving more spaciously. This aria makes no use of the intertwining cadences, nor really of the 5/3–6/3 coloratura sequences, but does open out the watery figuration with a new bass figure (see Example 4.7c).

Example 4.7c *Aci, Galatea e Polifemo*, 'S'agita in mezzo all'onde', bars 1–9

Poppea's 'Vaghe perle' draws freely on all those arias, using very fully the figuration that has hitherto served as water, birdsong and lover's flame; using also the 5/3–6/3 coloratura sequences and the intertwined cadence phrase (see Example 4.7d; also 4.7f).

Example 4.7d *Agrippina*, 'Vaghe perle', bars 1–9

After all of this, it is disconcerting to discover that it has to be accounted a 'borrowing' from Keiser. Octavia's 'Wallet nicht zu laut' indeed begins in a very similar way (see Example 4.7e):

Example 4.7e Keiser, *Octavia*, 'Wallet nicht zu laut', bars 1–8

and then later (as shown in Example 4.7f).

Example 4.7f Keiser, *Octavia*, 'Wallet nicht zu laut', bars 16–19

Moreover Poppea's cadence phrase remembers Keiser's too (see Example 4.7g).

I use the term 'remembers' deliberately, because to call such things 'borrowings' seems to me a slovenly use of language. What we are dealing with is a complex, perhaps rather sophisticated, and probably not entirely rational procedure, in which memory and association are certainly at work – more busily at work than any deliberate searching – and which I hope Handel

Example 4.7g *Agrippina*, 'Vaghe perle', bars 60–65

would have been happy to see described as '*Witz*'.[19] The word of course means Wit, but wit with rather specific connotations, as Johann Christoph Adelung's great Dictionary, published in five volumes between 1774 and 1786, makes clear: 'In the narrowest sense of the word, now the only one in general use, '*Witz*' signifies the capacity of the soul to discover similarities, and in particular hidden similarities.'[20]

All his life Handel was an attentive and observant listener, with a capacity to absorb and learn from everything he came across. Already by the end of the Italian period his mind teemed with memories and associations, between which cross-currents flowed incessantly, sometimes deliberately organised by *Witz*, sometimes, one might say, short-circuiting involuntarily.

[19] If we try to imagine Handel in Italy sitting at the harpsichord and recalling his days at the opera in Hamburg, as from time to time he must have done, would we be far wrong if we allowed a famous romantic tale to float into our minds? In E. T. A. Hoffmann's 'Ritter Gluck', the fictional revenant Chevalier Gluck sits at the 'Klavier' and from memory performs his *Armide* overture. He played 'the majestic march with complete fidelity to the original' reports the storyteller; 'but in the Allegro only Gluck's main ideas were woven in, and he introduced so many wonderful new turns of phrase that my astonishment grew and grew.'

[20] J. C. Adelung, *Grammatisch-kritisches Wörterbuch der hochdeutschen Mundart*, s.v. Witz. 'In der engsten, jetzt noch allein üblichen Bedeutung ist der Witz, das Vermögen der Seele, Ähnlichkeiten, und besonders verborgene Ähnlichkeiten, zu entdecken.' (Horace Walpole used the term 'Wit' to describe the way Sir Joshua Reynolds made use of famous prototypes in his own painting.)

Everything he heard was germane to his own musical language, his own inventiveness; everything helped him acquire greater mastery and range, and helped him to keep up to date. And by 'him' I mean Handel the composer-performer-improviser. Much of what he heard may have been no more than routinely competent, but sometimes the most unremarkable scraps of material needed only to be placed and coordinated by the organising mind of a master composer; sometimes he found good ideas crying out for a more effective context; and sometimes things stuck in his capacious memory with the classical rightness of a Latin tag. What is extraordinary – and not just in *Agrippina* – is how, time and again, Handel's 'borrowings' provide some of the most perfect matchings of music to dramatic situation in the opera: as they do, I would suggest, in the four pieces considered here.

A few pages back I quoted Goethe. It is worth quoting a fuller version of what Goethe was saying about the nature of his own achievement; any Handelian will find it remarkably suggestive.

> I have known artists who boast that they ... owe everything to their own genius. What fools! As if the world does not press in upon them at every step they take ... If one of these artists strolled through this room, casting fleeting glances at those sketches by the old masters which I have hung here, he must, if he had any talent at all, leave this place a different and a better man ... It's true, during my long life I have done and produced various things that I could certainly take some pride in. But if we are going to be honest, what did I have that was really mine, apart from the ability and the inclination to see and to hear, to discriminate and to choose, to animate what I had seen and heard with some spirit, and create it afresh with some skill.[21]

Another witness to Goethe's thoughts on that same February day in those last weeks of his life reports the following remark: 'Everything that I have heard and observed I have taken up and made my own ... My work is the work of a collective being who bears the name Goethe'.[22]

Rinaldo: virtuosity and expression

Since it is Handel's first London opera, *Rinaldo* marks another new beginning. But it is also a work of summation, a showcase for his gifts as a composer in the Italian style; and these are displayed with a youthful panache that has no parallel anywhere else in his work. Weaknesses, even asininities,

21 Eckermann, *Gespräche mit Goethe*.

22 The witness was Frédéric Soret, a painter friend of Goethe and Eckermann. He is quoted in R. Friedenthal, *Goethe: sein Leben und seine Zeit* (Munich: R. Piper, 1963), p. 729.

in the unfolding of the drama do not alter the fact that *Rinaldo* offers a sensational demonstration of those qualities of virtuosity and expressive flair for which Handel was already renowned. Flights of extraordinary brilliance are set off by passages of noble simplicity, by winsome and elegant dance strains, by sombre counterpoint, rich and complex beyond the imagining of any English composer of the age. For those with ears to hear, a new art was coming to birth in London.

One short passage from the second tableau of Act I (*Rinaldo*, Nos. 12–14), the scene of Almirena's abduction, epitomises the vast expressive range Handel now had at his fingertips. The abduction, accompanied by a tumultuous orchestral sinfonia (rather oddly, Handel calls it a Prelude), is preceded by a love-duet, 'Scherzano sul tuo volto', quite delicious in its light-heartedness; and it is followed by 'Cara sposa', a desolate elegy for the lost beloved, which Burney famously judged 'by many degrees the most pathetic song, and with the richest accompaniment, which had been then heard in England'.[23] And the emotional range goes even beyond that, since both duet and aria have strongly contrasting middle sections: an interlude of sweet mock-pathos in the former, an outbreak of frustrated rage in the latter. It is typical of the expressive virtuosity of *Rinaldo* that an unusually large number of arias and duets (some half dozen) have this kind of extreme contrast of mood and style between the principal and middle sections. And it is symptomatic of Handel's operatic acumen that such numbers are always placed at dramatically critical points.

The prodigality of invention is intensified by Handel's virtuosic use of the orchestra, another quality in which *Rinaldo* has no match among the later operas; it begins already with brilliant *concertino* episodes in the Overture. Of course *Rinaldo* is predominantly a work of continuo-accompanied recitatives and solo arias accompanied by an orchestra of strings, oboes and bassoons, and continuo. But its 'showcase' quality prompted Handel to break free from this norm more often than usual, for example by highlighting his star violinist, oboist or bassoonist in extensive solo passages. In arias for Argante in Act I (No. 5) and for Rinaldo in Act III (No. 38) he adds, respectively, three and four trumpets and drums to the standard orchestra. (Rinaldo's aria is preceded by a crusader march, similarly scored, which became popular enough to be adopted for a chorus of highwaymen in *The Beggar's Opera*.) The garden scene in Act I opens with a sinfonia for flageolet, recorders and solo viola, during which, in the words of the libretto, 'Birds are heard to sing' and live sparrows were in fact released over the heads of

[23] Burney, *A General History of Music*, vol. II, p. 674.

the audience at the premiere (good copy for the *Spectator*);[24] this sinfonia merges imperceptibly into Almirena's aria, 'Augelletti che cantate' (No. 11), during which the carolling of the bird-flageolet continues. Most thrilling of all, in the closing aria of Act II, 'Vo' far guerra' (No. 28), Handel himself took the audience by storm, breaking into the framing orchestral ritornellos with harpsichord improvisations of such startling brilliance that they have been claimed to have 'changed the history of keyboard music'.[25] Something of their character was preserved in transcriptions by William Babell, another virtuoso harpsichordist associated with the theatre orchestra.

Little of the opera's music is completely new; in much of it Handel takes up some of the best material he had invented and already worked over – sometimes several times – in the Italian years, or even in Hamburg. In almost all cases he gives it the finishing touch in *Rinaldo*: the perfect matching of proportions to material; the ideally judged context for an arresting idea; the final exquisite nuance for a melody. Three arias from the second tableau of Act II serve to show him at this kind of work.[26]

'Lascia ch'io pianga' (No. 22) evolved via 'Lascia la spina' (*Il trionfo*, No. 23) from the Act III sarabande in *Almira*. The sarabande provided the archetype (see Example 4.8a): the slowly moving blocks of harmony, the general melodic outline, the rhythmic strategy (defining the sarabande manner and then shifting from 1-bar to 2-bar segments in bars 5–8; an

Example 4.8a *Almira*, No. 52, 'Sarabande – Tanz von Asiatern', bars 1–8

[24] Addison's famous essay appeared in the *Spectator* on 6 March 1711; a large part of it is reprinted in Deutsch, pp. 35–6, and *Documents I*, pp. 204–6.

[25] G. Pont, 'Handel versus Domenico Scarlatti', *GHB* 4 (1991), 238.

[26] These and other reworkings are fully discussed in R. Kubik, *Händels Rinaldo* (Neuhausen-Stuttgart: Hänssler, 1982), pp. 70–106. Kubik helpfully provides many comparative music examples and a tabular overview of all the reworkings thitherto identified in *Rinaldo*.

almost identical strategy is followed in bars 9–16 to complete the design). The *Trionfo* reworking transformed all this.

The music of the dance becomes melody and bass in an aria, richly harmonised in four parts, framed by orchestral ritornellos, and reconfigured so as to form the Principal Section of a full da capo design; the rhythmic rigidity is softened, the melody shaped more expressively with passing notes and appoggiaturas (see Example 4.8b); and of course the completion of the aria form by the addition of a Middle Section provides the opportunity for a range of contrasting keys. If Handel had simply taken over the oratorio aria unaltered for *Rinaldo*, it would have been admired as one of the gems of the score. In fact there is not a phrase that is not in some degree rewritten: sometimes a matter of delicate nuance, sometimes a completely new idea.

Example 4.8b *Il trionfo del tempo*, No. 23, 'Lascia la spina', bars 23–30

First, to give greater directness to Almirena's appeal, Handel discards the Opening Ritornello. In the first phrase (bars 1–8) the rhythm becomes just a little more supple, the melody just a little more intense, thanks to the appoggiaturas in bars 4 and 7, the latter requiring a matching change in bass and harmony. (On the other hand, the changes of harmony which in *Trionfo* come on the second beats of the bars corresponding to 5 and 13 are for the moment held in reserve.) In the contrasting six-bar answering phrase (bars 9–14) the greater rhythmic suppleness continues, and the melodic climax (and the music's sarabande character) is reinforced by changes of harmony on the second beats of bars 9 and 11. At the reprise (bars 15–22) tiny changes in melody (bar 15) and in the bass (bar 17) preserve the expressive anxiety. The aria's B section distils into twelve bars what had occupied twenty-four in *Il trionfo*. Essentially these bars are modelled on the first eight bars of the B section of the earlier aria; but Handel treats the cadences more subtly, especially with the poignant disruption of the C major cadence at bar 38, and, sustaining the expressivity in this way, he spins out the melody for a further four bars.

'Abbrucio, avvampo e fremo' (No. 25) has, even by Handelian standards, an extended ancestry, some of which has already been recorded.[27] It derives from *Almira*, No. 43, 'Ob dein Mund', via the motet 'Saeviat tellus', *Rodrigo*, No. 2, 'Pugneran con noi', and *Apollo e Dafne*, No. 2, 'Spezza l'arco'. What distinguishes the *Rinaldo* aria from all those earlier versions is its focus on dramatic context – in musical terms its energy and density of material. The treatment of the Opening Ritornello, in which Incipit overlaps with Continuation (at bars 3–4), and Continuation overlaps with Cadence (at bar 5), sets the tone. It is trimmed from ten bars to seven by the excision of the coloratura that had run into the cadence in 'Pugneran con noi' and 'Spezza l'arco', and the cadence itself reverberates in humming rage until the voice begins to sing, Handel having shifted to this point the repeated chords he had cut from the cadence in the middle of the ritornello (it is the equivalent point to 'Pugneran con noi' bars 6–7 and 'Spezza l'arco' bars 5–6). Midway through the Principal Section, where 'Pugneran con noi' had lingered floridly in the tonic, 'Abbrucio' follows 'Spezza l'arco' in making an emphatic shift to the dominant key. There is no hint of a contrasting type of theme, as in 'Spezza l'arco bars 18–20, and the *Rinaldo* aria diffuses far less of its energy in coloratura. In the one passage where coloratura is dominant, Handel creates a graphically hostile effect by fracturing the flow of semiquavers and hurling the fragments backwards and forwards between voice and instruments (bars 19–20). The Closing Ritornellos in the *Rodrigo* and *Apollo e Dafne* arias are both full-length; in *Rinaldo* Handel abbreviates, essentially by omitting the Continuation – the quest for concentration never relaxes. And he modifies the Incipit by adapting it to the rhythm of the singing voice – a simple but clear instance of his habit of letting musical ideas evolve as he goes along.

The declamatory urgency of 'Abbrucio' is even more marked in the Middle Section of the aria. It is in continuo-song style, like the parallel passages in 'Pugneran con noi' and 'Spezza l'arco', but there is no trace of the relaxation into the flowing cadence phrases heard in the two earlier arias. This part of the *Rinaldo* aria looks harmless, but is in fact rather skilfully

[27] See pp. 105–6.

wrought. One notes how, in two unequal halves (B1, bars 32–35 and B2, bars 35–41), what was simply repeated in bars 32–33 (an arresting change of rhythm compared with all we have heard in the A section) is spaced out sequentially in bars 35–37, while bars 33–35 in B1 are stretched out by partial augmentation (bar 38) and an interrupted cadence with a touch of voice/bass imitation in bars 37–41.

Finally, 'Ah! crudel' (No. 27): the emotional model for the suicidal versus murderous impulses of this *scena* seems to come from the cantata *Agrippina condotta a morire*, No. 3, 'Come, o Dio'. From the opening bars of that aria Handel spins out a brief trio for oboe, bassoon and double bass to launch the Opening Ritornello. Out of that spare, acidulous start evolves an exceptionally rich seven-part texture (chiefly it comprises four parts against three parts in overlapping antiphony, and it has been developed out of the last movement, 'Si muora', of the cantata *Qual ti riveggio*), a fabric of broken, sighing fragments of motif which, after the ritornello has ended, continue to supply the accompaniment for Armida's song through much of the Principal Section. But the song itself comes from elsewhere; at least its opening phrase does. It is a reworking of what had previously formed the opening of the cantatas '*Un sospir*' (Florence 1707) and '*Ah crudel*' (Rome? August 1708), and had been used again in a cynically mock-pathetic operatic context in Nerone's 'Qual piacer' (*Agrippina*, No. 5). A phrase that Handel had designed and used three times, in slightly different forms, to stand out against bleakly stalking octaves (just continuo bass in the Florence cantata), in *Rinaldo* finds its ideal home embedded in an orchestral fabric of exceptional richness; and gradually the vocal line disintegrates to become one with the sighing antiphony of the orchestra.

The middle section of the aria – it is one of *Rinaldo's* radically contrasting B sections – comes from a different source, 'Parto, crudel' (*Rodrigo* No. 17). Typical is the recasting of the ritornello: the breathlessness that still affects some of the *Rodrigo* music gives way to Handel's mature spaciousness.

The mass of borrowings, revisions and recompositions stretching from *Almira* to *Rinaldo*, and on indeed to the next opera, *Il pastor fido*, provides extraordinarily interesting material for the study of Handel's ripening skills as a musical craftsman and as a composer of opera. Many of his *Rinaldo* reworkings – in so far as they were deliberate and fully conscious, as all the cases I have described clearly were – he seems to have regarded as definitive, and relatively little of this material recurs in later operas. Some was, however, fruitfully adapted in instrumental contexts. The reworkings of the principal section of 'Ah! crudel' in the first movements of the organ concerto Op. 4 No. 3 and the trio sonata Op. 2 No. 5 provide notable examples.

5 The music (2): its role in the drama

By the time he composed *Rinaldo* the still young Handel was a consummate master, and his operatic experience was already extensive and varied. Henceforth, for the next twenty-five years, whatever the financial and social and political complexities of the situation might be, his artistic purpose was largely stable: he would compose Italian opera for an English audience gathered in a public theatre in London. The fundamental musical question now was how he was to use his mastery to express and embody the dramatic themes that interested him.

The orchestra

The orchestra that played under Handel's direction in his London operas was a large and accomplished one; some of the men were real virtuosos. Eye- and ear-witness accounts of their playing are few, but all that do survive are admiring ones. The exact constitution of the orchestra at any particular time is never quite certain, but if we imagine a band of some twenty violins, four violas, half a dozen woodwind (oboes and bassoons), a continuo group of one or two harpsichords and theorbo, and half a dozen string basses (cellos and double basses) we shall not be far wrong.[1] Once or twice, in most operas, Handel found occasion to vary this palette by the addition of extra obbligato instruments: flutes or recorders; trumpets or horns. But even when he confined himself to the normal string and woodwind combinations with continuo, the scope for variety was considerable: strings could be used with or without woodwind doubling; the woodwind could operate separately from the strings, either in obbligato fashion or as a concertino group of oboes and bassoon. And the string ensemble could itself be variously divided and subdivided: into four or three parts; with *unisoni* violins above the continuo; or indeed *tutti unisoni*

1 Contemporary accounts of the opera orchestra survive from 1710 (Documents 95 and 96 of Vice Chamberlain Coke's theatrical papers); 1728 (Pierre Jacques Fougeroux); 1733 (Sir John Clerk of Penicuik); see Donald Burrows, 'Handel's London Theatre Orchestra', *EM* 13 (1985).

including the continuo. The two or three parts of the upper strings lent themselves to all manner of permutations too: unison violins with independent violas; violins divided, with violas doubling second violins; with a small group of third violins separated off from the rest to reinforce the independent violas; and so on. During the course of an aria such groupings are likely to be dissolved and then again re-formed, perhaps in some slightly different permutation. In some of the more delicately scored operas, *Flavio* being an excellent example, Handel seems to take a particular delight in such procedures.

Normally any extra instruments were used because of their traditional, symbolic associations: the military connotations of the trumpets, for example, or the pastoral connotations of the recorders. But very occasionally Handel did seem to be exploring the power of instrumental colour in a more than traditional way – to have had some intuition that there was more to timbre, to the colour of instrumental sound than could be rationally explained. There was nothing extraordinary about obbligato horns in hunting arias; but the use of the solo horn in 'Va tacito e nascosto' (No. 14 in *Giulio Cesare*) is decidedly unusual; the huntsman goes not clamorously and convivially in search of his prey, but furtively, and the softly stepping horn sounds a rare note of mystery. And when, in *Orlando*, in the aria 'Già l'ebro mio ciglio', No. 35, the deranged hero is being lulled into healing sleep, and Handel chooses to accompany the singing with two *violette marine* – sounding as one might imagine muted violas in an echo chamber – the aura of instrumental magic is strong indeed.

Memorable as such colours help make certain arias, the effect is of no more than local significance. But a larger claim can be made: that sometimes Handel employs the orchestra in a way that helps give a particular opera a character peculiarly its own, a unique *colorito* – to use the Verdian term. The most obvious, indeed sensational, example of this has already been discussed, for it is provided by his very first London opera, *Rinaldo*.

However, in *Rinaldo* the treatment of the orchestra is not really an integral part of a dramatic theme at all. That opera was a manifesto: it was designed to demonstrate the full expressive scope of Italian opera as an art form, and in particular the dazzling gifts of the young Handel. A carnivalesque prodigality of orchestral colour supplied much of the evidence. The *colorito* of later operas is more discreet. *Giulio Cesare*, sometimes linked with *Rinaldo* on the grounds of its orchestral richness, in fact has a far less varied instrumental palette, but uses it in a more dramatically pointed way. It has all the customary instrumental embellishments: the hunting horn in 'Va tacito e nascosto' has already been mentioned; flutes or recorders add their sighing plangency to several of the arias of regret or loss; No. 20, 'Se in fiorito ameno prato' is a birdsong aria with solo violin obbligato. But these are commonplaces; it is in the sumptuous colouring of the dramatic frame that this most epic of Handel's operas displays its distinctive grandeur: to be specific, with the four horns, which add lustre to the opening chorus, and which return in sinfonia and chorus in the opera's final scene. Furthermore, enclosed within the brassy panoply of victorious armies is the story of an erotic passion very different from the tender bonds of *promessi sposi* which form the emotional heart of so many other Handel operas. The world-historical consequences of the Caesar–Cleopatra relationship is brought to sounding life in the great scene at the start of Act Two. The double orchestra with harp and theorbo pulsating through it surely evokes more than a 'seduction' – a commonly preferred term for this scene – and quite overrides the ostensible bewilderment or uncertainty of the dramatic situation. It is rather as if the congress of the lovers has set the cosmos throbbing in a *musica mundana* not quite dissimilar from Orpheus's.[2]

An utterly different *colorito* distinguishes the operas on either side of *Giulio Cesare: Flavio* and *Tamerlano*, both of which do without brass instruments entirely. In *Tamerlano* this contributes to the claustrophobic atmosphere that both Dean and Keates have commented on. It is not that powerful, conquering warriors are lacking, simply that their power is manifest not in public show but in prison-cell sadism. Other features add to the 'sparse, bare, dark' atmosphere. Even when different instrumental colours are added – transverse flutes in 'Deh lasciatemi' (No. 9); clarinets in 'Pur che mi nasca' (No. 17) – they play next to nothing in the way of free-ranging obbligato parts, but simply touch in a nuance or two of light or shade. Only in the duet 'Vivo in te' (No. 29) do transverse flutes, doubled by recorders, sound a distinct note, shadowing the singing voices with melancholy echoes and antiphonies. 'Sparse and bare', too, is Handel's treatment of the standard string and woodwind tutti: in *Tamerlano* he prefers to mass them all together on a single line (considerably more arias have this two-part treble-bass scoring than have the 'standard' à4 texture; almost twice as many as are scored à3). The opera's metrical structure contributes its part to the austerity: 4/4 outnumbers all other time signatures put together.

In this last particular the likewise brass-less *Flavio* contrasts as sharply with *Tamerlano* as it does with *Giulio Cesare*, for here as much of the music

[2] See 'Possente spirto', the Act III centrepiece of Monteverdi's *Orfeo*.

is written in the light-footed 3/8 metre as in 4/4. The modest scoring also has a very different effect, one of delicacy and intimacy that plays in nicely to the ironies of the drama. In *Flavio*, even in the Overture, Handel prefers scoring à3 to scoring à4.

The shape of an opera: frames and points of articulation

How dramatic works begin and how they finish are vital matters, especially if they are dramatic works set in a social frame, as eighteenth-century operas were. Only slightly less critical is the placing of the intermediate marks of articulation – the handling of climaxes and points of repose along the way. So I shall investigate next the role of music in the overall 'architecture' of the opera: the way music is used to frame the drama in Overture and Finale, to get the action under way at the start of an act, and to bring it to some temporary climax at act ends. To examine the operas under these aspects is to find clear confirmation of the fact that such frames and points of articulation were one of the means by which Handel staked his claim to be the controlling creative intelligence in the whole enterprise. At each step of his career the tendency became a little more pronounced; and at each step he departed a little further from the presuppositions of those theatre poets of the day for whom it was axiomatic that the shape of the drama was the shape the poet gave it.

Early operas (1705–15)

The outer frame – Overtures and Finales:

Almost always in a Handel opera the starting point is an 'Ouverture' in the French style. *Almira* has a curious example of the type: the Presto being non-fugal, and the return of the Adagio – a frequent feature of these movements – coming not at the close of the Presto but in the middle.[3] In the operas that follow *Almira* several of the overtures include distinctive, and appropriately distinctive, features in the fugal movement: the melodramatic breaks in continuity in *Agrippina*, the highlighting of virtuoso soloists in *Rinaldo*, the French style woodwind trio in *Amadigi* are all features that play in nicely to the style of the operas they introduce. But it would be difficult to claim that such characterisation of the fugal Allegro in the spirit of what follows became an important principle for Handel. After *Agrippina* all the overtures are extended with extra movements; indeed, from *Rinaldo*

[3] There should presumably be another 'Adagio' at bars 48–49.

onwards they have turned into small-scale concertos, closing with a final movement which is dance-like in character and (in all cases but *Teseo*) labelled as such.[4] *Il pastor fido* has a whole suite of dances. It is very likely that such suite-like overtures originated as free-standing concertos composed for some different non-theatrical purpose.

But while the overtures have become sumptuous affairs, the finales in these early operas are very slight, with a short chorus following a denouement in simple recitative; in *Amadigi* the chorus is extended by a Trio section for the lovers and a short dance based on the same material.

Starting the dramatic action and articulating the acts:

In none of these early operas is there a link between the style of the overture or its final dance and the start of the dramatic action. In all but one of them the first scene starts from scratch with a simple recitative; for this is one place where, for a few years, Handel was prepared to continue to do what he had learned to do in Italy, accepting the respective roles of poetry and music in accord with the beliefs of the best 'reform' librettists of the age. The exception is *Il pastor fido*, which starts with a continuo song for Mirtillo which serves to identify the principal theme of the opera – his difficulty in winning the love of Amarilli. It is noteworthy that this first Handelian example of operatic action beginning with 'full music' should be in a pastoral drama. Second and third acts also begin, in the great majority of cases, with simple recitatives, and the exceptions in *Rinaldo* Act II and *Teseo* Act III seem largely accidental matters: the five-act structure of *Teseo* inevitably occasions a number of irregularities.

First and second acts always end with big arias, perhaps with obbligato instruments, perhaps with metaphor texts.

Excursus 5.1 – the overture to *Rodrigo*

I have said nothing yet about the overture to *Rodrigo* because it is such a curious case. Although Handel's autograph was probably written some time in 1707, its heading, spelt 'Overture', not 'Ouverture', suggests either that it was added after he came to England,[5] or that Handel, though still

[4] The English spelling 'Overture' in *Rinaldo* is perhaps no more than what Handel felt was a courtesy to his new audience. In a similar spirit he had called the overture to *Agrippina* a 'Sinfonia', without its French Overture character being much compromised.

[5] This is the suggestion in Dean and Knapp, *Handel's Operas 1704–1726*, p. 111.

in Italy, had some reason for addressing the music to an English audience.[6] What is more, this rather out-the-way piece enjoyed the surprising distinction of being the first music by Handel to be published in England. Several months before the composer reached London, it was issued by John Walsh as a 'New Set of Tunes compos'd by an Italian Master'; it formed part of a series of more than fifty sets of such 'tunes' taken from plays and semi-operas, and had apparently been performed in the centenary revival of Ben Jonson's *Alchemist* at the Queen's Theatre in January and February 1710.[7] Curtis Price notes the suggestive coincidence that Handel's *Rodrigo* overture forms exactly the sort of set of pieces required in a production in the English theatre: four of the eight tunes could have been grouped in pairs to form the First and Second Music, the remaining four could have served as Act Tunes, and the Overture itself would have followed any Prologue, immediately before the rise of the curtain on the first scene of Act One.

To the best of my knowledge there is not a shred of evidence that Handel designed his 'Overture' with such considerations as these in mind. Nevertheless, someone must have delivered it to London long before Handel arrived there. To conjecture: the situation seems to depend on some Englishman who met Handel during his years in Italy, admired his music, perhaps chatted with him about the sort of theatre music cultivated in London, and then took back home with him a copy of one of Handel's most suite-like concertos, composed, or adapted, or merely entitled ('Overture') for an English audience, perhaps partly to encourage the growing partiality for Italian music in London ('compos'd by an Italian master'), and partly to whet theatre audiences' appetite to hear more of this particular Italian master.

None of this has any bearing on the question of whether or not the music was played at the Florence premiere of *Rodrigo*.[8]

The Royal Academy operas (1720–28)

The outer frame – Overtures and Finales:

With *Radamisto* a new level of framing organisation is immediately apparent. The Royal Academy years may have been the time when opera projectors

[6] That Handel was a man known about and talked about in London well before he came to England is suggested by the account of *Agrippina* which appeared in the *Post-Boy* for 28–31 January 1710. See *Documents I*, pp. 175–6. See also p. 16 in Chapter 1.

[7] C A. Price, 'Handel and the Alchemist', *MT* 116 (1975), 787.

[8] See Chapter 4, p. 102.

in London looked most admiringly at Italian *opera seria*, but as far as Handel was concerned, it marked a phase where his music's precedence over his librettist's poetry was to be asserted a little more emphatically. *Radamisto* in this respect marks a notable advance. The Overture makes no return to the opening style at the end of the fugue; instead, it closes in the tonic key, without a concluding dance, and leads directly not into a recitative but into full music, an *arioso* scene-opener, 'Sommi Dei', which identifies a central motif of the opera: that suffering humanity is in the hands of the gods. Can it be chance that its opening vocal phrase echoes the opening of the Overture? Ballets close each act, following directly on substantial vocal numbers: aria in Act One; duet in Act Two; chorus in Act Three. The procedure is particularly notable in Act Three, for there the ballet forms a pair of instrumental variants, in the manner of a Variation Partita, on the large-scale *coro*.

In the second version of *Radamisto* all these ballets are omitted: but Handel preserves the effect of an imposing finale by preceding the *coro* with a second large-scale duet (No. 36, 'Non ho più affanni'),[9] and preceding that by a quartet (No. 35, 'O cedere o perir'). Most Royal Academy operas follow this second version of *Radamisto* in including a (second) big duet in the final scene to give musical weight to the denouement.

Continuing from the Overture; articulating the acts:

After *Radamisto*, *Muzio Scevola* and *Floridante*, Handel returns in *Ottone* to the practice of adding dance movements or airs to the overtures: *Tamerlano*, *Rodelinda*, *Scipione* and *Siroe* all have them. In *Giulio Cesare* we find a striking variation on the idea: the final dance movement of the Overture (a grandiose minuet) follows the rise of the curtain, and by the addition of chorus and resplendent orchestration is turned into a Triumph Scene. Moreover, it leads directly into an *arioso*, which differs from earlier examples in being richly scored and full of extensive bravura passages – being, in fact, exactly like the Principal Section of a full-scale da capo aria.

Tamerlano is (apart from the untypical *Flavio*) the first Royal Academy opera to discard the Act I *arioso* starter, having instead a free mixture of recitative and instrumental music – a *scena* in fact – that coordinates the music with the start of the dramatic action in an even more direct manner. This becomes the common practice in the later Academy operas: the action may be claustrophobically gloomy, as here; or solemn (*Admeto*, *Siroe*); or thrillingly spectacular (*Alessandro*, *Riccardo primo*).

[9] There has already been one, 'Se teco vive il cor', at the end of Act Two.

Once the opera has been launched in such ways as these, the formal articulation remains, for some years, the standard *dramma per musica* procedure: nothing much is made of the start of an act, but it comes to a rousing conclusion. Either in Act One or Act Two the rousing conclusion will include a grand duet; the exception is *Flavio*, where the off-beat plot requires a duet, after a short recitative, at the very start of the opera. The vast and magnificent first act of *Alessandro* comes to a fittingly impressive close in a temple scene. This begins with what sounds like the start of a French-style Overture (though it is labelled 'Sinfonia'); between that and the start of a fugal Allegro a brief recitative intervenes; and the fugal Allegro, after some fifteen bars of serious contrapuntal business, is gradually metamorphosed into the introduction to a solemn *accompagnato*; the unique Cuzzoni–Faustina duet, 'Placa l'alma' follows; and the act ends with 'Da un breve riposo', one of the most grandiloquent of Handel's arias for Senesino.

By this time, after Faustina joined the company, Handel had decided that acts needed not only impressive closing movements but musically significant starts too. The third act of *Scipione* was his last to open with simple recitative. After *Scipione*, accompanied recitative or *arioso* is used for the opening of Acts Two or Three rather than Act One. In two operas, *Scipione* and *Admeto*, freestanding overtures are used to start the second acts.[10]

Lotario and the 'Second Academy' operas (1729–34)

Again, the opera that initiates a new phase of Handel's career marks a new stage in the richness of the musical framing. The most important feature, all but ubiquitous in the later operas, is the use of sinfonias to introduce the second and third acts. Both *Lotario* examples could be mistaken for the opening ritornellos of arias, and do in fact run on directly, not into arias, but into accompanied recitatives, and do therefore have a strongly scenic character. Soon, however, Handel came to prefer a type of sinfonia which has often been compared with a Purcellian act-tune, sonorously harmonised, often allemande-like in character, in a binary form of two roughly (or exactly) equal halves, but rarely with any obvious bearing on the scene introduced. Purcell comes to mind in *Lotario*'s fine Overture, too, where, in the principal Allegro movement, the vaguely fugal procedures that do from time to time make their presence felt are upstaged by a quasi-ostinato

[10] This was the first time since *Almira* that Handel had started an act in this way: in the Hamburg opera, however, it had been for Act Three.

ground bass motif. This recurs in many of the keys through which the music modulates, but is suspended to manage the modulatory episodes themselves, to cadence, and to enlarge the breathing space at climactic points.

In other respects, too, the musical framing in *Lotario* is notable: an *arioso* at the start of Act One proclaims the theme of the opera; splendid metaphor arias on the grandest scale conclude the first two acts, and the final scene in Act Three has both duet and chorus, with only four bars of simple recitative to separate them. While relatively brief, this gavotte-like final chorus is a striking conception where the first violins play an instrumental 'double' on the gavotte theme which, simultaneously, the sopranos are singing.

After *Lotario*, overtures are generally of the small-scale *concerto da camera* kind: in the French style for two movements with, at the close of the fugal movement, either a coda returning to the 'over-dotted' style of the opening movement, or a link into a concluding dance. The exceptions are *Sosarme*, which has an unusual opening movement in 3/2 time, and the two Metastasio operas, *Poro* and *Ezio*, where only a two-movement overture is supplied, though *Ezio* has a concluding Gavotte in some sources; and in any case, after the rise of the curtain there follows a March, serving to launch the stage action to the strains of orchestral music, in the manner of *Giulio Cesare*.

Sosarme follows *Lotario* in having something of a composite Act Three finale in which a duet for the two principals runs, after only the shortest of recitatives, into the closing chorus. Other operas mix soloists and full ensemble in a freer way, basing the chorus on a preceding aria (*Arianna*) or duet (*Poro*), or providing a whole series of solo verses, culminating in the choral finale (*Ezio*).

Covent Garden and later (1734–41)

By this stage Handel seems to have felt that his French Overtures (with suite-like extensions available if required), his act-tune-like sinfonias, his action-launching accompanied recitatives or *ariosi*, his climactic (often metaphor) arias, his strategically placed ensembles and his variously elaborated final scenes provided him with all the means he required for giving his opera an 'architecture' in which the unfolding of the dramatic action could in its broadest terms be articulated by the music. His framing resources had, in short, all been displayed by the time of *Lotario*, and for the later operas it will be sufficient to comment on the unusual cases.

Clearly the most interesting come from his first season at Covent Garden, when a small chorus and Marie Sallé's ballet group formed part of the company: in 1735–36 Handel's operas came closer to the spirit of masque than they had ever been. Ballets were added to the Covent Garden revivals of *Arianna* and *Il pastor fido*, and *Ariodante* and *Alcina* were planned from the start with ballet forming an integral part of the action. In *Ariodante* ballet gives emphasis and distinction to the ends of each act: convivial social dance in Act One, symbolic-psychological dance in Act Two, courtly ceremonial dance in Act Three; and the framing function of the dances is underlined when the gavotte from the Overture returns as part of the courtly dance sequence in the *scena ultima*.

In *Alcina* the frame is necessarily a little more complicated because, within the customary outer frame of Overture and closing chorus or finale, there is an inner frame by means of which the action is shifted into and out again from Alcina's enchanted realm. Instead, therefore, of a masque-like conclusion to Act One, the equivalent scene of *Alcina* is shifted back almost to the start of the act, where a sequence of chorus, gavotte, sarabande, menuet and second gavotte follows (after only a short recitative scene and an aria for Morgana) the musette and menuet that concluded the Overture. The closing scene of Act Three mirrors this arrangement, just one recitative and aria being placed in the midst of a denouement containing three quite distinct choruses, a terzetto, an *entrée* and a *tamburino* (this last providing the material for the last of the three choruses). In Alcina's great *scena* at the end of Act Two the psychological symbolism of the ballet – of *songes agréables* and *songes funestes* and of their '*combat*' – is even clearer than it would have been in *Ariodante*, the opera for which they seem originally to have been composed.[11]

Next season, though Sallé had now left, *Atalanta* also had a masque-like finale, inspired by the fact that the opera was composed for the Royal Wedding in April 1736. The splendour here, however, is less of song and dance than of song and spectacle: a *deus ex macchina* in the person of Mercury descending in a cloud, a richly adorned Temple of Hymen, and a firework display: 'there is a row of blue fires burning in order along the ascent to the temple; a fountain of fire spouts up out of the ground to the ceiling, and two more cross each other obliquely from the sides of the stage; on the top is a wheel that whirls always about, and throws out a shower of gold-colour, silver, and blue fiery rain.'[12] For some years this 'celebrated Fire Music', as it came to be called, enjoyed an independent existence as a concert item.

[11] On the rather confusing matter of the ballet music Handel composed for the 1735–36 season, see Donald Burrows' Preface to his edition of *Ariodante*, *HHA*, II. 32, especially at pp. xxii–xxiii.

[12] Letter of 11 June 1736, Thomas Gray to Horace Walpole; in Deutsch, p. 410.

The *Atalanta* finale also marked 'the hilarity of the occasion'[13] by adding to the scoring a single trumpet, to be played by the great virtuoso Valentine Snow. With arresting effect Handel also adds this single trumpet to all movements in the Overture.[14] He takes the matter of *colorito* no further than that, but, setting aside the special case of the opening scene of *Giulio Cesare*, *Atalanta* also provides the first, indeed the only case of Handel's beginning a new act with a chorus (Act Two). In the last operas, *Imeneo* and *Deidamia*, unsurprisingly since Handel's thoughts were by this time so much occupied with oratorio and ode, the chorus became as important a part of his operatic architecture as the overture and act-tune sinfonia.

Verse and music: metre, rhythm, rhetoric: *Rodelinda*

At school in Halle, Handel would have studied rhetoric, and before he left school he would have been familiar with the academic exercise of analysing poetic texts in the formal terms of rhetoric. This must have had a deep-seated, if not always fully conscious influence on his understanding of his own art of music. For he lived in an age which, in trying to deepen its understanding of the venerable aesthetic principle of 'imitation', was becoming increasingly thoughtful and therefore increasingly self-conscious about the relationship between the arts: between music and painting; between music and architecture. There was no doubt, however, that the crucial relationship was that between music and poetry. Had Handel been a man more disposed to analytical speculation, had his creative urges been less exuberant, he might have joined the ranks of the several Lutheran cantors who, out of their practical musical experience, were moved to publish textbook treatises on musical rhetoric.[15] That was not his way; but that does not mean that he did not understand perfectly well the intimacy of the relationship between poetry and musical expression. That understanding can only have been deepened by his experiences in the Hamburg opera house, and his friendship with Mattheson. And while, already in those years and forever afterwards, he was to grant a fuller role to counterpoint and to orchestral

13 The phrase is Burney's: *A General History of Music*, vol. II, p. 800.

14 It is more immediate in impact than the horns of *Giulio Cesare* (or *Ezio* or *Arianna*), which are held in reserve for the extra-curricular movements (the minuets in *Giulio Cesare* and *Arianna*, the march in *Ezio*).

15 D. Bartel, 'Rhetoric in German Baroque Music: Ethical Gestures', *MT* 144 (2003), 15–16, cites several of these. It was a particular enthusiasm of Lutheran musicians because the eloquence with which the word (the Word) was proclaimed was so central a concern in Lutheran theological education.

colour than Mattheson or the more 'progressive' opera composers of the day would have done (it is probably an echo of Handel's voice that can be heard in Mainwaring's observation that Hasse's operas were 'remarkable for his fine elevated air, with hardly so much as the shew of harmony to support it'[16]), nevertheless, at least since the time of his friendship with Telemann,[17] he would have recognised that the kernel of the whole matter was to be found in melody, in the way in which the singing voice utters the poetic text. For our purposes, therefore, the term 'rhetoric' may be understood in its plain English dictionary sense as 'the art of persuasive (musical) speech.' The corollary of that is that to perform this music well, we must understand what it means to say.[18]

Rodelinda, for many Handelians the most beautiful of all his operas, provides an excellent focus for examining how intimately his music feeds on the verses written by his librettist. It is a balanced and spacious work, with nothing of the frantic scrambling through the action which mars some of the librettos prepared for Handel, but even in *Rodelinda* (comparing the libretto set by Handel with the Florence libretto on which it was modelled) cuts in the recitative were drastic: approximately half of it (close on 650 lines) was removed. Of Salvi's aria texts, on the other hand, three-quarters were kept (twenty-one out of twenty-eight). Moreover, those that were not kept were not simply cut out; they were replaced by different aria texts, and this was done not to improve the poetry but to give the aria a different expressive or dramatic point. Other arias were added where Salvi had none. Given the probability that these changes were made under instruction from Handel himself,[19] the arias, particularly those added in previously aria-less passages as opposed to those that replace Salvi's own aria texts, make an interesting group:

In I.i. No. 1, 'Ho perduto il caro sposo'
In I.vi. No. 7, 'Dove sei, amato bene?'
In II.vi. No. 22, 'Ritorna, o caro e dolce mio tesoro'
In III.ultima. No. 34, 'Mio caro, caro bene'

16 Mainwaring, *Memoirs*, p. 117; cited in Deutsch, p. 372.

17 See Telemann's memories of his early meetings with Handel published in Mattheson's *Ehrenpforte*; in *Documents I*, p. 31–2.

18 I am paraphrasing an idea of Nikolaus Harnoncourt, whose topic, however, ranges well beyond my immediate concern with music and verse. See Nikolaus Harnoncourt, *Musik als Klangrede: Wege zu einem neuen Musikverständnis* (Munich and Kassel, 1985), pp. 25–6.

19 See A. V. Jones, 'The Composer as Dramatist: Handel's Contribution to the Libretto of *Rodelinda*', *ML* 87 (2007).

What is immediately striking when one lifts out these four arias for separate consideration is that each of them has been designed for a quite specific musical need. The first two complement one another, 'Dove sei' being the matching response to 'Ho perduto il caro sposo'. Just as No. 1, the wife-to-absent-husband lament, provides the emotional keynote for the opening group of scenes, so No. 7, the husband-to-absent-wife lament, supplies the lyrical heart to Bertarido's solemn ruminations in the royal cemetery-cum-cypress grove. In the case of 'Ritorna o caro e dolce mio tesoro', it must surely have been a request from the composer that prompted the unusually long, hendasyllabic lines, which Handel uses to achieve an exceptional breadth of phrase. Of No. 34 the opposite seems to be true, the music suggesting that what above all things Handel wanted here was a text in which key words or tight little knots of three or four words could be repeated and juggled with and danced with more or less *ad libitum*: that at least is what, with the ostensibly feeble opening line in 'Mio caro, caro ben', Haym provides. The aria rolls back the mood of Rodelinda's previous aria, 'Se'l mio duol', in a lyrical discharge of personal joy before the more formal celebration of the finale.

Once the placing of the arias, their dramatic function and form have been settled, composition can begin. It is a principle of Handel's musical rhetoric that the sense of the words must be absolutely clear; such poetic beauty as they may possess can always be savoured, because the melismas, the word repetitions, the fragmentation of phrase that often obscure the text in later stages of the aria, never take over until the words have been heard once without any such adornment or dislocation. It is also the case that the general rhythmic character of the aria arises very naturally from the metre. This is clearest with the more extreme metres. I have already cited 'Ritorna, o caro e dolce mio tesoro': for several passages in this aria Haym's *endecasillabi* prompt Handel to compose music which, despite the time signature, is in 18/8 time. *Quinario* metres, though not, as it happens, the example in *Rodelinda* (No. 26, 'Quanto più fiera') tend to be reflected in paratactic accumulations of short musical phrases.[20] In fact, while Handel's mastery of large-scale rhythm was exceptional and very personal, on a small scale he did not really need to invent rhythms at all when he was composing Italian verse; for there was already available for each poetic metre a range of natural musical matches. The examples at Example 5.1 show some very simple but characteristic instances.

[20] A good example is 'So chi t'accesi', No. 9 in *Ezio*.

(a)

Example 5.1a *Rodelinda*, No. 14, 'Confusa si miri', bars 28–32. *Senari*: the syllabic delivery of the verse is unaffected by the few passing and auxiliary notes

(b)

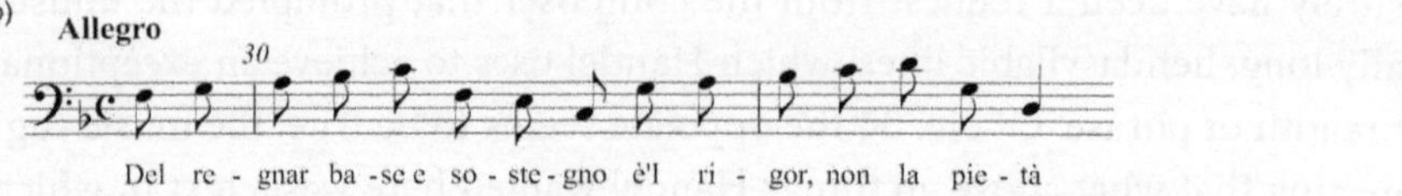

Example 5.1b *Rodelinda*, No. 18, 'Tirannia gli diede il regno', bars 29–31 (middle section). *Ottonari*: see also Example 5.3a[21]

(c)

Example 5.1c *Rodelinda*, No. 20, 'Con rauco mormorio', bars 11–13. *Settenari* (with *quinari* final lines in each half): there is a shift of scansion to match the shift of accent in line two of the verse – a typical feature of *settenari*

Example 5.1b is taken from the Middle Section of the aria, where such correspondences are often clearest. But the crucial issue really is how the sung part of the aria begins: this is where Handel will give the singer an opportunity to arrest and direct the listener's attention by the rhetorical flair with which, first time round, the verse is presented. It is the point where, in his early operas he had often proclaimed the theme of the aria with a *Devise*. And although that particular pattern was uncommon in the later operas, the juncture remains critical. The presentation will be essentially syllabic (as in the examples already cited); passing and auxiliary notes are used, sometimes abundantly, provided they do not compromise the clarity of the text, and provided they enhance its sense expressively: the quivering rage in No. 2, 'L' empio rigor del fato' (see Example 5.2) – the confident facing of the tempest in No. 26, 'Quanto più fiera'.

[21] Verdi was still complaining about 'those damned notes on the upbeat' that tradition required of a composer setting *ottonario* verses (Letter to Boito, 10 January 1881).

Example 5.2 *Rodelinda*, No. 2, 'L'empio rigor del fato', bars 21–28

Within this opening line the very first words may be further singled out for expressive emphasis, usually by prolonging or augmenting them (as in Example 5.2) in relation to the predominant rhythmic match of verse and music. In Garibaldo's two arias this procedure becomes an aspect of characterisation, sounding from the outset a strutting, muscle-bound note of menace (see Examples 5.3a and 5.3b).

(a)

Example 5.3a *Rodelinda*, No. 5, 'Di Cupido', bars 31–35

(b)

Example 5.3b *Rodelinda*, No. 18, 'Tirannia gli diede il regno', bars 7–9

Once the first exposition of the idea expressed in this fusion of music and poetry is complete, the poetry is likely to be dissolved into sound – Apollo yields to Dionysus – and quite commonly the beginning of the process comes at the close of the opening chunk of text: its final syllable will break loose, and the melodic and/or rhythmic style of that breaking loose will be a first intimation of the delights to come: in No. 31, 'Se fiera belva ha cinto' (in *settenari*), it is a florid symbol of freedom; in No. 30, 'Se 'l mio duol' (in *ottonari*), a cry of bewildered despair. In No. 23, 'Tuo drudo è mio rivale' (in *settenari*), blunt declamation breaks into hectoring coloratura, as if an execution warrant were being signed with a flourish. Sometimes, provided the clarity of the text is not compromised, a word falling a little earlier in the verse lends itself to this kind of treatment. A good example in No. 12, 'Sono i colpi della sorte', is the 'forte' that explodes into coloratura in

Example 5.4 *Rodelinda*, No. 12, 'Sono i colpi', bars 8–12

the midst of regular phrases of *ottonario*-conditioned declamation (see Example 5.4).

None of these things affects the prompt delivery of the text in a musical rhythm closely dependent upon poetic metre: the more, therefore, the declamation does break free from such metrical-rhythmic intimacy, the more striking can the effect be. Excellent examples are to be found in Grimoaldo's music: No. 3, 'Io già t'amai', has a rhythmic counterpart to the contrapuntal symbolism: Grimoaldo's love versus Rodelinda's defiance. Here, a standard quaver treatment of the *settenari* for lines 2–3 of the verse throws into relief the rhythmically augmented and partly reiterated setting of line 1 (see Example 5.5).

Example 5.5 *Rodelinda*, No. 3, 'Io già t'amai', bars 10–16

No. 17, 'Prigioniera ho l'alma in pena' makes a standard *ottonario* start, but with the second line loses control: erotic torment becomes a sweet self-indulgence, and Grimoaldo takes nearly twenty bars to deliver the text completely. In No. 33, 'Pastorello d'un povero armento', trance-like repetitions of line 2 in both orchestra and voice before the text is completed enhance the dream-like mood.

Perhaps because he was not much of a singer himself – to return to a point that Mattheson occasionally made about him[22] – Handel was rarely satisfied by this rather one-dimensional kind of musical rhetoric. Before leaving *Rodelinda*, I cite just a few of the ways in which he used texture and colour to bring to vivid expressive life the characters, the situations they find themselves in and the verses they speak, sometimes earning – though to modern ears certainly not deserving – the rebuke that his music was over-complex for the theatre.

[22] See Chapter 1, p. 6.

The contrapuntal elements in No. 3, 'Io già t'amai' have already been mentioned: in them are expressed Grimoaldo's bitter memories – 'once I loved you; you scorned to be my wife'. But Grimoaldo warms up these memories from his current position of power – 'now that I am king.' It is surely this perspective (even though those last words come only in the Middle Section of the aria) that prompts Handel to compose so many menacingly uprearing phrases. Another Grimoaldo aria, No. 23, 'Tuo drudo è mio rivale', also makes rhetorical use of counterpoint, here to articulate the two facets of a single mood – the indictment in declamatory style, and the dangerous rage which the accuser feels in savage coloratura.

Rhetorically effective textures need not be complex; they may be of extreme spareness, as in No. 14, 'Confusa si miri', where much of the desolation of the mood is owed to long stretches of bare octaves, especially when, as at bars 5–7 and 32–34, the phrases die away in single-line echoes. Suitably ethereal is the texture of No. 21, 'Scacciata dal suo nido', where, no doubt with an eye on the symbolic association of the swallow with loyal companionship, the first violin shadows the singing voice at the upper octave throughout the principal section, and the pair of them – voice and violin – start their journey (bars 10–14) without the solid ground supplied by the basso continuo. The circling through an extensive range of keys in this aria may be another image of flight. For imaginative strokes of harmony were another resource that Handel held always at the ready: witness, in No. 4, 'Lo farò,' the sudden plunge into the tonic minor at bars 25–26, as if Handel felt that the indignant energy, vividly enough expressed in the earlier part of the aria, was becoming too generalised, and needed a fresh charge of bitterness; or in No. 28, 'Chi di voi', where a profusion of interrupted cadences – 'deceptive cadences' as they are sometimes called – symbolise the deceptions of which Bertarido feels himself to be the victim.[23]

The power of the unexpected: atypical scenes

Listening to the quartet 'O cedere o perir' in Act Three of *Radamisto*, or the trio 'Non è amor' in Act Three of *Alcina*, critics have often regretted that such movements do not feature more frequently in Handel's operas. They

[23] See Reinhard Strohm, *Dramma per musica: Italian Opera Seria of the Eighteenth Century* (New Haven and London: Yale University Press, 1997), the chapter entitled '*Arianna in Creta*: Musical Dramaturgy', for a discussion of the relationship between musical figures and the poetic ideas of which they are the counterpart – what Strohm calls 'the glue of communication in the theatre'.

have not always made it clear that the regret is for a musical treat foregone, not for a dramatic opportunity missed. Such movements, during which a single dramatic situation or stage picture is stretched out with no essential change are, compared with solo arias, not differently dramatic. Nor is the trio 'Voglio strage' in Act Two of *Tamerlano* significantly different, though a more excruciating complexity and variety of feeling is compressed into a smaller space.

If it is the interlacing of music with the course of the dramatic action that one is seeking, it is to be found, not in these ensembles, but in the numbers – rarely more than one or two in any opera – that take their starting point from the accompanied recitative: that is to say, in the dramatic *scena*, the first fine Handelian example of which, the prison scene in *Almira*, has been discussed in Chapter 4.[24] Handel's exploration of the theatrical potential of the *scena* memorably culminates in two famous episodes: the death scene of Bajazet in *Tamerlano*, III.x, and the mad scene in *Orlando*, II.xi. To the classic accounts of Dean[25] little need be added – except perhaps to underline the fact that at the heart of both is an aria.

In the case of *Tamerlano*, Bajazet's 'Figlia mia' is a miniature da capo aria, its reprise written out rather than indicated in the usual shorthand. As so often, lost love (his farewell to his daughter) prompts the adoption of the siciliana manner, but it is a siciliana from which the lyrical impulse has almost entirely withered away, from pain and exhaustion. So has all trace of rhythmic elegance; only in the final cadence (at bar 5, repeated at bar 17) is there even the slightest hint of the swaying grace we commonly find in Handel's sicilianas.

The centrepiece of Orlando's mad scene is a gavotte *en rondeau*, with two strongly contrasting episodes, one a lament, the other an outburst of frenzy. The gavotte theme 'Vaghe pupille', in which Orlando makes to console the weeping Proserpina=Angelica is less warmly smiling than at first it looks; in fact it derives a slightly weird hollowness from the fact that, above the continuo bass line, the simple tune is played by all the instruments in unison with the voice (in octaves at the second and third recurrences). The lament episode is a richly textured series of eight variations over a chromatic ground bass, the vocal phrases stretched in torment well beyond the regular four-bar patterns of the ground.[26] The pattern of episodes and refrains continues into the orchestral postlude, which accompanies one of

[24] See Chapter 4, p. 100.

[25] Dean and Knapp, *Handel's Operas 1704–1726*, pp. 542–6; Dean, *Handel's Operas 1726–1741*, p. 245.

[26] 'Regular' except that the ground moves in alternation between the upper and lower octaves.

the opera's many spectacular *coups de théâtre*: first (bars 178–186), to the accompaniment of vigorous concerto-like music, Orlando 'rushes furiously into the cave, which bursts open';[27] and then he is borne through the heavens in Zoroastro's arms, and the gavotte theme recurs for a last time (bar 187), now fully harmonised. I shall return to the irregularities of *Orlando* later in this chapter.

A comparably astonishing *scena* is that at the end of Act II of *Alcina* (II. xiii). Here the resources of the *scena* are weighted more towards the aria, 'Ombre pallide', the originality of which is perhaps less immediately obvious than is Orlando's. But no one has ever doubted that the *accompagnato* with which the *scena* begins is extraordinary, and the more striking because it is the only one in the whole opera. It moves through three contrasting phases: first (bars 1–14) Alcina mourns the loss of Ruggiero's love, her vocal phrases set against richly and strangely harmonised string chords, modulating eccentrically, with 'Neapolitan' progressions in every phrase, and two disconcerting lurches when the key simply drops, from B minor to A minor (bar 4) and then from C sharp minor back to B minor (bars 10–11); second comes a relatively conventional *concitato* invoking the Furies (bars 15–27), which, having failed to rouse them, is followed finally (from bar 27) by a passage thrillingly evocative of Alcina's loss of her magic power, a series of desperate rhetorical questions hurled into the silence, some with upward leaps of as much as a tenth, the whole passage unsupported by any harmony or any regular rhythmic pulse.

The aria itself veers strangely between grave polyphony (a symbol perhaps of the mysterious secrets with which Alcina is occupied), weird unison melisma ('errate'; addressed to the pale spirits who, having abandoned her, now wander in the void), declamatory rhetoric ('perchè, perchè?') and frustrated vehemence (the *concertato* reiterations in the second half of the principal section). All this, very clearly, constitutes what Burney (speaking of 'Empio perverso cor' in *Radamisto*) called an 'acting song'; and if it is to create its full theatrical impact, it would need to be performed in a way distinct from almost all the other arias which are not 'acting songs'. The *scena* is finally crowned by a dramatic ballet of *songes agréables* and *songes funestes*, which plays out in dance the conflict in Alcina's tormented heart.[28]

Scenes such as these rank with Handel's finest achievements as a dramatic composer. *Orlando* in particular owes much of its power and fascination

[27] This music derives from the 'outburst of frenzy' episode, bars 127–67.

[28] See, however, the comments on these ballet movements at p. 136 above.

and not a little of its beauty to the unexpected, the sheer waywardness of Handel's imaginings throughout the opera. There can, however, be no ducking the fact that, if he is really one of the supreme masters of opera, the key to understanding his greatness will have to be found in what have often been called his 'ubiquitous da capo arias'. If we had to wait for the dramatic *scena* before the dramatic interest quickened, then watching or listening to a Handel opera would be a penitential experience indeed.

The infinite variety of the da capo aria: *Ariodante*

Convenient as the term da capo aria is, there is no doubt that it has obfuscated more than it has illuminated in the understanding of Handel's operas. But that can easily be put right if we recognise that, to be appreciated fully, Handel's da capo arias deserve every bit as much close study as, let us say, sonata form movements in Haydn's string quartets. They are no less sophisticated in design, and they are no less various in their beauty. And because we are dealing with opera, these sophistications and beauties and variousnesses might prompt us to ask ourselves why they are there in quite the way they are. To be sure they are there for the delight of the musicians and the more attentive listeners; very likely they are there too (as Haydn would certainly have pointed out) to the Glory of Almighty God. But is there anything more? Do they perhaps suggest to us something about how, in his mind's eye, Handel imagined the characters who inhabit his operas and the situations they find themselves in? Is it not very possible that he would have endorsed with enthusiasm Verdi's exclamation, 'Do people suppose I write my music by chance'? I shall use *Ariodante* to investigate.

Two points of departure for the variety in these arias have been identified in earlier sections of the book: the variety of dramatic function which an aria may perform has been discussed in Chapter 3, in a consideration of the working relationship between composer and librettist; and something of the range of musical resources with which Handel addressed this multiplicity of purposes was outlined in Chapter 4. As he matured, the constituent elements in Handel's musical language became more fully coordinated; the various types of aria were no longer quite so obviously differentiated as they had been in *Almira*. Nevertheless, most are still here: in the best years of his operatic career Handel continued to address his audience in chamber music mode, in dance music mode, in concerto mode – especially perhaps in concerto mode. So the first musical variable to be considered is the constitution of the orchestra.

Viewed superficially, there is less variety in *Ariodante* than is usually the case with Handel. We do not find, for example, the continuo songs, or the continuo songs with solo obbligato instrument that are still to be found in *Orlando* and *Alcina*. Scoring that is more extravagant than the standard is also employed sparingly. To generalise, we can say that the scoring of the opera is notably full and notably consistent. Nearly two-thirds of the arias have four-part scoring with divided violins and independent violas; of these, approximately half are with oboes, approximately half without. Given this consistency, we can be sure that any exceptional scoring will have a clear purpose; here are some examples:-

In No. 8, 'Voli colla sua tromba', Fame's trumpet is represented by two horns. Burney thought Handel chose horns rather than a trumpet because he had lost Valentine Snow from his orchestra. But it is entirely appropriate: the aria embodies something more than majesty. We might define its governing passion as 'Majesty Rejoicing, with Convivial Overtones', and the horns, 'richer and better at filling out the sound than the trumpets', suited that best.[29]

The bassoon obbligato in Ariodante's 'Scherza, infida', No. 23, undoubtedly suggests a malign presence. Among Handel's earliest operatic memories must have been the sound of Keiser's bassoon parts. Kleefeld, writing in the days when there were more Keiser scores to consult than there are today, observed that their 'muffled, creeping, tonal character [der dumpfe schleichende Klangcharakter] ... most often ... appears in scenes of unhappy or unlawful love'.[30]

The scoring of Ginevra's 'Si, morrò', No. 39, might be described as archaic – appropriately, since, instead of being set as a da capo aria, this text is treated like a *sonata-da-chiesa* movement, in which the principal allegro section is preceded by an adagio introduction. The instrumental provenance of the style is underlined by the scoring, with violin and cello solos in addition to a five-part string ensemble. And the outcome of this – because of its rhythmic relentlessness – is that the orchestra less supports Ginevra's song than sweeps her along on its own momentum. It reinforces the dramatic point: namely, that she feels herself utterly powerless, utterly at the mercy of fate.

In the king's 'Al sen ti stringo', No. 38, the flutes do not have obbligato parts; they are used simply to colour the standard four-part texture, and give the siciliana a touch of tender melancholy.

29 Johann Mattheson, *Das Beschützte Orchestre*, Hamburg: Schiller, 1717.

30 W. Kleefeld, 'Das Orchester in der Hamburger Oper', *SIMG* I (1899); cited in McCredie, *Instrumentarium and Instrumentation*, p. 184.

The standard layout of a full-scale da capo aria has been described in Excursus 4.2 in Chapter 4.[31] It does not preclude an extraordinary variety of outcomes, and *Ariodante* provides some extreme examples. In 'Dopo notte atra', No. 41, we hear over forty bars of heroic vocal-orchestral concerto before the music reaches the final line of the first tercet of verse; in 'Io ti bacio', No. 37, the whole text of the Principal Section has been sung in the space of two bars, before the orchestra even enters. Some of these matters will be taken up again later in this chapter; here, however, I propose to examine just one particular detail of the arias, because how Handel engaged his architectural imagination in matters dramaturgical is best seen from his treatment of the ritornellos. That is only right for a dramatic composer; because the Opening Ritornello is, according to Strohm, the 'neuralgic moment' in the unfolding of the drama. Typically it forms the gateway from the world of action to the world of feeling, and commonly it provides in summary form a preview of the whole expressive and performerly range of the aria. Conversely the Closing Ritornello marks the return, from the character's inner world to the world of action. Although accounts of the da capo aria commonly speak of a ritornello 'returning' at the end of the Principal Section, there is in *Ariodante* – and how different this is from, let us say, the contemporary cantatas of J. S. Bach – no single example of an aria in which the Closing Ritornello simply reproduces the opening one. The relationship between them is often dramatically suggestive.

A simple but beautiful example is provided by the king's 'Invida sorte avara' (II.vi),[32] where the characteristic siciliana-like broken half-phrases in the Opening Ritornello, hovering between tonic minor and would-be modulation to the relative major, are, in the Closing Ritornello, in response to the deepening darkness of the mood, extended into one long, unbroken dying fall.

Even when the recomposition of the Closing Ritornello is plainer than that, it is likely to reward a moment's reflection. In the Closing Ritornello of Polinesso's 'Dover, giustizia, amor', No. 36, the weight of the music has been shifted: the opening of the Incipit has been cut, while the Cadence has been drawn out by further repetition. There is no longer any need for this unsavoury man, *Devise*-like, to display his fraudulent credentials; but it is wholly in keeping for him to prolong the bragging reiterations of bar 44 (cf. with bar 7).

[31] See that Excursus for what one might call a 'normal' procedure – also for a reminder of the terminology I am using.

[32] In the *HHA* edition of *Ariodante* this aria is in the Appendix, at No. 26a.

All Polinesso's arias are worth examining from this point of view. In No. 25, 'Se l'inganno', the canonic imitation and the self-hugging *pp* counterpoint that, in the Opening Ritornello, so vividly suggest his practised deceit, return in the Closing Ritornello only very briefly and quite transformed: the canonic theme, filled out harmonically and loudly accented, disappears almost as soon as it begins, its Continuation (which had been in ominous octaves in bars 3–4) becoming simply the bass for the clamorous, *furioso* repeated semiquavers in the upper strings. 'Coperta la frode', No. 4, is an unusual case. It is surprising that Handel accepted the text of the aria in the first place, because it is surely unsatisfactory: its climax – its recommended course of action, so to speak ('if deceit is your intent, dress it up boldly') – is confined to the Middle Section, and cancelled out by the da capo. What Handel does, it seems to me, is to ignore the structure of the verse entirely (there is not the slightest trace of 'more beauteous vestment' in the Middle Section), and turn the whole aria into one single reflection on how to conceal treachery. Given that topic, Polinesso is hardly going to put all his cards on the table at once, in the Opening Ritornello. In fact, only in the Closing Ritornello do we hear the material in full: (bars 54–58) an Incipit (perhaps a quickish sarabande in style: it would be suggestive of Polinesso's respectable courtly face; or would be were it not for the slithers on three of the main beats), followed by (bars 58–62) a Continuation based on the melisma to which, at considerable length, he has sung 'inganno'; this 'inganno' melisma also infects the Cadence (bars 62–66). In the Opening Ritornello, however, only the Incipit had been played, with, moreover, a different harmonisation, in which no fewer than ten of the twelve beats are on C major chords. Polinesso is, one might say, 'concealing his treachery' assiduously indeed.

One last example may be given of the purposeful imaginativeness with which Handel composed the ritornellos of these arias. After Ginevra has been denounced as faithless and unchaste, the grand *scena* that closes Act Two expresses her despair in an *accompagnato* recitative, 'A me impudica?', suicidally-mythological in manner, leading into a da capo aria in austere, intermittently polyphonic style (No. 30, 'Il mio crudel martoro'). It forms an instructive parallel with Alcina's *scena* already described at p. 145: for it is a mad scene 'fuelled by defiled innocence rather than guilt'.[33]

Very full instrumentation has been used throughout Act Two, with, in Handel's original version, only one aria (Lurcanio's 'Tu vivi', No. 22) using less than a four-part orchestral texture. It is therefore more striking that

[33] Dean, *Handel's Operas 1726–1741*, pp. 293–4.

'Il mio crudel martoro', which is in Handel's richest, most serious style, preceded by an *accompagnato* and placed at the emotional climax of the opera, should have the act's thinnest scoring, of *violini unisoni* and continuo. The purpose is surely to draw us into the realm of chamber music, into a more intimate sympathy with the afflicted heroine.

The Opening Ritornello is not thematic; instead the violins play a series of austere instrumental patterns, which, in a space of eight bars, suggest grandness of scale: slow harmonic movement; tonal juxtaposition; faster moving harmonies as the violins break into semiquavers – so that these mark expressive intensification, not just surface animation. Throughout the sung parts of the aria the violins continue with these ritornello materials, creating an obbligato, sometimes as a backcloth, sometimes in antiphony with the voice, sometimes reinforcing it, but at all events making of the aria the very image of an interior dialogue. This dialogue quality informs Handel's Closing Ritornello, which bears only the slightest resemblance (in the cadence) to the Opening Ritornello. It has been composed in a form in which, surely quite spontaneously, the most poignant interval of the opening vocal phrase has been reduced to a motif set in broken dialogue with the bass, before tapering away in melodic ornamentation of the same idea, then a passage which dissolves it into the style of figuration with which the Opening Ritornello began. So, during this Closing Ritornello, memories of 'crudel martoro' reach out in imagined dialogue, then are transformed into tuneful memory, then fade away into the bleak background patterning (see Example 5.6).

Example 5.6 *Ariodante*, No. 30, 'Il mio crudel martoro', bars 8–9, 46–49

Resources for characterisation

In this repertory the dramatic interest does not depend much on 'what happens' – on how the flow of the music is coordinated with a storyline. Winton Dean's writings on Handelian opera always insisted that, if this is great dramatic art, the key to its greatness is to be found in Handel's sense of character. It is a claim that deserves more specifically musical investigation than it has received, and the three Ariosto operas, *Orlando*, *Ariodante* and *Alcina*, offer an ideal field: they are close to one another chronologically, and come from the ripest period of Handel's work as an opera composer; the principal soprano roles were all written for the same singer, Anna Maria Strada (so any particularities that we find in them have nothing to do with the different qualities or accomplishments of different singers), and although the operas all stem from the same literary source – Ariosto's *Orlando furioso* – and have the same central theme of erotic, romantic love, they treat this theme in strikingly different ways.

First, in *Orlando*, the story of Angelica, whose beauty turns the heads of all the men who set eyes on her. She occasions much bewilderment among the knights of Charlemagne, and the greatest of them, Orlando, loses his senses altogether. But finally she falls in love herself with the simple soldier Medoro.[34] Then, in *Ariodante*, the story of Ginevra, whose love is strengthened and deepened by the ordeals of betrayal and misunderstanding to which she is subjected. And finally *Alcina*, who is like some figure from the darker (or jollier) recesses of ancient mythology; for together with her all but irresistible sexual allure she has magical powers which enable her to turn those lovers of whom she has wearied into beasts or trees or rocks or streams.

Alcina, which is the simplest case, may serve as a model for how an operatic role works when, as is usual, it is conceived as a parade of passions. Like the important characters in all Handel's operas, Alcina is brought before us in many different moods: sometimes introvert, sometimes extrovert; sometimes overwhelmed by her passions, sometimes able to stand back and survey them objectively; sometimes she is alone, sometimes the arias are addressed to others, in a tone of voice that may be insinuating, or threatening, or seductive. Each of these aria functions – to return, from a different perspective, to something already touched upon – has its own repertory of musical resources, and it would be scarcely an exaggeration to claim that they comprise all the musical riches of the age. So, 'Di' cor mio', No. 7, in which the musical phrases are shared almost conversationally between the singing voice and the instruments, is chamber music-like in character, as befits the intimacy of its mood; 'Sì, son quella', No. 12, is a continuo-song,

[34] In the libretto Medoro is called an 'African prince'; in Ariosto on the other hand (Canto XVIII, Strophe 165) he is one of two 'Mori … d'oscura stirpe'.

aptly used when a character feels vulnerable, lonely or abandoned, and the role of the orchestra is limited to playing a postlude at the end of the principal section. Concerto-like energy and virtuosity play their part in 'Ma quando tornerai', No. 34; while the romantic connotations of dance song are sounded in the middle section of the same aria, and in 'Mi restano le lagrime', No. 37. From a dramaturgical perspective the treatment of Alcina is typical for Handel's practice: each of her appearances on stage – two in each act – closes with a da capo aria on a generous scale.

The plot of *Orlando* is more confused, and the opera has a looser, more inconsequential shape. Besides the three characters from Ariosto – Orlando, Angelica, Medoro – two further characters appear who have little or nothing to do with the Italian poet: the shepherdess Dorinda (whose role is at least in part 'comic'[35]), and the prophet-magician Zoroastro, who presides over the whole bizarre affair. The general bewilderment mirrors the disorder in the mind of Orlando himself, whose role comes to its climax in the great mad scene discussed earlier in this chapter. And the distribution of the music in Angelica's role also participates in the general confusion, as the following table shows:

Table 5.1 The distribution of the music in Angelica's role in *Orlando*

Act I		
No. 10	'Ritornava al suo bel viso'	– an *arioso*-like piece which towards the close is taken over by Medoro
No. 11	'Chi possessore'	– follows No. 10 after a short recitative
No. 14	'Se fedel vuoi ch'io ti creda'	
No. 16	'Consolati, o bella'	– terzetto with Dorinda and Medoro
Act II		
No. 22	'Non potrà dirmi ingrata'	
No. 23	'Verdi piante'	– the two full-scale da capo arias are separated by a recitative of some 20 bars
Act III		
No. 29	'Così giusta è questa speme'	
No. 33	'Finchè prendi'	– duet with Orlando
No. 38	'Per far, mia diletta'	– sung at first by Orlando, the piece is taken over by Angelica in its final phrases

[35] See 'Comic traditions in Handel's *Orlando*' in Strohm, *Essays on Handel and Italian Opera*, pp. 249–69.

While some of these numbers are relatively normal da capo arias, introduced by passages of simple recitative in the customary manner (and therefore no comment is made on them in the table), others, especially the ensembles, are decidedly not. They comprise a substantial trio at the end of the first act, and an extraordinary group of duet-like pieces.

In the two movements Nos. 10 and 38, the procedure, though unexpected, is straightforward enough: the voice which started the song is not joined by the other voice; it is simply replaced by it. In 'Ritornava al suo bel viso' Angelica's beautiful melody is claimed by Medoro as the perfect expression of his own feelings; in 'Per far, mia diletta', on the other hand, Orlando sings in a mood of suicidal despair; but he is silenced and the whole character of the music changes abruptly when Angelica consoles him with a simple phrase of tender cantabile.

Rather more complicated and startlingly original is the duet 'Finchè prendi', which one might describe rather as a contested aria. Angelica believes that Medoro is dead, and prepares for her own death at the hands of Orlando by beginning to sing a gentle, elegiac cavatina. The text is composed, not in da capo form, but as a two-part structure. The music for the first two lines modulates to the relative major key (bars 1–14), and the music for the last three lines returns, more indirectly, to the home tonic, F minor (bars 20–45). As we would anticipate, each half is rounded off by ritornellos in the appropriate key. The unanticipated thing is that, when we reach the intermediate ritornello in A flat, the raving Orlando bursts in, singing a kind of vocal obbligato to the ritornello, and turning it into an expression of his own bloodthirstiness (bars 14–19). In the second half of the duet Angelica's music is challenged, phrase by phrase, by Orlando's; finally she can only weep, while his last phrase, still raging and threatening, is not superimposed on the ritornello, but reiterated and reinforced by it (bars 42–47). A piece of music which began as Angelica's lament ends as the song of Orlando's madness. The movement does not express a single passion; it becomes, so to speak, a psychological field of influence, in which the passions are divided or contested or redirected. One recognises the contribution made by the librettist: Handel's brilliant setting must have been in part stimulated by the fact that the single lines which Orlando sings at the end of each part are in a different metre from those sung by Angelica: calm *ottonari* yield to galloping anapaestic *decasillabi*.

So Handel's operas commonly use a dramatic structure in which the passions of the characters are presented in a clear but highly stylised form (as in *Alcina*). Thanks to this stylisation the composer always has the opportunity, when there are good dramatic grounds for doing so, to confound the audience's expectations (as so often in *Orlando*). Moreover, he has at his disposal the whole range of current musical styles and genres to be employed or adapted or alluded to in order to express the passions in an appropriate fashion. Turning to *Ariodante*, one finds that the role of Ginevra is conceived from another perspective again.

The dramatic action of *Ariodante* is unusually simple and clear, and Handel makes very deliberate use of that in his treatment of Ginevra. At each of her appearances on stage she sings not one aria, but two. The first is sometimes very short and simple in design, sometimes broken off prematurely; the second is an aria on the most generous scale.[36] It is of course common enough for a single scene to be designed in this way (the opening scene of *Rodelinda*, discussed on p. 86 has already provided an excellent example); it is the all-pervasive, systematic use of the pattern that makes the case of Ginevra special. For by this means Handel creates a musical portrait which is richer in nuance than that of almost all his other heroines. The two arias can be used, sometimes to stake out the furthest poles of her emotional life, sometimes to explore introvert and extrovert facets of a single passion.

Such two-fold presentations of Ginevra are seen directly at the start of the opera (Act I, Scenes i–iv), where we meet her before her character has been ripened and purified by suffering. In 'Vezzi, lusinghe, e brio', No. 1, she sits in front of a mirror, thoroughly pleased with her own beauty, because it is the thing that has made Ariodante fall in love with her. In the closing aria of the scene 'Orrida agli occhi miei', No. 2, she expresses her detestation of Polinesso, who sees himself as Ariodante's rival.

The charming picture that meets Ginevra when she looks in her mirror is the topic of the opening aria; and since the mirror is part of the stage set, the opening ritornello (bars 1–13) functions in part as a tone-painting prelude or sinfonia. The threefold, comma-ed-off articulation of the first line of text ('Vezzi, lusinghe, e brio') prompts a three-bar Incipit, and since the aria is a kind of love song, its underlying musical style is that of a dance (a slightly quicker than usual sarabande). A large part of the ritornello is occupied with decorative triplet figures, full of changing notes and springing octaves (bars 3–12), and when Ginevra begins to sing, these decorative elements recur frequently, with different effects: sometimes they supply an

[36] To be more strictly accurate, in Act II Ginevra does leave the stage between her miniature aria 'Mi palpita il core', No. 27, and her *accompagnato* and full-scale aria 'Il mio crudel martoro', Nos. 29 and 30; but she remains the subject of the all the recitative and of the aria 'Il tuo sangue' that between them fill her absence.

easy-flowing continuity to the short vocal phrases; sometimes a calm background against which she can give a simpler lyrical expression to her love. In the coda-like bars 56–73 the triplets create a musical stasis of decorative repeating figures, in the midst of which she sits becalmed.

The change of tone between this and her second aria, 'Orrida agli occhi miei', is extreme. Here the enunciation of the text is abrupt and obsessive. The thematic material grows out of the snapping declamation of the first word, 'orrida', which is continually repeated: ten times in the first part of the aria. So exasperated is Ginevra's mood that she can sing nothing but short, breathless phrases, which only gradually – really only in the Middle Section – acquire some measure of poise.

Important aspects of the garden scene have been already discussed in Chapter 3.[37] Ginevra's music comprises the duet 'Prendi da questa mano' and the aria 'Volate amori', Nos. 6 and 7. The duet, minuet-like in character, is more closely integrated into the stage action than usual, since it begins without introductory ritornello, and ends when it is interrupted by the arrival of the king. It is notable for what one might call its psychologically realistic disposition of the voices. The opening (bars 1–17), set out in the manner of Subject and Answer, gives priority to the princess; after Ariodante has answered her principal theme, he steps forward to join with it (bars 17–30), and then to imitate it (bars 31–34); only in the second part of the duet does his voice take over the leading role. In this duet the two lovers exchange vows: for Ginevra it represents the intimate expression of the emotions which will overflow in its extrovert counterpart, the aria 'Volate, amori'.

The aria is composed in concerto style, and forms an instructive contrast with the earlier 'Orrida agli occhi miei', likewise in concerto style. Indeed, a starker contrast could scarcely be imagined than that between the obsessive repetitions of small figures in the one and the gracious charm of this other. A large part of its good humour comes from the melismas on the word 'volate', imaginatively varied, often with contrapuntally enriched details. But before we reach the melismas, the whole text of the first part of the aria has been sung to a melody which mirrors very vividly the sense of its words: the flying cupids ('volate amori'), the boundless joy ('la gioia immensa'), the celebration, in the form of a definitive cadence ('a celebrar'). One notes too how the little exclamations of 'amori' and 'volate', which to begin with form a nippy counterpoint to set off the melismas (bars 17–18), later develop into a complete melody (bars 37–39).

[37] See pp. 76–7.

After this brilliant aria, because of the near-tragic course of the action that follows, Ginevra sings not a single melismatic phrase until almost the end of the opera. She has three more of these double-aria scenes; but only in the last of them, in her final duet with Ariodante, 'Bramo aver mille vite', (No. 44) does her radiant *joie de vivre* return.

Of course, all this does not mean that Handel had a completely distinct tone of voice for all his heroines, in the way that one might claim Shakespeare did have for his. What it does show, I hope, is the scope and variety of the choices he had at his disposal every time he sat down to compose an opera, and how clearly he understood that these choices could be used to reflect a particular character in a particular situation in a particular kind of drama. Because there is surely no doubt, whatever may have been the origins of his personal style of musical rhetoric back in the Halle days, that he had long since, in Silke Leopold's phrase, 'exchanged the pulpit for the stage ... the portraiture of humanity takes the place of the expounding of a text'.[38] Beyond that generalised humanity, the individuality – if desired – was a matter for the performers.

Old and new in *Serse*

After *Ariodante* and *Alcina*, the unfolding tale of Handelian opera rather lost its way. Consistently the later operas were commercial failures; Handel himself was seriously ill towards the end of the 1736–37 season; as far as we can see he had no trusted librettist colleague to assist him, and it is difficult to perceive any common theme or tendency in the texts he set; musical influences continued to wash in on all sides. Out of this confusing and – as far as his operas were concerned – melancholy scene, towers one of Handel's very greatest. *Serse* is at least the equal of the finest Royal Academy operas of the mid 1720s and of the three Ariosto operas. Indeed, if one rates the gift of melody as a first prerequisite for opera, it might deserve to be ranked as the finest of them all.

Serse was not unaffected by the conditions under which it was written. And Burney's complaint, already quoted in Chapter 2, that 'this drama ... is one of the worst that Handel ever set to music', a deplorable 'mixture of tragi-comedy and buffoonery',[39] suggests that for some eighteenth-century judges it seemed a ramshackle sort of confection. But the judgement of

[38] Cited in Poppe, 'Geniestreich oder Werk eines unerfahrenen "Pedanten"?...', p. 287.

[39] His comments on *Serse*, here and in the following paragraph, are from Burney, *A General History of Music*, vol. II, p. 822.

history is rather that Handel somehow succeeded here in bringing together in one musico-dramatic conception all that he had ever learned about opera and all that he was continuing to learn: a rich and beguiling brew of old and new, of the virtuosic and the simple, of the high style and the homespun.

In his commentary on the music, Burney remarked how modern many of its features still seemed. In 'Se bramate', No. 28, he noted 'a base in iterated quavers, very much in the style of Hasse and Vinci', and declared, 'no music fifty years old can have a younger appearance.' 'Anima infida', No. 31, on the other hand, was 'a fine mixture of new and old passages and effects, with a Corelli base, and a modern accompaniment'. We may add that Handel never dipped deeper into the pre-classical style than in 'Crude furie', No. 51, where, through great stretches of music, the slowly moving harmonies are invigorated by repeated notes in the bass and scrubbing inner strings, and where the midpoint dominant cadence in the Principal Section is approached by a bar's worth of seventh chord harmony on the sharpened fourth (at bar 28).

In their musical architecture, too, several *Serse* arias are more 'modern' than anything we have hitherto come across. An incipient sonata style makes some telling appearances, telling not only for the expressive richness it gives the arias in question, but also because it strongly implies a loosening up of the way in which the singers presented themselves to the theatre audience.[40]

In this respect the closing aria of Act I, Atalanta's 'Un cenno leggiadretto', No. 19, is an exemplary *Serse* piece. Handel first sets the whole of the first part of the text:

Un cenno leggiadretto / Un riso vezzosetto, / Un moto di pupille / Può far innamorar[41]

like a simple song (bars 6–11). Then, as the music modulates to the dominant key, he decides to make rather more of the third and fourth lines with a new kind of theme, full of dotted rhythms and with some teasing vocalisation in the cadence phrase (bars 14–19). Especially after the orchestral-vocal exchanges of bars 12–13, there can surely be no question but that Handel envisaged Atalanta acting this music in character. The contrasting dotted theme recurs firmly in the tonic key from bar 36. If it is legitimate to describe this as a 'second subject', what one might call the 'first subject', the simple song-like theme, also plays a notable role. Only the beginning

[40] The pattern is not unprecedented in Handel's operas; but no earlier work uses it so frequently or in such developed and suggestive forms.

[41] Expansively rendered in the 1738 libretto as: 'A graceful and consenting nod, / Alluring smiles, and rowling eyes, / Assisted by the wanton god, / May, with soft love, his heart surprize'.

returns after the Intermediate Ritornello, and it returns in the orchestra, as if for Atalanta to mime to, as she tosses in the occasional detached phrase, 'un vezzo', 'un riso'.

A tendency towards 'acted song' had often been evident in the music Handel wrote for soubrettish characters like Atalanta. 'Se bramate' explores the scope of the incipient sonata style in a would-be heroic context. The aria is in Handel's grandest (as well as most modern) concerto style, with many typical features. Its Opening Ritornello is compact, with the florid Continuation and the Cadence phrase fused into one (bars 5–8); but its architectural function is strongly emphasised, for it is only slightly trimmed at its later recurrences, at the dominant midpoint (bars 29–34), and to round off the Principal Section (bars 64–69). The boldly rising Incipit, suitably paraphrased, is used to launch all the main vocal sections of the aria, at bars 9, 35 and 70, and the semiquaver scales of the Continuation supply the raw material of the orchestral fabric as the voice rises to its cadenza-like climaxes in A, at bars 21–25 and 51–54. All that is time-honoured Handelian practice. The extraordinary feature is a more than embryonic Second Group of themes, with no fewer than three distinct elements: thematic, virtuosic, pathetic (bars 19–28, recapitulated at bars 49–58).[42]

As one would anticipate, the formal distinctiveness is prompted by poetic, characterising considerations:

> Se bramate d'amar chi vi sdegna,
> Vuò sdegnarvi, ma come non so.
> La vostr'ira crudel me l'insegna;
> Tento farlo e quest'alma non può.[43]

Each half of the text ends with half a line expressive of Serse's inability to do what he knows he ought to do: 'ma come non so' in A; 'e quest'alma non può' in B. The musical setting of these two phrases is held back until the first one-and-a-half lines of the verse have been set and reset very thoroughly, and then it is brought in to round off each phase of the design (A1, A2 and B) with a new idea of great poignancy. While the ritornello theme and everything that has evolved out of it has proclaimed purposeful outward-looking energy, here, at the last of the three stages of the 'second group', the energy is exhausted and the music turns inward in a series of

[42] To be quite clear and avoid any danger of confusion: these features of 'incipient sonata' are all contained in the Principal Section A. In this particular aria, exceptionally, similar qualities are found in the Middle Section B.

[43] If thou with love do'st meet disdain, / I'd slight thee too, but know not how. / Your anger teaches me in vain; / My heart can't e'n the thought allow. (1738 libretto).

slow, rich and dissonant chromatics. We have heard one energetic and purposeful theme (bars 19–21); one in which energy is reduced to ineffectual bluster (bars 21–25); now (at the adagio) all collapses into pathos.

To suggest that there are sonata-ish elements in several of the *Serse* arias is not in itself a value judgement. Sonata form is not intrinsically more virtuous than da capo ritornello form nor aesthetically superior to it. But in a dramatic context it is, perhaps, more psychologically lifelike; it brings us a little closer to the emotional world of the young Mozart, and specifically to his *Idomeneo*, a world in which many modern opera singers and almost all stage directors feel more comfortable than they do with the Metastasian model of heroic opera. Other features of the score link it with quite different tendencies in mid eighteenth-century music.

I mentioned in Chapter 1 the curious reactions of some of Handel's contemporaries to his last operas. For instance, we learn from a letter written by Lord Shaftesbury that some people talked of *Serse* as a 'ballad opera': 'my own judgement' wrote Shaftesbury, 'is that it is a capital opera notwithstanding tis called a ballad one.'[44] To use that term for an opera which is 'all-sung' and in Italian, and which is so rich and subtle in every musical respect, is certainly an odd misnomer. But perhaps it would make some kind of sense if it were meant simply to draw attention to the fact that, at the time he was composing *Serse*, Handel seems to have been warmly sympathetic to some aspects of contemporary English musical taste: things like an attachment to the great old songs of Purcell, to the new songs of Arne and to the treasury of national song tapped in the ballad operas. For a large number of the arias in *Serse* are not really arias at all; they are songs: simple, tuneful, technically undemanding songs, of a kind scarcely heard in Handel's operas since *Almira*, and they use the simplest binary and ternary and even strophic forms. Fully half of them make no use of the da capo/dal segno convention. And they are not confined to minor characters; Serse and Romilda sing several of them. The prevalence of these little songs has two important musico-dramatic consequences. First, the full-scale virtuoso da capo arias such as 'Più che penso' and 'Se bramate' stand out boldly and vividly; and second, Handel can find room for a very large number of arias, more than in any other of his operas since the Hamburg years.

With so large a number of arias, a high proportion of them discarding the da capo reprise, *Serse* might be supposed to be breaking new ground. But mention of Hamburg and *Almira* is not fortuitous. These particular apparent innovations in fact mark a return to the past: Handel's opera is a

[44] See Chapter 1, footnote 116.

resetting of a libretto which Nicolò Minato had originally written for Cavalli as long ago as 1655. And even though Handel got there, not directly, but by means of a *rifacimento* undertaken by his old rival Bononcini in Rome in the 1690s, *Serse* preserved more of the mid seventeenth-century Venetian spirit than any other of his several operas whose roots reached back so far.

Handel had been dipping into Bononcini's score, of which a copy had found its way to London, for some years. By December 1737 he could no longer withstand the fascination exerted by this 1690s update – by Stampiglia – of a brilliant operatic text from the greatest age of Venetian opera, and began to recompose it, making further extensive use of Bononcini's score as he did so.[45] Lindgren has suggested that this very early Bononcini opera was so congenial to Handel precisely because he found in many of its airs the kind of brevity and simplicity which the 1730s enthusiasm for ballad opera had brought back into fashion.[46] Be that as it may, *Xerse* (Bononcini's title for the opera) certainly provided Handel with dozens of good musical ideas set in a fast-moving and effective dramatic framework, and he proceeded to make brilliant use of them.

The flexibility of form and style in *Serse* is one of its most endearing qualities: an unusually large number of arias are broken into by phrases of recitative; an unusually large number of recitatives are broken into by stretches of song. But nothing shows the flexibility more strikingly than the opera's duets. The first of them, No. 6, 'Io le dirò,' is really a simple strophic song, in Handel's most popular vein, of which Serse sings one verse and Arsamene the other; another, No. 27, 'L' amerete?', tiny in scale, consists largely of a string of recitative clichés, broadened out in slow 3/4 time, in conversation between the two singers. A third, No. 40, 'Gran pena è gelosia', is in a more laboured declamatory style; in fact it is uniquely brooding for a duet, since at least one of the singers – probably both – doesn't realise the other is there. The final lovers' duet, No. 49, 'Troppo oltraggi la mia fede', is sung while Romilda and Arsamene are still at loggerheads, and breaks out again, without orchestra, in the middle of the following recitative.

[45] The relationship between Handel's *Serse* and Bononcini's *Xerse* is the topic of a number of studies; see particularly H. Powers, 'Il Serse trasformato', *MQ* 47 and 48 (1961 and 1962); John H. Roberts (ed.), *Handel Sources: Materials for the Study of Handel's Borrowings*, 9 vols. (New York: Garland, 1986). vol. VIII; W. Dean, 'Handel's *Serse*', in Thomas Bauman and Marita P. McClymonds (eds.), *Opera and the Enlightenment* (Cambridge University Press, 1995); Dean, *Handel's Operas 1726–1741*; L. Lindgren, 'To Be a Bee in Eighteenth-Century England, as Exemplified in Handel's Xerxes', *GHB* 7 (1998); D. Kimbell 'Operatic Variations on an Episode at the Hellespont', in E. Bridges, E. Hall and P. J. Rhodes (eds.), *Cultural Responses to the Persian Wars* (Oxford University Press, 2007).

[46] Lindgren, 'To Be a Bee'.

The ultimate effect of all these things was to make this late opera a work in which lively stage action and superb musical inventiveness are coordinated so incomparably well that it has few equals between *L'incoronazione di Poppea* and *Le nozze di Figaro*. The claim can be made with respect both to individual numbers and to the general musico-dramatic conception of its various tableaus. We may take our leave of it with a quick glance at its opening scene.

While Serse's *recitativo accompagnato* and aria are remarkable only for their extraordinary beauty, the scene that follows sets the tone for the whole opera, preparing us for a treatment of the operatic convention that is freer – because more old-fashioned – than anything we have hitherto met in Handel. It fuses sinfonia, recitative and song in one single imaginative vision in which the unfolding dramatic action (in recitative), and the feelings and reflections of a central character (in Romilda's songs) are all perceived, as Serse perceives them, through a haze of enchantment conjured up, and then sustained, by a sinfonia of recorders and muted strings. The design is that of a mid-seventeenth-century *scena*, mediated via Bononcini; and it permits and is partly stimulated by a use of the aria that is more multifaceted than was normal in the 1730s. In 'Voi che penate', No. 4, Romilda is offering advice on unhappy love. But instead of this being done in a detached or generalised reflective manner, it is drawn closely and wittily into the stage action we are watching by her satirical observations on Serse and his plane tree, and by the snatches of recitative between Elviro and Arsamene as they draw near.[47]

I have made no attempt in these last two chapters to provide a comprehensive or systematic analysis of the music in Handel's operas, or even to suggest what methodology might appropriately be used for such an analysis. My object has been to highlight a number of matters which seem to me particularly germane to his achievement as a musical dramatist, and to the potential effectiveness of his music on stage. Necessarily, I have investigated only a few scenes in a few operas from a few perspectives. All the same, I believe that, for anyone thinking to perform one, whether on the stage or in concert, it would be rewarding to explore any of the operas in these ways. A delighted fascination with their many-faceted inventiveness can be guaranteed; what above all such an exploration would show was that, indeed, Handel did not 'compose his music by chance'.

47 I have discussed this scene rather more fully in 'Operatic Variations on an Episode at the Hellespont'.

6 | Aspects of the performance of Handelian opera in his time and ours

Hamburg

Handel's first four German operas were all performed at the Theater am Gänsemarkt in Hamburg, a theatre erected in the latter part of 1677, on plans by Girolamo Sartorio, architect at the Hanover court, who modelled it on the Venetian Teatro dei SS. Giovanni e Paolo. It was large and horseshoe-shaped with, it is said, space for between 1,800 and 2,000 spectators, accommodated in parterre, two tiers of boxes and a gallery; audiences were socially mixed; educated, but not exclusive; boxes could, on the Italian model, be hired for the season. The stage was very large – some thirty metres deep in Handel's time – and with its fifteen pairs of sliding flats, practicable machines and much admired resources for lighting, it was able to stage opulent performances of ambitious operas. From 1703 until 1705 or perhaps 1706 Handel worked in this theatre as orchestral violinist, harpsichordist (therefore someone with a primary responsibility for the musical direction of the opera) and composer. These were the crucial formative years for him as a man of the theatre.[1]

We are fortunate to possess fascinating, if not exactly objective accounts of the style of opera performance with which Handel first became professionally involved, thanks to Mattheson. Handel's closest friend in these Hamburg years, Mattheson was himself composer, harpsichordist and leading tenor at the theatre. He had emerged from the student ranks of the chorus to assume leading solo roles during the brief period in the mid 1690s when Johann Sigismund Kusser, a pupil of Lully, and similarly fiery and authoritative in temperament, was directing the theatre's fortunes. After Mattheson retired from the stage he went on to write a uniquely illuminating series of books and pamphlets – theoretical, practical, analytical and historical – in which, among much else, opera and the performance of opera are thoroughly examined.

[1] Chapter 3 of Dean and Knapp, *Handel's Operas 1704–1726* provides an invaluable introduction to most aspects of the Hamburg opera. It is best supplemented, particularly for details on performance, by H. J. Marx, 'Die Hamburger Oper zur Zeit des jungen Händels', *HJb* 36 (1990).

Performers were assembled from the most heterogeneous sources. Later, in London, Handel was to work with a small group of virtuoso singers and a first-rate professional orchestra: an arrangement which seems quite natural to us today. Hamburg could not afford to import such singers as London did, and had no system for training them. Very rarely indeed did castrati sing there, until Campioli was engaged for a few seasons between 1725 and 1728. Its small stock of professional soloists could be supplemented with singing actor-comedians (for such roles as that of Tabarco in *Almira*) and with students from the Gymnasium, who might have taken on the smaller roles in *Nero*, *Florindo* and *Daphne* and supplied any chorus that was required. The orchestra was a similarly mixed body: something between fifteen and twenty players, of whom only the eight *Ratsmusiker* were fully professional, the balance being made up by apprentices and/or students.[2]

It had been Kusser's genius to weld these motley elements into a unified Hamburg ensemble style, and he did this in a manner, doubtless much influenced by Lullian practice, that sounds prophetic of what Weber was to do more than a hundred years later. For, as Mattheson reported, it was Kusser's practice, in any opera which he was supervising, 'to require all the people involved, from the greatest to the least, to come to his house, where he would sing and play every note to them to demonstrate how he wanted it performed'.[3]

Hamburg performances aimed at the 'textually intelligible, theatrically exciting communication of a story'.[4] Feind still commended the English theatre as a suitable model; and to keep alive that quasi-Shakespearian vitality and variousness which had been brought to the city long before by English travelling theatre companies, the opera employed three groups of stage performers: professional actor-singers, vagabond comedians and amateurs. Each had its own repertory of movement and gesture. From the students came what was, at the turn of the eighteenth century, the deportment demanded by social etiquette; from the comedians a vigorously

2 Marx describes the constitution of the orchestra as follows: 'The most important were the eight Ratsmusikanten [city council musicians] under whom were placed two Adjuncti or Expectanten [apprentices] who, on the death of one of the Ratsmusiker, moved up. Next in rank after the city musicians, and subordinate to them, were the so-called 'Roll-brothers', a confraternity whose rights and privileges were recorded on a roll. A third group included the unorganized musicians, the Greens, who in 1691 had received from the Hamburg Senate the privilege of playing at dances in the suburbs and in the open air … The Roll-brothers and students were brought in to strengthen the Ratsmusiker, functioning in effect as ripienists; while some of the wind players seem to have been engaged from the ranks of the Greens' (Marx, 'Die Hamburger Oper', 121–2).

3 Mattheson, *Der vollkommene Capellmeister*, III, pp. 480–1.

4 K. Zauft, 'Zu den Inszenierungsformen der Hamburger Barockopern', *HJb* 36 (1990) 130.

physical style probably related to contemporary *commedia dell'arte*; from the small group of professional singers such as Madame Conradi (probably Handel's first Almira) and Mattheson himself (Handel's Fernando) the stylised gestures and facial expressions to be found in the manuals of classical rhetoric. It was this last that was Mattheson's particular concern.

Rather surprisingly, he begins his discussion of the accomplishments demanded of the 'complete Capellmeister' with a consideration of the arts of posture and gesture (*Von der Geberden-Kunst*), telling us that it was an art which, in classical times, Cassiodorus had defined as 'silent music', because of its expressivity. Anyone who composes for the theatre, declared Mattheson, needs, if not a professional mastery of it, at least a clear working knowledge of its principles, because without it he may well make the singer's task more difficult. And however fine his music may be, it is ultimately the singer on whom the success of his opera will depend.[5] So a real master of opera (he singles out Heinichen for praise) must have the gift of turning into music not only the expressive and rhetorical sense of the words, but all the movements, postures and gestures of the singer too. The fact that so few composers since Lully have really understood dance is the reason why the music of the ballet episodes is so often not written by the composer of the opera, but selected or written by some dancing master. (Here, no doubt, one hears the voice of Kusser; if it is true, it sheds interesting oblique light on the Handel/Sallé collaboration.) No one, Mattheson declared, would dispute the close kinship of *Tonkunst* and *Redekunst* (the art of tones and the art of speech); vocal music is both beautiful sound produced by the voice (the choicest of musical instruments) and speech articulated. Performance demands that music, poetry and action should work together – this was the nature of the art of opera.

That was the aspiration, and we may be sure that Mattheson himself, when he took the leading roles in both *Almira* and *Nero*, did them in style (a few months before the premiere of *Almira* his performances in his own *Cleopatra* had had audiences shrieking in terror). So, without doubt, could Madame Conradi have done. In Mainwaring's *Memoirs* Handel remembered her as being as fine an actress as singer, and, in his translation, Mattheson added that she was endowed with 'an almost complete personal beauty' and 'an exceptionally splendid voice' of very extensive compass.[6]

In general, however, Mattheson was scathing about the calibre of German opera singers, above all because of their woodenness on stage: they took far

[5] Mattheson, *Der vollkommene Capellmeister*, I, Chapter 6.

[6] Mainwaring/Mattheson, p. 41.

too little care over matching gestures and the play of features to the expression of the music. He was also sympathetic about the unusual difficulties they had to contend with. While he welcomed the use of women in all the principal female roles, he acknowledged frankly both the low social status from which they suffered and the moral dangers to which actors had always been subject: it was not so much a question of the temptations to sinful living as the danger to the integrity of one's personality (he recognised the problem in his own experience of *hypocrisis* – the playing of a role). His writings on behalf of singers helped to make Hamburg a city in which, during the following decades, theatre came to be tended more responsibly than in most places in Germany: the first national theatre was established there (under Lessing), and a state theatre academy; and pensions were paid to old performers.

Italy

Both the theatres where Handel's operas were first staged survive, albeit much altered. They were very different. The Teatro del Cocomero in Florence, built to designs by Niccolò degli Ughi, originally opened in 1648; reorganised in 1699 (and redeveloped again and renamed the Teatro Niccolini in 1861), it was a small building with seating for just over 500. In Handel's time it belonged to the Accademia degli Infuocati, really more a society than an academy, whose particular interest was drama and whose particular policy was that of bringing the latest style of opera to their city. Salvi was a member. Nothing is known of its facilities in the early eighteenth century. The Teatro San Giovanni Grisostomo, the largest and most fashionable theatre in Venice, was erected in 1678. Some 1,400 or more spectators could be accommodated, in parterre and five tiers of twenty-one boxes; four additional boxes of great luxury were built into the thickness of the proscenium arch.[7] The theatre aimed for a superior clientele by charging high prices and favouring erudite plots. (It was drastically reconstructed in 1834, and the following year renamed Teatro Malibran.)[8]

Handel was now writing for casts of star singers: all or almost all of them, both in Florence and in Venice, were artists who sang under the protection of and by permission of royal or aristocratic patrons; indeed, they formed part of a 'ducal circuit' of singers which Ferdinando de' Medici had set up in

[7] *Mercure galant*, March 1683, quoted in N. Mangini, *I teatri di Venezia* (Milan: Mursia, 1974), p. 78.

[8] *Ibid.*, pp. 206 and 207. It had previously, for just a few months been renamed the Teatro Emeronittio.

the late 1680s to provide Florence and other north and central Italian courts with music to compare with that of Venice, Naples and Rome.[9] Evidently Handel enjoyed good relations with several of them, and they went on to play important parts as he established himself as an opera composer in London.

While he had doubtless learned much from working with Mattheson, the Italians transformed his understanding of the singing voice and what could be done with it. With Stefano Frilli in *Rodrigo*, and with Valeriano Pellegrini in *Agrippina*, he had his first experience of the operatic potential of fine castratos; Pellegrini worked with Handel again for some years in London. Giuseppe Maria Boschi, one of the two basses who sang in *Agrippina*, was also to come to London, and enjoyed a long period of productive work with him there; but it was Boschi's more experienced colleague Antonio Francesco Carli, in the important role of Claudio, whose music shows how much Handel's appreciation of what might be done with the bass voice had developed. While the roles of Consalvo and Raymondo in *Almira* suggest that he saw the bass voice as a quite straightforward vehicle for singing 'naturally', the Claudio role shows the bass transformed into a virtuoso performer with a huge range, the extremes of which could easily, sonorously and athletically be ventured. And that has implications for dramatic characterisation: dignified, grave and tender where need be – as Consalvo and Raymondo had been – but capable too of bullying and blustering and comic caricature. Then there was Margherita Durastanti: as a young singer she had joined Ruspoli's establishment in Rome at the same time as Handel turned up there. Three years later she starred in *Agrippina*, and she was to become his most dependable trooper in the early Royal Academy years.

From these fine singers Handel would have learned all that he needed to know in order to address his composing skills to the art of Italian opera: two things in particular. First, as Mattheson will already have tried to persuade him, the essential unity of poetry and music – in Italian vocal music as in ancient Greek drama, to declaim poetry was to sing[10] – a unity which made the idiomatic performance of recitative uncapturable in standard musical notation, and which made good diction the first foundation of the singer's art. And then, secondly, what has become the ticklish topic of vocal ornamentation. That is a matter better discussed later in the chapter (see Excursus 6.1).

[9] R. L. Weaver and N. W. Weaver, *A Chronology of Music in the Florentine Theater, 1590–1750* (Detroit: Information Coordinators, 1978), pp. 65–6.

[10] See the discussion in Harnoncourt, *Musik als Klangrede*, p. 64.

No less epoch-making would have been Handel's experience of Italian string playing. The purity and refinement of the string ensembles with which he worked in Rome (with their *concerto grosso* and *concertino* groupings) had evolved over a period of some twenty years under the guidance and inspiration of Corelli, and the great man continued to preside. The anecdote recorded of the rehearsals for *Il Trionfo* need not be doubted,[11] but any suspicion that Handel may have underestimated Corelli's art is surely answered by the sublime solo *obbligato* in the closing aria of that same oratorio (where Arcangelo on his violin escorts the soul heavenwards), and by the fact that the Italian works regularly make more technical demands on the string players than anything in *Almira* had done.

Where to look for the best information on production styles in Italy in the period 1706–10 is not quite a simple matter. The 'reform' that led to the emergence of *opera seria* (of which *Rodrigo*, if not *Agrippina*, is certainly an example) was in large part an attempted reassertion of the primacy of the poet, and it is probably to the views of the poets one should ideally look, especially to those associated with the Arcadian movement and those whose librettos were collected and later used by Handel himself: men such as Pariati, Stampiglia, Zeno and Salvi.

But there is no escaping the fact that by far the best source of understanding is the correspondence of Metastasio. Though he was a mere boy when Handel was in Italy, there are no grounds for believing that production style changed significantly between 1710 and 1725; Metastasio's teacher, Gravina, had been a founder member of the Accademia degli Arcadi; and Metastasio's sense of being Zeno's heir was strong. In his letters one finds the fullest, most thoughtful and most experienced reflections on how Italian opera of Handel's period was best staged (though there is no evidence that he knew Handel's own settings of his or anyone else's work). As Handel's operas came closest to the Metastasian ideal in his Royal Academy years, it seems sensible to defer this question, too, for a little later.

London

In London Handel came to work in a brand-new theatre, the Queen's Theatre in the Haymarket, which had been erected by Vanbrugh in 1705 with the specific object of giving a home to the brand-new art form. During the vicissitudes of the following five seasons it had regularly been refurbished,

[11] The story is told in Mainwaring, *Memoirs*. See Deutsch, p. 17, or *Documents I*, p. 70.

improved or extended, so that by the time it became the opera house definitively and finally, for the 1710–11 season – the season of Handel's operatic debut in London – it had the facilities to present the most splendid scenic displays.[12] The auditorium was, however, modest in size compared with those in Hamburg or at the Teatro S. Giovanni Grisostomo in Venice. Attendance records suggest that 670 people could be accommodated in comfort, and more than 900 when they were really packed in.[13] The orchestra was a little smaller than it became in the Royal Academy years, when the number of violins was significantly increased and the oboes were generally doubled up,[14] but it had enough outstanding players for Handel to feel confident that in *Rinaldo* he could use it to help him take the city by storm, writing a large number of vivid orchestral sinfonias and accompaniments for the arias more varied in colour and more ostentatiously virtuosic than London audiences had ever experienced in the opera house, or indeed than he was ever again to write.

In the opera house in London Handel found a state of affairs different from anything he had hitherto experienced: an alien, Italian art form, performed by almost exclusively Italian singers in the Italian language, to an audience only a small number of whom would have understood it fluently, idiomatically or with any degree of sensitivity. He was to find his own way of dealing with this curiously unnatural problem during the Royal Academy years. What he at once understood and exploited brilliantly in *Rinaldo*, *Teseo* and *Amadigi* was that, under the circumstances, glorious singing of glorious music was the key to success. Three singers in particular helped him concentrate his mind on this truth.

Handel evidently hoped that Boschi, whom we have already met in *Agrippina*, was ready for better things – ready to out-Carli Carli one might say – and Handel wrote for him the brilliant bass role of Argante in *Rinaldo*, with all the features I have described as characteristic of Carli's role in *Agrippina*. Perhaps, as Argante, Boschi was over-parted: at any rate Handel never wrote another such plum part for an operatic bass, whether for Boschi or anyone else. But he was happy to recruit him again when the opportunity arose, and Boschi remained a dependable, integral member of the ensemble that presented the great repertory of Royal Academy works,

12 Excerpts from the celebratory poem are given in Stanley Sadie and Anthony Hicks (eds.), *Handel Tercentenary Collection* (Basingstoke: Macmillan Music Division, 1987), pp. 95–6, and in *Documents I*, p. 194.

13 J. Milhous and R. D. Hume, 'Handel's London – the Theatres' in *CCH*, p. 56.

14 Orchestra lists for the period are given in D. Burrows, 'Handel's London Theatre Orchestra', *EM* 13 (1985), 355, and M. W. Stahura, 'Handel and the Orchestra', in *CCH*, p. 243.

their 'blustering Polyphemus' character singer, a limited star, but certainly a star of a kind.

A singer whose art must have had a particularly powerful effect on Handel's imagination in these years was Elisabetta Pilotti-Schiavonetti, whom he will have known and perhaps already have worked with during his months in Hanover, for she was a singer in the service of the Dowager Electress Sophie; she returned to Hanover after 1717. It is curious that her London performances left so little trace in contemporary criticism and literature. We deduce from the roles Handel wrote for her between 1710 and 1715, especially the three enchantress roles of Armida in *Rinaldo*, Medea in *Teseo* and Melissa in *Amadigi*, that she was one of the most brilliant, certainly the most dramatic, and perhaps the most intrepid of all his sopranos. In the first of these roles her top C in 'Molto voglio, molto spero' – a note Handel very rarely used at all – has to be plucked out of thin air; and it was she whom Handel chose to challenge – one imagines to some kind of emulation – with his keyboard improvisations in the climactic aria at the close of Act II, 'Vo' far guerra'.

The supreme opera singer working in London in those pre-Royal Academy days was the castrato Nicola Grimaldi (Nicolini), one of the great artists of the century. A musician sufficiently fastidious to love best of all the music of Alessandro Scarlatti, and intelligent and gentlemanly enough to be entrusted with the choosing and arranging of Italian operas for staging in London, Nicolini enjoyed a long and glorious career embracing the music of Provenzale at one end and of Pergolesi at the other. He had made his debut in his native Naples in the year of Handel's birth, and died in the same city forty-six years later during rehearsals for Pergolesi's *Salustia*. In England even those disquieted by castrato voices respected the man and venerated the artist: perhaps 'the greatest performer in dramatic Music that is now living, or that perhaps ever appeared on a stage', thought Addison; 'a person whose action gives new majesty to kings, resolution to heroes, and softness to lovers.' 'I have often wished', Addison continued,

> that our tragedians would copy after this great master in action. Could they make use of their arms and legs, and inform their faces with as significant looks and passions, how glorious would an English tragedy appear with that action which is capable of giving dignity to the forced thoughts, cold conceits, and unnatural expressions of an Italian opera![15]

[15] *Spectator* No. 13, 15 March 1711.

And Algarotti, who can only have seen Nicolini at the very end of his career, if at all, was to suggest that he should be remembered and emulated in the same way as in Paris the great French tragedians and tragediennes of the age of Corneille and Racine were remembered.[16]

Singing – the art of song – was the gateway to great music-making, to brilliant characterising 'turns' and to supreme tragic acting alike. As soon as the opportunity arose, as soon as the necessary authority had been vested in him, Handel made choosing his own casts of singers an integral part of his work.

The Royal Academy of Music

The terms of Handel's employment with the Royal Academy have few if any parallels in the history of opera. In effect, one composer was given responsibility – of course subject to the approval of his directors – to choose an ensemble of the best singers money could buy, to compose for them – with contributions from a small group of hand-picked colleagues – a varied repertory of operas, to supervise their rehearsal and direct their performance in a first-rate, purpose-built theatre. Working with this small company of the finest singers of the age and with an orchestra of matching excellence, he could match his music perfectly to the particular qualities of their voices and to their particular musical and theatrical skills. Under such circumstances, in the course of nine seasons, Handel composed thirteen new operas and the single act of *Muzio Scevola*. The singers who chiefly helped give them their character were the already familiar Boschi (every season) and Durastanti for five seasons; and the new singers Cuzzoni for six seasons, Faustina for three and, most crucially, Senesino for eight. 'The significance of the cast to his opera composition was fundamental, and the nature of his artistic relationships to his singers was neither compromising nor trivial.'[17]

Singers of this calibre did not come cheaply, and the emphasis on historical subjects during the Royal Academy years was certainly in part due to the need to economise on spectacle – to 'exclude those various Embellishments of Machinery, Painting, Dances' precisely because of the 'vast Expence

[16] F. Algarotti, *Essay on the Opera*, English edn., London, 1767. Cited in R. King, 'How to Be an Emperor', *EM* 36 (2008), fn. 2.

[17] Larue, *Handel and His Singers*, p. 7. One can think of only one other operatic repertory of comparable distinction created under comparably extraordinary circumstances: that formed by the nine operas composed for Naples by Rossini between 1815 and 1822.

of procuring Foreign Voices'.[18] No doubt the standard sets – courtyards, throne rooms, prisons, gardens, and so on – were handsomely designed, for good artists were employed. But the reliance on a limited number of fixed locations meant that, particularly in the eyes of those with a more international experience of opera, the Haymarket Theatre now offered relatively drab fare. P. J. Fougeroux, a French visitor to the theatre in 1727, summed up his impressions thus (*Siroe*, *Tolomeo* and *Admeto* were the operas he saw): 'since there was no spectacle in the form of dances or decorations or machines, and the stage was denuded of choruses and the multitude of performers who adorn the scene, one can say that the name of opera is ill-applied to such a spectacle; it is rather a fine concert given in a theatre.'[19] The 'best depiction we have' of a Royal Academy staging – and it is really not very good – is the familiar caricature of Senesino, Cuzzoni and Berenstadt, probably performing in Ariosti's *Coriolano*.[20]

With scenic marvels temporarily reduced in importance, the operas were now presented as a picturesque exhibition of living statuary. Occasionally, in the grander operas such as *Radamisto* or *Giulio Cesare*, supernumeraries will have been used to animate the scenes of pageantry or battle.[21] But the chief thing was that, as Cuzzoni and Senesino and the rest sang their arias, they should present a picture as elegant and as heroic as a canvas by Poussin or a Tiepolo fresco; that, as was said of Nicolini a few years earlier, there should be 'scarce a beautiful posture in an old statue' which they did not 'plant [themselves] in, as the different circumstances of the story give occasion for it'.[22] And the sight was as anachronistic as Tiepolo too. Male costume derived from classical Roman styles of armour were obligatory, even for mythological and allegorical principals, a character being identifiable – like a saint on an altarpiece – only by the appropriate attributes. Women wore fashionable eighteenth-century court costume, complete with high nodding tufts of feathers and trains which required pages to control them. Nor did Cuzzoni and Faustina appear on stage with empty

18 The words are from Lewis Theobald's *Rape of Proserpine*, 1727, quoted in L. Lindgren, 'The Staging of Handel's Operas' in Stanley Sadie and Anthony Hicks (eds.), *Handel Tercentenary Collection* (Basingstoke: Macmillan Music Division, 1987), p. 117.

19 The French text is given in W. Dean, 'A French Traveller's View of Handel's Operas', *ML* 55 (1974), 177.

20 For reproductions see Deutsch facing p. 129, or *Documents I*, pp. 647–8.

21 It has been calculated that at least twenty-six of them were involved in the original *Radamisto*. J. Milhous and R. D. Hume, 'A Prompt Copy of Handel's *Radamisto*', *MT* 127 (June 1986), 317. If they did, as Milhous and Hume suggest, have something of a 'semiotic' function, they would have been a highly desirable adjunct in any opera.

22 R. Steele, *Tatler*, no. 115.

hands: handkerchieves and fans were the standard accoutrements, but in certain roles a wand might have been judged more fitting. With such dress, and the dignified and constrained style of movement such dress dictated, the sensation caused by Sallé's skimpy outfits in the 1730s is readily understandable.[23] The acting, in the sense of what Nicolini had done to win the admiration of Addison and Steele, and what Senesino was now doing, really began only after the tableaus had been formed.[24]

In short, though all contemporary critics emphasise the importance of acting, for English audiences this meant acting perhaps less in the sense of animating a text urgently and thrillingly than in the sense of creating an emotionally moving picture. London audiences will not – many of them – have been great connoisseurs of Italian literature, but they were often connoisseurs of fine art, and they will have known how to read the movement, the deportment, the pose and the gesture of the singers. It is time to introduce Metastasio.

Metastasio claimed for himself responsibility and authority in matters of stage direction; the claim was rooted in his belief that it was the poet who was the dramatist.[25] The evidence is unmistakable that while he was writing, he envisaged very clearly in his mind's eye exactly how his dramas should look: how the set would be designed; how the characters would be grouped for best effect; how the demands of stage decorum and dramatic vividness could best be reconciled; and so on. And these writing-desk visions he expected to see realised in the theatre. Two brief excerpts from his extensive correspondence give us some impression of the scope of his concern (and the scope of the concern of his correspondents). First, from a letter to Abate Pasquini about the staging of *Demofoonte*:

If you ask me who should be placed on the right hand, and who on the left, I must tell you I never meant to regulate that by the dignity of the personages, but by the convenience and necessity of the action. And if, in favour of such convenience and necessity, the superior personages chance to be on the the left of the inferior, they may be respected and distinguished in various ways; for example: by being a little forwarder on the stage and facing the audience, while the subaltern characters are further on the stage, with their sides to the audience and faces towards the principal

[23] Opera costume is discussed in Dean and Knapp, *Handel's Operas 1704–1726*, p. 27. A fuller account is given in Barbara Purrucker, 'Das Bühnenkostüm des Barock', in B. Siegmund (ed.), *Gestik und Affekt in der Musik des 17. and 18. Jahrhunderts*, Michaelsteiner Konferenzberichte 63 (Blankenburg: Stiftung Kloster Michaelstein, 2003).

[24] See Joachim Eisenschmidt, *Die szenische Darstellung der Opern Georg Friedrich Händels auf der Londoner Bühne seiner Zeit* (Inaugural-Dissertation), Halle, 1940, vol. II, p. 32.

[25] See Metastasio's comments quoted in Chapter 3, p. 82.

personages. And indeed by a thousand other expedients they may be distinguished, without having the right side of the stage assigned to them.[26]

Second, to Farinelli, about the staging of *Alessandro nell'Indie* (= *Poro*):

The last scene of the third act … would entirely languish, if the architect did not contrive a decorous and probable skreen on the right hand side, near the orchestra, to conceal *Porus* and *Gandarte* from all the other actors, and yet leave them visible to us spectators. I have imagined for the purpose, the temple to be wholly adorned with very rich carpets, hanging from the architraves, pilasters, and columns.[27]

Equally fascinating are his opinions on matters of singing and acting, which ideally were not two things but two complementary aspects of a single accomplishment. What must be particularly gratifying for Handelians (whose composer was never quite satisfied with merely 'dressing' the poetry) is that Metastasio believed the key to doing both well was to be found in a singer's understanding of character. A famous, long letter on the matter was written to Hasse in 1749 about the staging of *Attilio Regolo*;[28] but in a Handelian context still more to the point is a letter he wrote about the opening scene of *Alessandro nell'Indie* (*Poro*), in which Metastasio's description of the scene, his glosses on his own poetry and his reflections on Poro's psychology turn his advice into something 'quite novellistic' in its insight into the character's state of mind. Summarising his remarks he writes:

from which account, esteemed sir, you will understand well enough that the actor who plays the part of Porus should not say 'To whom am I speaking?' to the fleeing soldiers, but to himself, or – by theatrical licence – towards the audience, and not in an imperious tone, but rather that of a man who blames himself for having made a useless attempt.[29]

It was natural that Metastasio should be principally concerned with production matters that related directly to the organisation of the plot, and to the effective delivery through the music of the poetry he had written. But the idea that the singer's business was 'to imitate the speech of man with numbers and harmony' was not just the wishful thinking of a self-willed poet.[30] For a more music-centred endorsement we may turn to Pier Francesco Tosi, our best authority on the matter. Dean and Knapp are right

26 Letter of 16 February 1748, in Burney, *Memoirs of Metastasio*, vol. I, pp. 225–6.

27 Letter of 4 February 1754, in Burney, *Memoirs of Metastasio*, vol. II, p. 114.

28 See Burney, *Memoirs of Metastasio*, vol. I, pp. 315–30.

29 Letter of 24 June 1764, more fully discussed in R. Savage, 'Staging an Opera: Letters from the Cesarian Poet', *EM* 26 (1998), 592.

30 Cf. Chapter 3, p. 82, and fn. 16.

to remind us that Tosi was a singer – a castrato at that – and a generation older than Handel; but he spent many years in London (1692–1705, and again in the mid 1720s); his *Opinioni* appeared originally in Bologna in 1723 when Handel had just reached the high noon of his operatic career and Metastasio was on the point of launching his; and they were evidently felt to be still pertinent for the London musical scene in 1742 when Galliard, a good judge, Englished them. If we are looking for someone to counsel us, these are surely the best credentials we can hope to find. It is Tosi who provides us with some sense of the changing vocal style during Handel's career, by remarking that the ancients were better at cantabile, the moderns at brilliant allegros;[31] and his is the familiar classic (and satirical) account of the role of ornamentation in the performance of the da capo aria.[32] But I would see his emphasis on two humbler excellences as being what modern performers most need to take to heart. The first is diction:

> let him take Care that the Words be uttered in such a Manner, without any Affectation that they be distinctly understood, and no one Syllable be lost: for if they are not distinguished, the Singer deprives the Hearer of the greatest Part of that Delight which vocal Musick conveys by Means of the Words. For if the Words are not heard so as to be understood, there will be no great Difference between a human Voice and a Hautboy.[33]

Along with that emphasis on clarity of diction must go the ability to give dramatic vividness to the recitative, without which gift 'I would advise you to renounce the Name and Office of Master'.[34]

Changing circumstances: 'Second Academy' and after

During the Royal Academy years Handel would have had every opportunity to decide how most effectively Italian opera should be presented to London audiences: what the best balance of voices and instruments was; what role the spectacle – considered both in terms of the stage-sets and of the comportment and grouping of the singers – ought ideally to play; how best to use the musical and theatrical skills of a superb body of performers so as to give delight to an audience very different from the audiences among

31 P. F. Tosi, *Opinioni de' cantori antichi, e moderni*, Bologna, 1723, tr. J. E. Galliard as *Observations on the Florid Song* (London, 1742) (hereafter Tosi/Galliard), p. 87.

32 *Ibid.*, pp. 93–4. It is quoted in, for example, D. J. Grout, *A Short History of Opera* (New York: Columbia University Press, 1947), pp. 192–3.

33 *Ibid.*, pp. 58–9.

34 *Ibid.*, p. 71.

which they had first learned their arts. For the latter part of his operatic career, from 1729 to 1741, from *Lotario* to *Deidamia*, only a few changing circumstances need be noted.

For most of the period, the five seasons of the 'Second Academy', 1729–34, and the season 1737–38, Handel presented his operas at the Haymarket, in the theatre that had been his operatic home since he arrived in England in 1710. But three seasons were spent in the new Covent Garden theatre, and his last two operas, *Imeneo* and *Deidamia* were first staged at Lincoln's Inn Fields. While this last was probably a makeshift arrangement in the absence of anywhere better to take them,[35] to perform in Covent Garden proved enormously stimulating.

The operas of the 'Second Academy' suggested a gradual decline of interest in the star singer and a reawakening enthusiasm for more flamboyant staging, perhaps stimulated by English pantomime.[36] Covent Garden was the High Citadel of this pantomime tradition, and John Rich, who had built the theatre only a few years earlier in 1732, was its master showman. Covent Garden was therefore designed from the first to be home to the most sensational spectacle the English theatre had to offer, and a surviving inventory of its 'effects' shows that Handel happily availed himself of them in his operas: rolling billows for *Ariodante*, falling rocks for *Alcina*, oxen and plough furrows for *Giustino*, and so forth.[37] But what most distinguished the Covent Garden operas, sadly for the 1734–35 season only, and made them a landmark – if at the time a little-appreciated landmark – in the history of eighteenth-century opera, was that Marie Sallé's team of dancers formed part of Rich's company. So, as in *Almira* and the first version of *Radamisto* but far more thrillingly, ballet music integral to the drama was composed for one of the most influential dancers of the century: in the Covent Garden revivals of *Arianna*, *Il pastor fido* and the pasticcio *Oreste*, and in the new operas *Ariodante* and *Alcina*. It is in these two new works that something quite different from the usual decorative framing of the action appears. For Sallé's genius and boldness, her readiness to use her whole body as a means of mirroring the irrationally veering impulses of her character's predicament and the passions of her heart gave a tangible physical form to some of the operas' dramatic crises, matching the expressive power of Handel's

35 Indeed, the third and final performance of *Deidamia* was transferred to the Little Haymarket theatre.

36 See Lindgren, 'The Staging of Handel's Operas', p. 102.

37 More details of the inventory are given in Dean and Knapp, *Handel's Operas 1704–1726*, pp. 24–5.

music and perhaps more than matching the constrained stylisation of such action as the singers could encompass.[38]

If there were no divas in later seasons quite to compare with Cuzzoni and Faustina, and if the often brittle relationship between Handel and Senesino eventually snapped irrevocably after *Orlando*, great singers continued to sing in his operas. His relationship with them was rather different from what it had been with his previous stars. His principal soprano throughout the 'Second Academy' and the Covent Garden years was Anna Strada del Pò, who, more than any other Italian artist he worked with, seems to have been moulded and refined into a great singer by Handel himself. 'She came hither', reported Burney, 'a coarse and aukward singer with improvable talents, and he at last polished her into reputation and favour' – and this notwithstanding her uningratiating appearance, for 'her person is *very bad* and she makes *frightful mouths*'.[39] Burney's comment possibly sheds light on one surprising fact about Strada: most of the principal singers with whom Handel worked in London were, on their English debuts, and often in subsequent operas too, given small-scale arias with continuo-only accompaniment at their first appearance on the stage.[40] Partly, perhaps, this was to sing themselves in, but partly, and more importantly, one feels sure, it was to give them the opportunity to show what they could really do: unconstrained by an orchestra, they could sing with such fancy and freedom and ostentation as was theirs to command. Strada was never given such an aria.[41]

After the departure of Senesino, Handel's leading castratos – Carestini, Conti, Annibali and Caffarelli – belonged to a younger generation, and had been formed in a more modern repertory. The most interesting of them was Carestini: Burney reported him to be 'tall, beautiful, and majestic … a very animated and intelligent actor, and having a considerable portion of enthusiasm in his composition, with a lively and inventive imagination, he rendered every thing he sung interesting by good taste, energy, and judicious embellishments'.[42] The music Handel wrote for these men, particularly for the first two, shows that he was, predictably enough, keen to

[38] On this topic, see S. Henze-Döhring, 'Zur Gattungstradition von Händels "Ariodante"' *VIHAK* (1992), especially at 44f.

[39] Mrs Pendarves, in a letter written in November 1729, when Strada was new in London (Deutsch, p. 247).

[40] For details see below at p.191. Faustina seems an exception; but the circumstances of her debut in *Alessandro* perhaps made it difficult for her to be singled out in such a way.

[41] For more on this topic, see Excursus 6.1.

[42] Burney, *A General History of Music*, vol. II, pp. 782–3.

pick up what he could from them and to put their particular skills to good effect. Ariodante's arias, for Carestini, made that role the most expressive, inventive and energetic of all Handel's castrato roles, and the same kind of virtuosic energy – if in a more one-dimensional way, with more touches of contemporary musical styles – is typical of Conti's roles in *Arminio* and *Giustino*.[43] Perhaps with these younger singers he also picked up a note of 'Pergolesian pathetic', sensed its affinity with Arne's new English lyricism, and fused them in the entrancing ditties which from time to time punctuate the series of grand da capo arias in his late operas.

The rediscovery of Handel's operas

One takes an interest in what actually happened in Handel's theatre, not necessarily as a guide to what ought to happen in our own theatres, but because, when an art of exceptional beauty has been rediscovered, it seems urgent to try to understand it as fully as possible. Handel's operas occupy a relatively small part of the repertory in modern opera houses, but it is now, in most places, an indispensable part. This circumstance has a most singular history.

Admeto was the last Handel opera to be staged in London during the composer's lifetime, at the King's Theatre in 1754. Thereafter no other Handel opera was staged anywhere until after the First World War, a period of almost 170 years.[44] Nowhere had there been a continuing tradition of Handel opera performance; when the exploration of the repertory began in the 1920s an unmarked *tabula rasa* lay before the revivalists.[45]

Oskar Hagen, who was assistant professor of the History of Art at Göttingen University between 1918 and 1924, and who had also studied *Musikwissenschaft* with Hermann Abert in Halle, began the theatrical rediscovery with a series of productions – *Rodelinda* 1920, *Ottone* 1921,

43 Before he wrote these, however, Handel showed a touching fatherly concern for young Conti, only twenty-two years old at the time and a 'courteous and modest' youth. See Chapter 1, p. 38 on his *arie di baule*.

44 A partial exception might be made for four stagings – three of them in Hamburg, and all of them drastically abbreviated – of *Almira*. They were given on three celebratory occasions: in 1878 (the bicentenary of the Hamburg opera house), repeated in Leipzig in 1879; in 1885 (the bicentenary of Handel's birth) and in 1905 (the bicentenary of his operatic debut). Except for the 1885 performance, each was part of a double bill, either with Gluck or with Mozart. (Manfred Rätzer, *Szenische Aufführungen von Werken Georg Friedrich Händels vom 18. bis 20. Jahrhundert: eine Dokumentation* (Halle an der Saale: Händel-Haus, 2000), p. 19).

45 Dean's essay 'Production Style in Handel's Operas' in *CCH* surveys the ensuing saga.

Giulio Cesare 1922, *Serse* 1924 – in his own adaptations. These adaptations survived in the repertories of some German opera houses into the 1960s.[46] They had been well received in the 1920s and they were proving durable; for Hagen had done a serious job, inspired by his conviction of Handel's greatness as composer and man-of-the-theatre. His adaptations were, however, heavy-handed, and the musical consequences – to a later taste – were dire.

All the same, Dean's judgement, likening Hagen's efforts to 'a grinning parody', is surely unfair:[47] neither grinning nor parody seems quite the *mot juste*. As far as the staging and costumes were concerned, Hagen's revivals appeared to have been inspired less by the neo-classical ethos of the period than by a lingering devotion to Expressionism.[48] They were heavily cut, not just to clarify and speed up the plots, but also to reshape the arias. Da capos were eliminated and the arias were commonly reorchestrated, or assigned to different characters, or transposed. This was especially the case with castrato parts, which had to be turned into baritone or bass-baritone parts, since high-voiced, soprano or alto heroes were as unthinkable in the 1920s as low-voiced heroes had been 200 years earlier. All this was done in the interest of an emotionally charged expressivity – in itself an entirely legitimate aim. Hagen was, one feels, eager to make Handel a more central and integral part of the great classical canon of music, as Bach had long been, and he interpreted the music in the retrospective light shed by that canon.

A few popular arias from the operas had always been much loved. But it was only as the Early Music movement became a regular presence in modern musical life that the abundance and energy and the sheer beauty of Handel's operas could be fully appreciated. The performance of early opera often became a strand in a well-rounded musical education in colleges and universities, and proselytising groups of enthusiasts sprang up: in the Handel Opera Society, at the Unicorn Theatre in Abingdon, and elsewhere. Rather more hesitantly, established opera houses began to explore a few of the operas which seemed to have the stuff of popularity in them, and several of which, it may be noted – *Giulio Cesare*, *Rodelinda*, *Serse* – overlapped with Hagen's choice; *Agrippina* and the Ariosto operas were also viewed as potential winners. But this is a story that has been told well elsewhere and I do not propose to retell it here. Nor is it necessary to enter the debate

[46] Full details are to be found in Rätzer, *Szenische Aufführungen von Werken Georg Friedrich Händels*.

[47] Dean, *Handel's Operas 1726–1741*, p. 447. He is writing of *Serse*, but his comments on Hagen's other adaptations are not more cordial.

[48] See the discussion following E. Kohlhaas, '"Prima la musica, poi le parole" oder Händel zwischen Wort und Ton', *VIHAK* 5 (1994).

on the 'authentic', or 'historically aware' performance of eighteenth-century music. The desirability, let alone the attainability, of 'period performance' may have become more problematic than it seemed fifty years ago.[49] But at least some of the musical insights afforded by the movement are things that almost no one would today care to relinquish: the pacing of the recitative – free and fast-moving; the effectiveness of Handel's balance of voices and instruments; the appropriateness of the voice-type to the music composed; the use either of period instruments (provided they are played with the same mastery as we expect from modern instrumentalists) or, if modern instruments are to be used, a way of playing them that is at the very least courteous in respect of their older colleagues.

On the musical front much has been achieved: instrumental playing (even in many of the opera house orchestras with little experience of early music) can, under firm direction, be stylish as well as accomplished, and there are many first-rate singers for whom Handelian opera is a fundamental part of their repertory. What used to be called the castrato problem no longer exists: it has been more than adequately solved, both by distinguished mezzo-sopranos (historically the more authentic choice) and a superb generation of male altos who have learned, when appropriate, to instil into their voices a steely heroic timbre, without losing the poignancy and pathos that had always been the mark of the finest exponents of this type of singing.

The reappearance of Handel operas in established opera houses coincided with the arrival of *Regietheater*, of which 'producer's opera' is an apologetic and scarcely adequate English rendering. Since the operas had played no enduring part in European civilisation (and in that respect were quite different from the operas of Gluck, which were scarcely less remote, or from the French classical dramatists, who belonged to an even more distant world), the debate about how they should be done tended to polarise: in colleges of music and universities they were commonly seen as ways of understanding and enjoying the way things had been done once upon a time; while in the professional theatres there was simply no received wisdom, no routine, no sense of how now they 'ought' to be done.

Lest some of the comments that follow suggest that I have forgotten or deplore the fact, let it be said at once that the performance of Handelian opera requires a stage director. To say that there was not one in the theatres Handel knew is true only in the rather limited sense that there was not

[49] An admirable survey of the question is N. Kenyon (ed.), *Authenticity and Early Music* (Oxford University Press, 1988).

one specifically identified professional figure who did the job. The opera's 'production values' would, however, have been part of the responsibility of one of the senior wise heads involved in the enterprise, ideally and most commonly the poet. In Handel's lifetime those who wrote about the performance of opera – from Perrucci in 1699 to Algarotti in 1755,[50] and plenty more besides – were in no doubt that such a figure was indispensable. And though they all discuss the matter from slightly different perspectives and with different degrees of thoroughness, it is certain that each of them would broadly have endorsed the programme of the '*Corago*' (perhaps to be identified with Pierfrancesco Rinuccini), who wrote a small treatise on the staging of opera in *c.*1630.[51] His recommendation was that a *corago*, a producer-director, should be the man in charge of all that pertains to the staging of opera – the acting and dancing and fencing; the lighting; the dressmakers and carpenters and masons – and that he was to perform this role in the service of the poet. His top priority, therefore, was to be to tell the story intelligibly, and to ensure that the grouping of the characters into stage pictures and all the movements that led into and emerged out of these stage pictures should be helpful, 'readable', readily understandable for the spectators.

Coming to these matters, as most of us presumably do, via the music, we may feel a momentary discomfort at the idea that the service of the poet was the top priority. But the discomfort is assuaged the moment we reflect that, simply by virtue of dressing the poetry, the music had taken it over – had interposed itself with glorious self-assertiveness between the poet's writing desk and the presentation of his work in the theatre, especially when singers and orchestra alike had been coached and rehearsed in their duties by the composer. Besides, if one takes the high classical line that *opera seria* took, poetry and music were hardly to be put asunder anyway. No one in Handel's day would have disputed the inseparably close kinship of *Tonkunst* and *Redekunst* (the art of tones and the art of speech); for, to reiterate Mattheson's claim, 'vocal music is both beautiful sound produced by the voice (the choicest of all musical instruments), and speech articulated'.

An observation by Strohm has often been cited, to the effect that, if we seriously wanted to revive the art of *opera seria* today, we should concentrate

50 A. Perrucci, *Dell'arte rappresentativa premeditata ed all'improviso*, 1699; F. Algarotti, *Saggio sopra l'opera in musica*, 1755.

51 See R. Savage and M. Sansone, '*Il Corago* and the Staging of Early Opera: Four Chapters from an Anonymous Treatise *circa* 1630, *EM* 17 (1989), 495–511. The full Italian text is in P. Fabbri and A. Pompilio (eds.), *Il Corago* (Florence: Olschki, 1983).

less on what Handel or Hasse wrote than on what Senesino or Farinelli did with the chief role … if we had a Senesino, who had a deep understanding not only of singing but also of reciting Italian verse and not least of how to be an Emperor it might not matter so much that some of his arias were by Harnoncourt and not Handel. In fact they could even be by Penderecki.[52]

Well, indeed they could, and we might – if we had superlative Italian dramatic poetry to deal with and an audience that was in a position to appreciate it. But the revival of *opera seria* is not what I am primarily concerned with. Handel's operas matter to us (to most of us anyway) for the simple reason that the music is by Handel, that much of it is of supreme beauty, and that all of it was composed with a dramatic purpose. It might have been different if Handel had ever had an invitation to compose an opera for the Viennese court in the 1730s, and had – *per impossibile* – enjoyed an entirely harmonious working relationship with Metastasio. But as it is, the only material question is how we might most effectively (that is to say in a way that places Handel's work most vividly and expressively before us) perform his operas now.

A good starting point, something to be tried at least as a working hypothesis, might be to suppose that Handel, who spent close on forty years working in opera houses, and whose understanding of music and poetry and human nature shines through virtually every operatic scene he wrote, could be trusted to make effective use of the theatrical practice of his age, and that we might therefore be well advised to try it ourselves. And indeed, many of the Handel productions from the 1960s onwards which have been informed by an understanding of stylish 'Early Music' performance practice have also experimented with a period style of staging. There are overwhelmingly good reasons for continuing these 'experiments', and plentiful evidence to show they are experiments no longer, since they work so well. Handel, like all the other great composers of opera one can think of, 'saw' the scenes as he composed them – and this is not simply a trivial psychological tic; the consequences of it permeate the fabric of his music. As a result, the music typically comprises not just the rhetorical and affective setting of the poetry; there are cues for gesture and movement too, and plentiful clues as to how the most important part of the music – the arias and occasional duets – might best be placed in the picture presented to the spectator. The musical and poetical and theatrical elements of the opera comprise one single vision.

52 'Towards an Understanding of the *Opera Seria*' in Strohm, *Essays on Handel and Italian Opera*, p. 98.

If that vision is to be shared effectively with a theatre audience, it needs the support of appropriate stage-settings and costumes, and it requires that the singers comport themselves in a congruous style. Andrew Jones has remarked on how, when everyone involved acknowledges the same ideal, the discipline and apparent circumscription of the acting style provides a perfect complement to the particular kind of formality found in Handel's music. And he speaks from experience when he underlines the fact that the stage director who has taken the trouble to master the rules of this game need be no more inhibited by that knowledge than the musicians who sing and play are inhibited by the insights they have gained from their Early Music studies.[53]

For the stage directors who recognise that how singers act is an intrinsic part of the performance of a Handel opera, there is evidence enough – literary, critical, theoretical and iconographical – as to how Handel himself would have expected it to be done. The way singers moved about the stage, the groups into which they formed themselves, the postures they adopted, the gestures they employed, the play of eyes and face: these are richly documented things which could be taken seriously. And in an intriguing essay, Richard King takes the reader through a scene of *Alessandro*, doing just that, drawing on the best painted and sculpted images of the age – the sorts of images that Handel's London patrons would have collected for their own galleries and drawing rooms, and might have hoped to see and recognise once more on the stage.[54]

King would go further: he would like to see the reported and easily recognised idiosyncrasies of such historical figures as Alexander (his tilt of the head, for instance) reproduced on the stage, but doubts whether producers can be expected to study such things. Most of us, I think, could do without Alexander's tilted head, but – without expecting an eighteenth-century staging or stage picture to be slavishly reproduced – we might regard it as obligatory for the stage director to do his homework on all aspects of the multimedia work he is helping perform. Performance in Handel's day demanded that music, poetry and action worked together – this was the nature of the art of opera. Indeed, unless that expressive-rhetorical-visible unity is preserved, one is not performing an early eighteenth-century opera at all – which is not to say that one may not be doing something admirable and worthwhile, perhaps even more worthwhile than performing an

[53] A. V. Jones, 'Staging a Handel Opera', *EM 34* (2006). Jones was the musical director of Cambridge Handel Opera from 1985 to 2013.

[54] King, 'How to Be an Emperor'.

eighteenth-century opera.[55] And that brings us, I think, to the crux of the matter.

Werktreue and the composer's 'real intentions': *Verwirklichung*

The triumph on the musical front of *Werktreue*, by which I mean the serious and well-informed determination to perform Handel's music as he might have hoped to hear it performed, has, in the professional theatre, rarely been matched by a comparable triumph in the realisation of Handelian production values. This may be due simply to what has sometimes been seen as the abject failure of stage directors to take the trouble to understand the art they practise; their unwillingness to recognise how deeply the theatre practice of Handel's age worked its way into the fibre of his music.[56] But it will sometimes be due to their doubts about the philosophical plausibility or desirability of *Werktreue* as a performing ideal at all. And even if the production team does in some measure acknowledge the ideal, they may question whether the staging or spectacle is a constituent part of Handel's operas in quite the same way as the music and the words are. It may, for instance, be argued that staging and spectacle were never recorded with anything like the same exactness; and it is sometimes claimed that to try to make them constituent and integral parts of an opera has really never worked. Attempts in the second half of the nineteenth century to preserve the repertory of the Paris *Opéra* in the 'correct' style by issuing definitive production books, or stagings of *Parsifal* in the early decades after its premiere, or the weariness of the old D'Oyly Carte G&S seasons half a century or so ago may be held up as warnings.

But surely no one who has ever been involved in an attempt to stage a Handel opera in something like period style supposed they were making an exact copy of what went on in the Haymarket Theatre in the 1720s, or that it would be a good thing if they had been. For when sensitive and accomplished performers are at their best, great music – whether it be in an opera house, or a concert hall or some intimate room with a few friends – transforms them into magicians, able to make of each performance a spellbinding

[55] In 1693, for instance, it was more admirable and worthwhile (I would think) for Purcell and (?)Betterton to create and stage *The Fairy-Queen* than it would have been to stage a merely 'faithful' revival of Shakespeare's *Midsummer Night's Dream* (which they would never have thought of anyway).

[56] See, for example, the references to Sigiswald Kuijken's complaints in Wolfgang Ludewig, 'Die Oper – eine Schau der Welt', *VIHAK* 4 (1994), 133.

and unique occasion. And however much their sensitivity and accomplishment may take a twenty-first-century colouring, many of them feel that the more humbly they try to serve the composer, the more powerfully their own musicianship expresses itself. It is difficult to see why stage directors should be denied this magical privilege. Staging a new production of a Handel opera in response to ideals of *Werktreue* is not like switching on fairground automata; it is more like the budding and leafing of this year's spring as compared with last year's, and it brings its own fresh, unique epiphany.

What I suppose makes that simple idea problematic is the fact that these works of art do themselves change. To see that, it is not necessary to go into abstruse theoretical questions about whether the staging of a work can be regarded as an integral part of it, or whether it must necessarily be some kind of hermeneutical exercise addressed to our contemporary circumstances and needs. It is enough to consider what did actually happen when, after a lapse of some few years, composers took up their works again to revive them. Even the composer, it transpires, when he restaged an opera, may have come to be unsure, not just whether he had got it quite right first time, but even what had really been in his mind – what really had been his intention – when he wrote it. *Der fliegende Holländer* provides a particularly interesting illustration: what began, and was first performed, as a picturesque dramatisation of a romantic, balladesque ghost story, over the years was partly transformed by the transformation of Wagner's own imagination into something different: an embryonic mythic music-drama in which a few not-quite-digested anachronistic relics got left behind.[57] Handel's own re-stagings of his operas in later seasons provide teasing examples of a very different kind (as do some of the operas of Mozart and Verdi). No doubt what changed generally had more to do with the words and music of the opera than with the question of how to perform it; but the one can hardly have been changed without having an effect on the other. In any of these cases, for whatever reason, the work changed as the world changed; and that being so, when we come to perform them ourselves, we may feel that the unique once-and-for-all commitment to *Werktreue* is called into question. We are faced with what James Hepokoski calls the Myth of Recoverable Immediacy,[58] and fundamental choices have to be made.

[57] The matter is discussed by Carl Dahlhaus, *Richard Wagners Musikdramen* (Velber: Freidrich, 1971), pp. 156–7.

[58] James Hepokoski, 'Staging Verdi's Operas: the Single, 'Correct' Performance', in Alison Latham and Roger Parker (eds.), *Verdi in Performance* (Oxford University Press, 2001), pp. 11–20.

It is sometimes proposed that, instead of even attempting to stage an opera exactly as Handel and his contemporaries would have staged it – what one might call the 'archeological' approach – a production might aspire to present us with the work's 'real intentions'.[59] However, a more flagrant instance of question-begging would be difficult to conceive; and one might doubt whether it were possible to find any useful meaning in an aspiration at once so ambitious and so vague.[60] Roger Savage, in the exhilarating finale of his chapter on the staging of opera in the *Oxford Illustrated History of Opera*, does make a heroic attempt to umpire fairly the debates around the matter.[61] But I shall choose the simpler path of putting forward two – as it seems to me – legitimate alternative approaches; one of them might be described as growing out of the opera that is to be performed, the other as coming at it from a new perspective. Those who choose the former course, working outwards from their historically informed understanding of 'the work', are seeking not so much 'what the composer intended' as the idea of *Verwirklichung*: an excellent Wagnerian term which signifies realisation or materialisation or, to put it in suitably non-abstract terms for Handel, how to bring music and poetry to tangible, sensuous life in the theatre. The alternative strategy might be described as that of deliberately choosing to make something new. In practice it is rare if either of these approaches does not borrow at least something from the other.

For Wagner of course, *Verwirklichung* was the final stage in the creation of his own operas. If we are seeking it in the staging of 'early opera', the situation is rather different; Savage's formulation 'the proper modern way to animate the proper period style', though perhaps not entirely free from question-begging itself,[62] is a helpful paraphrase. In the case of Handelian opera, nothing is more fundamental to the 'proper period style' than making the most of the particular skills of the performers one is working with. And as far as production values are concerned, these will, among other things, nowadays almost certainly include the ability to sing beautifully while engaged in more fluid movement about the stage than an eighteenth-century singer would have used. Whether or not that is therefore a desirable thing to do is a separate matter. My readers will, I think, sense that we are moving into subjective zones.

59 See, for example, Strohm's contribution to the discussion in E. Kohlhaas, 'Prima la musica, poi le parole oder Händel zwischen Wort und Ton', in *VIHAK* 4, 1994, 108–9.

60 Nevertheless, not infrequently stage directors will volunteer, in their programme notes, to tell us what the opera they are staging is 'really about'.

61 Roger Savage, 'The Staging of Opera', *OIHO*, pp. 350–420.

62 And though Lucchino Visconti seems to be putting the words into his mouth. *Ibid.*, p. 409.

Where exactly the balance should fall between 'the proper modern way' and 'the proper period style' is the critical question; I find I can only try to answer it by considering how things have sometimes been done in recent years. And as, of all Handel's operas, *Serse* – for reasons some of which I have sketched out in Chapter 5 – provides the gentlest, least dogmatic and most enjoyable induction into the aesthetics of the *opera seria*, a good place to start reflecting on the question is an admired staging of *Serse* by English National Opera – so much admired in fact that more than a quarter of a century after its first appearance it was still (2014) in the repertory.[63] It intends no belittlement of Hytner's achievement, nor of his singers', to say that *Serse* is the easy one. *Serse* lends itself better than any other Handel opera to that intermixing of first-rate music-making and continuous stage activity that comes most naturally to modern performers; it doesn't always require – often it scarcely even allows – the stylised separation of recitative and aria which modern singers find difficult and stage directors seem to deplore. Many of the arias are short enough and free enough in form to be dissolved into the surrounding action; the characters can 'live through' them, almost as if they were conceived by Puccini; they do not necessarily require to be presented in the high style. Above all, perhaps, the spirit of the opera is a gently humorous one; an audience's sympathy is soon engaged, and the stage director needs strain neither for solemnity nor uproarious laughter.

While Hytner's staging provided a few off-the-ball incidents – contrived attempts to keep non-singing characters involved in the arias; a few perplexing choral routines – for most of the more substantial musical numbers he found a style which came close to the ideal that Savage's form of words suggests. The singers stood still enough (they did generally stand – a touching relic of a dying era) to form well-composed stage pictures; but this stillness was combined with naturalness of posture and liveliness of gesture (and of movement when required), all coordinated aptly with the music, and admirably performed by the singers.

The chorus has a non-avoidable if hardly significant part in *Serse*. To turn that minor element into a proper framing device, and to create

[63] At ENO it is, of course, called *Xerxes:* stage director, Nicholas Hytner. In the original 1988 transmission, which was the one I saw, Ann Murray sang Serse, and Valerie Masterson Romilda; Charles Mackerras conducted. All the stagings discussed in this chapter are currently available on DVD: from ENO, *Serse* (stage director, Nicholas Hytner) and *Ariodante* (s.d. David Alden); from Glyndebourne Festival Opera, *Giulio Cesare* (s.d. David McVicar) and *Rinaldo* (s.d. Robert Carsen). I have not supplied a discography-like list, for that might be taken to imply all-embracing commendation.

something formal and decorative out of what was merely inconsequential, was wholly in the spirit of eighteenth-century opera. And that being the case, to incorporate within the formal and decorative frame a 'wheeze' was nicely judged too, and the chorus' umbrellas and their deckchairs, whether laid out in Vauxhall Gardens or in the street of some 'Persian' city while the winged bull of Assyria was towed in for Ariodate's triumph scene, were charming wheezes. Maybe they slightly outstayed their welcome, but only once – regrettably it was in the opening scene – was the sense of the opera spoiled: to make the plane tree the focus of a tree-planting ceremony, and to turn Romilda's arias into a musical entertainment laid on for the guests misconstrues the meaning and/or the spirit of each of the first two arias in the scene: 'Ombra mai fù' and 'O voi che penate'. A clever idea is given priority over making clear to the audience of what is going on.

The thoughts raised by the ENO *Serse* are the questions addressed in the rest of this chapter. If one is convinced of the vitality of the conventions of Handel's own time, how creatively can modern performers work within the constraints they impose? What kinds of thing which are taken for granted in the modern theatre, but which one knows to be anachronistic in Handel, can one nevertheless appropriately employ? What details in the text and music of the opera offer pretexts for a stage director's *jeux d'esprit*? How far can one stretch the ostensible meaning of something without falsifying it completely?

For close on thirty years, under the musical direction of Andrew Jones, the productions of Cambridge Handel Opera emphasised the proper period style, and despite the modesty of their resources, did so eloquently and persuasively. But the audiences who saw these performances were relatively small, and most people's notions of how Handel opera is staged today will derive from what they have seen from the established professional companies. Of these, as far as England is concerned, both English National Opera and Glyndebourne Festival Opera have recognised that Handel ought to provide a regular element in their repertories. But the company with the most distinguished Handelian record is English Touring Opera. Over a relatively brief period they have staged at least seven Handel operas, and some of these have been outstandingly good. The singing and playing is usually excellent, and some productions, like the recent baroque-Byzantine *Ottone*, have been beautifully designed too.[64] However, precisely because in

[64] Hence the choice of illustration for the cover of this book: Richard Hubert Smith's photograph of Louise Kemeny as Teofane in English Touring Opera's production of *Ottone* (2014), directed by James Conway, set and costume design by Takis.

many ways their Handel productions are among the most stylish one could hope to see, it seems a pity that they give space to so many of the clichés of contemporary theatre: rolling in the dust, eyeball-to-eyeball confrontations, spitting at and clouting one another. Despite all of which, they do evidently understand the shape of a Handel opera, and when it comes to arias, the characters (emphasis on character is one of the strengths of ETO stagings) are allowed to sing their hearts out unmolested – unmolested, that is, except by the da capo ornamentation under which they too often labour (see Excursus 6.1).

A famous Glyndebourne staging of *Giulio Cesare* by David McVicar also makes brilliant, if spasmodic, use of the opera's recitative-aria shape, when, having staged the early scenes with relatively little gratuitous distraction, he devises show-stopping spectacles to mirror the elements of artifice and play in two of the big metaphor arias. 'Va tacito e nascosto' is embodied in what one might describe as a faintly sinister court dance with touches of parade-ground manoeuvres, beautifully hitting off the cagey diplomatic bluffing of the scene; while in 'Se in fiorito ameno prato' the little bird with which Cesare duets is there in person, as an immaculately attired on-stage violinist – and Cesare whistles a bit himself-herself. In fact many of the arias are brilliantly done; what distinguishes the two I have mentioned is that the brilliance is, one might say, in 'high style', and the artifice arises from the text. The staging of many of the others is less in the spirit of heroic opera than of circus or cabaret, and that contributes to the fact that, overall (and only in part because a contrast is being drawn between Romans and Egyptians), the production suffers from the common blight of frenzy. A new plague has descended on Egypt, and everyone has St Vitus's dance. There is no keeping still; if the singers are not hopping or gyrating or fidgeting or wriggling or stroking themselves (and others) or practising their swimming strokes as if they hope to soar into the ether, they will at the first opportunity head for the floor, where they promiscuously crouch, lie, roll, crawl and grovel. Moreover, no passion that can be depicted as negative or corrosive will pass without gross over-egging, the consequences of which tend to poison the music too. 'Non è si vago', one of the more ingratiatingly simple songs in this opera, is re-conceived to provide dirty laughs for the mess-mates, and has to linger to make the most of it. In 'V'adoro, pupille' the endless writhings, the come-hither semaphoring of Lidia/Virtù/Cleopatra (it's not as if it's particularly difficult to get the idea) are matched in the da capo by obtrusive ornamentation which quite drowns out the beckoning allure of the music. As in too many modern stagings, silly props are de rigueur. In 'L'angue offeso', for example, Sesto waves his gun about with fetishistic obsessiveness, as if an audience can't be expected to know what a gun is for, or that you point it at people to shoot them.

But it is still recognisably Handel's *Giulio Cesare* that is being performed; it remains *Verwirklichung*, and for all the nonsense has some wonderful scenes.

It also got to grips with what, as I have already suggested, seems one of the most intractable problems for stage directors: how to deal with the distinction between recitative and aria. To refuse to acknowledge the problem, to try to stage an aria as if the action were still continuing at the same pace as in the recitatives, or as if the singing character were continuously experiencing something fresh during the course of it, has become one of the commonest solecisms. Characteristic manifestations are the way directions for exits and entrances are ignored: characters are kept on stage to react to what is being sung, distracting goings-on in the background (sometimes even in the foreground) can be dreamed up for them. And then the crowning absurdity: to ask singers to perform a full-scale da capo aria with all its vocal-instrumental interplay and its myriad repeated words, while refusing to recognise that the opera has stepped out of anything resembling a realistic time-scale, is to reduce the characters to gibbering maniacs. The fact that some singers are able to achieve astounding gibbering-maniac feats makes it no less preposterous to require them.

Excursus 6.1 – vocal ornamentation

Thirty years ago Dean and Knapp complained that too many performances were being ruined by the inept and pretentious ornamentation of the da capos.[65] This abuse has now reached epidemic proportions; and a word about the matter might be appropriate.

I would question their view that, without ornamentation, the arias sound 'bare, flat and tedious', and indeed – to be obtrusively personal for a moment – often wonder during the performance of an ornamented da capo if I can be alone in longing for it to be over – not quite wishing for the return of Karl Richter, perhaps, but certainly wishing that more conductors and singers shared Steffani's coolness about ornamentation.[66]

[65] Dean and Knapp, *Handel's Operas 1704–1726*, pp. 30–1. But the complaint is already in the earlier 1987 edition.

[66] Steffani's reported veto on ornamentation seems to refer only to duets, but see further below. On Richter's Handel (*Giulio Cesare*) see Dean and Knapp, *Handel's Operas 1704–1726*, p. 28.

However, Handel will have shared the view that certain modest types of ornamentation, most obviously the cadential trill, were obligatory, and – a little more speculatively – that the best singers were in some measure creative artists, who could be trusted to let their creativity emerge out of the dramatic situation and the mood of the poetry and the song, and yet remain entirely at one with the orchestral music in which it was embedded. Sometimes, at 'adagio' cadences, and far more rarely at *ad lib.* junctures in arias, they could be handed a little more freedom.[67] But while stylish ornamentation can enhance the beauty and expressiveness of the music in moods both jubilant and grave, it ceases to do that, either if it has been (very obviously) composed in full by some musical adviser who thinks it incumbent on him to replace the original melody with a completely new one, or if it has not been very carefully matched to the singer's quality of voice and technical skill. The best singers handle florid song quite beautifully; but not all of them have that gift, and then it is an unkindness to inflict it on them (and us).

A good starting point might be one of the maxims which Dean deduced from the ornamented arias that survive from *Ottone*: namely that [ornaments] 'should never mask the melody'.[68] While I think that is perfectly true, I would gloss it in a number of ways, because as it stands it sounds both vague and discouraging. One could, for example (perhaps very rarely, but surely not never), imagine a performance in which it might be musically exhilarating and dramatically effective if the singer did – metaphorically – don a mask for the da capo, and ornament the music accordingly. More to the point, however, is to consider what 'not masking the melody' actually means. It means, obviously, that the expressive intent should never be distorted, nor should Handel's melodic phrases be hidden away behind something else, an additional strand in the texture of the music, as if the ornamentation were a kind of descant. And it means, surely, that the music's architectural strategy, as far as it concerns the voice – its rises and falls and episodes of calm – must be respected. It would, for example, be intolerable if any ornamentation for Rinaldo's 'Cara sposa' obliterated the way in which Handel controls the slowly intensifying emotion in a series of rising and subsiding waves, set off by episodes of stasis, and finally ebbing away in despair. And I would tentatively suggest that the maxim might encourage one further

[67] See, for example, 'Come, se ti vedrò', *Muzio Scevola*, No. 9, or 'Sì, tornerò a morir', *Faramondo*, No. 9.

[68] Dean and Knapp, *Handel's Operas 1704–1726*, p. 447. For further on these ornamentations and their authenticity see Fiona McLauchlan's edition of *Ottone*, *HHA*, II. 12.2, pp. 398–9.

aspiration: to see to it that the audience wasn't quite sure whether ornamentation was taking place at all, but was simply conscious of the growing exuberance, or deepening melancholy – or whatever – of the music.

That suggestion is prompted by a second factor. Handel's use of continuo-song to introduce a major character has often been remarked upon; such arias are particularly associated with Senesino: 'Cara sposa, amato bene' in *Radamisto;* 'Alma mia' in *Floridante;* 'Ritorna, o dolce amore' in *Ottone*; 'Bella Asteria' in *Tamerlano.* What is striking is how many of the other Italian singers Handel brought to London were introduced to their new public with similar continuo-accompanied arias: Durastanti in the original *Radamisto;* Cuzzoni in *Ottone*; Bernacchi in *Lotario* and *Partenope*; even Baldi in *Scipione.*[69] Although they normally have an orchestral ritornello to round them off, these arias are only very loosely comparable with the continuo-songs with ritornellos in *Almira.* And most of them are love songs, so they are being used for a purpose very different from the expression of isolation that I suggested was often their chief *raison d'être* in Handel's mature operas. Is it not very possible – I cannot supply the evidence to assert it more strongly than that – that one of the things integral to introducing a new singer to London was a first entrance that enabled him to display in one brief, concentrated episode the beauty of his voice, his technical mastery and his imaginative creativity? The moods of these tiny arias are intimate and overwrought, and no duetting instruments stand in the way of a presentation that is as personal, as subtle and as free as art and imagination (and Handel) permit. Senesino sang these arias so beautifully – we may speculate – that they remained for some years treasured items in his roles.

There are not many Handel arias offering such freedom; which brings me to a related question. In his *Observations* Tosi wrote, 'All Compositions for more than one Voice ought to be sung strictly as they are written; nor do they require any other Art but a noble Simplicity.' Just after that passage, Galliard added to his translation, 'The renowned Abbot Steffani, so famous for his Duetto's, would never suffer such luxuriant Singers to perform any of them, unless they kept themselves within Bounds.'[70] Would Handel have been so strict? And if we think he might have been, then could not Steffani's reported veto on ornamentation in duets be more widely applied, to cover, as well as Handel's duets, many of his arias too? For there are few of them in which the relationship between voice

[69] Cf. the earlier mention of this matter at p. 176.

[70] Tosi/Galliard, p. 151, cited in Timms, *Polymath of the Baroque*, p. 304.

and violins does not resemble duetting – the duetting of, say, violin and oboe in a trio-sonata. In the introductory continuo-accompanied arias that Steffani-ish constraint would not apply.

Making things new – the 'Konzept'

The ideal of *Verwirklichung* demands, first, a certain humility on the part of the stage director: a performer alongside the musicians, or – better – an enabler whose principal responsibility is to help the musicians do what they have to do. And it presupposes, secondly, sensibility and wit on the part of an audience. Many stage directors lack the first and do not recognise the existence of the second. By contrast, 'making things new' accords them the status of creative artists. The underlying presumption is that unless radical steps are taken to restore an opera's urgency, it will lack the immediacy – the 'relevance' – that poet and composer intended it to have; and that it is the director's prime task to decide what form that relevance must take.

Both the ENO *Serse* and the Glyndebourne *Giulio Cesare* were, in their different ways, distinguished demonstrations of *Verwirklichung*, of how to stage a Handel opera for a modern audience. That cannot be said of much of what has passed for Handel opera over the last thirty years or so. A Pope or a Swift might possibly have found apt terms to describe the inanities with which one has sometimes been met; as it is, however, nonsense, far from being excoriated, has been accorded metaphysical grandeur in the 'Konzept'.

The Hamburg Staatsoper recently staged *Almira*. For anyone consulting the theatre website to help decide whether a trip to Hamburg was likely to be worthwhile, enlightenment was rapidly forthcoming. 'Our concept', explains one of the production team, 'was' … etc. What the concept was doesn't much matter;[71] what matters is that when audiences have what for most of them will have been a once-in-a-lifetime opportunity to hear and see the opera with which one of history's great opera composers had made his debut (his only surviving German opera at that), the production team had no doubt that their concept was the first important thing to be remarked on. Does anyone care tuppence for their concept? Evidently someone does.

[71] It entailed among other things setting the opera in four different periods, from Marie Antoinette via Downton Abbey and Elizabeth I to the present day. The 'Konzept' was of course rationalised, but with the kind of pseudo-profound banalities, about the 'carousel' of love, power and jealousy, that could be equally well applied to hundreds of other operas. The production appears also to have included 'Lascia ch'io pianga' from *Rinaldo*, as if the fifty-odd arias *Almira* already contains (not to mention all the duets and instrumental movements) needed eking out to furnish a sufficiency.

A very large number of the world's opera houses seem perfectly comfortable with the idea that the stage director's concept takes precedence over any concept that Handel and his librettists might have had.

Though, in principle, a more or less infinite number of options must be open to an imagination that chooses to work along those lines, and though, in principle, one could imagine some of them enabling Handel's music to speak with real power (a concept is not by definition absurd), the choices embraced tend to be limited and repetitious. Commonly two resources are pressed into service.

The first is anachronism and its inseparable companion anatopism: the piece will be 'staged as a modern piece naturally' or 'whatever you do on stage must = the public at the time you stage it'. 'Naturally', 'must' – such views[72] are deemed so self-evidently true that they need not be argued. It seems rather quaint to reflect that in nineteenth-century Italy anatopism was a favourite prerogative of the censor's office (so that, for example, William Tell could be transported to Scotland or Joan of Arc to Lesbos). But it isn't really quaint at all because censorship is what it remains, even if the game is played, so to speak, backwards. The audience must, for whatever reason, be protected from what the composer and poet actually said (like commending virtue), and the person to exercise that censorship is the stage director.

Alongside anachronism + anatopism, 'irony' is commonly enlisted; for some stage directors it seems a permanent state of mind. Let David Alden be their spokesman: 'you have to cast a very cold eye on the score, however much you may adore it … [my hope is that audiences] are getting something that is emotionally committed and emotionally daring on the one hand, and they're also getting a completely ironic, 20th-century searchlight thrown on this thing at the same time.'[73]

Irony is a notoriously elastic thing, its literary embodiments running the whole gamut from the gentlest of humorous verse to the novels of Thomas Mann. When it is claimed as the appropriate tone of voice for a re-creative engagement with early opera, one might anticipate some kind of 'romantic irony', that irony in which the creative artist steps back and objectifies the experience into which he and his audience are being drawn. There is, I suppose one could say, romantic irony in the treatment of Cesare's metaphor arias in the Glyndebourne *Giulio Cesare*, as there is in the Vauxhall Gardens deckchairs in the ENO *Serse*.

[72] I am quoting Harry Kupfer and Peter Sellars respectively – in turn from Savage, 'The Staging of Opera', pp. 412 and 414.

[73] Quoted in Savage, 'The Staging of Opera', p. 414.

Two other widely viewed productions – again I am referring to work at Glyndebourne and ENO – give us some sense of what else might happen when 'irony' is drawn into a 'concept'.

Glyndebourne *Rinaldo* (2011, 2014)

Robert Carsen's concept is a schoolboy's fantasy: a tale of bullying and flogging, of earning the adoration of a bespectacled and pigtailed lovely by setting out on his bicycle for deeds of heroism, resisting a shiny black-leather dominatrix, and triumphing in a final battle – not quite on the playing fields of Eton, rather in a tarmacadamed cage which does service both as handball pitch and bicycle shed. Several of the arias are reconceived to amuse us by being performed in situations that want us to cry out 'impossible!': slumped against a wire fence in the playground for 'Cara sposa'; singing the da capo of 'Venti, turbini' from a flying bicycle; repairing a puncture during 'Siam prossimi al porto'. It is only fair to report that the sillier the show became, the more it was enjoyed. But once you have established the fact that 'ironic' laughter is the summit of your ambition, that you are not actually producing an opera but staging a foolish spectacle which happens to be going on while some Handel is playing in the background, and which is funny simply by virtue of the incongruity, then it isn't too difficult to keep folk laughing.

Rinaldo, it must be conceded, is not a convincing example of Handel's art as a composer of musical drama. If one has no interest in the stylish staging of opera, and simply wants a soundtrack for one's own concept, it is probably the best one to choose. But it is not trash. It has a number of deeply impressive episodes and much of the music is magnificent. A good concert performance would give an immeasurably fuller impression of its power and beauty, which one might think was the point of performing it. Better still would it be if the concert were set against a series of stylishly designed backdrops that helped group its various scenes into sustained tableaus, deepening the flavour of the music and giving variety to the pace with which it moves past us: *Rinaldo* might prove the ideal opera with which to explore the scope of semi-staged presentations.

ENO *Ariodante* (1996)

The key to David Alden's concept of *Ariodante* is the sexualisation of everything that can be sexualised; it hinges round the person of Polinesso.

In the opening scene, as Ginevra, on the floor (of course) in her underclothes, insultingly rebuffs him ('Orrida agl'occhi miei'), he prods at her *décolleté* with a cane, while Dalinda undergoes surrogate ecstasies on the bedroom chair. When Dalinda in her first aria sings 'Open your eyes', he opens his mouth instead, and grazes on her neck, arms and wrist. While Lurcanio sings his love song to Dalinda, 'Del mio sol', Polinesso is left on stage to observe, sneer and then drag Dalinda away to make love to her. During his Act II aria, 'Se l'inganno', he rapes her (she is not supposed to be on stage at all). In the love duet for Dalinda and Lurcanio in Act III, Polinesso's dead body lies between them and is propped up to stare at her. In the joyless staging of the final joyful chorus Dalinda is still weeping over Polinesso's armour. Particularly nasty are the ballets in the three finales: there is no trace of pastoral in Act I; it is set at some kind of gathering in the palace, and Polinesso, disguised perhaps as a footman, glides about, fingering miscellaneous bosoms. In Act II Ginevra's dreams are enacted by a double, who is sexually abused by her father, and then – after a spasm of apple fetishism – stripped naked by a coven of crones and tipped into a glass tank. The Act III finale comprises grotesque and sinister dances; Ariodante ends the opera looking terrified and Ginevra utterly fed up. A nadir of cynicism came a little earlier with the duel, won not by Lurcanio but by Polinesso. When, however, Polinesso is about to deliver the *coup de grâce*, he is distracted by a ghost, so Lurcanio can treacherously run him through while his back is turned.

Irony doesn't seem quite the term for all this. An observation of William Empson's hovers in the mind, about a 'revisionist' Shakespeare critic who was 'ridiculously indifferent to the Letter of the play, and laboured to befoul its Spirit'. The eighteenth-century *opera seria* aspiration of making some contribution to mankind's enlightenment is tossed aside like so much junk: far easier to reduce us all to grubby voyeurs.

This will seem no very enthusiastic endorsement of a style of operatic production I earlier described as potentially as worthwhile as any 'authentic' revival could be. But that is because these particular stagings leave an important question unaddressed.

Is the love-adoration-admiration-devotion of-for-to Handel which is commonly professed by the ironists and conceptualists really compatible with contempt for the value system out of which Handel composed these pieces? Is it the presumption that Handel didn't really mean what he said, or that he was too simple to realise how silly it all was? Might one not hope, perhaps even require, that a stage director would acknowledge, if only for the duration of the work and if only on the imaginative level, some plausibility, some merit, some purpose in that value system – that Handel himself and his poets also had a concept, and that it is part of their work? If in fact our stage director feels confident that his own humanity is so much truer than Handel's, his perception of the human condition so much sharper, let him not simply turn his 'ironic, 20th-century searchlight' on it, winking and leering at us from behind the composer's back; let him spend his energy staging the contemporary operas that will prove his conviction to be true. Or if he cannot keep his hands off Handel, let him at least advertise his wares honestly.

And then, if stage directors are to be allowed to claim authorship of their stagings (how often do we read of 'stage director A's *Alcina*' or 'stage director B's *Rodelinda*'?), a more fundamental shift is certainly required. An audience should know that what it is being offered is not so much a performance of a Handel opera, rather an evening of music-theatre, conceptualised by such-and-such a stage director, with accompanying music by Handel. But under those circumstances there seems no reason why stage directors should confine themselves to music from just one opera; still less is it clear why, in a contemporary concept-based music-theatre event, they should set particular store by a musical performance rooted in eighteenth-century practice. The time has surely come to consider whether some types of staging do not also demand a radical rethinking of how to perform the music. One commentator, Barry Emslie, has already suggested this, making great play with the fact that in Handelian opera the climactic musical feature, the ornamented da capo repeat, 'isn't there'; and he urges the adoption of glorious 'post-modern' rejoicings in which we supply types of ornamentation that are 'contemporary to us'.[74] But this is pusillanimous counsel. What excuse can there be for leaving it at that? The continuo backbone of the music is also, in Emslie's sense, 'not there', nor are all the passages in which, say, the oboes play '*coi violini*' or '*colla voce*'. Let the continuo player improvise in his own genuinely modern style, especially as Handel gives so few guidelines in his figuring. He might like to take inspiration from David Wilde's modernist improvisations on the 'Sphinxes' in his fine recording of Schumann's *Carnaval*, or from the thought of Richard Strauss (according to Wolfgang Sawallisch) dropping in allusions to his own pieces in his piano-accompanied recitatives in *Così fan tutte*. And let the oboes adorn their *colla parte*s with all the fervour of a Gaelic psalm-singer at work on the Old Hundredth. 'What larks, Pip!'

But to return to the proper modern way and the proper period style: much of the authority usurped by the modern stage director can be traced back to

[74] Barrie Emslie, 'Handel the Postmodernist', *COJ* 15 (2003), 190.

the revolution at Bayreuth in the 1950s led by Wieland Wagner. One aspiration of the New Bayreuth was to universalise an operatic repertory which was in danger of being tied too closely to one time and one place. That corrective impulse makes no sense for Handel. Though his characters may bear familiar historical names, they are in fact remote, archetypal and comprehensively anachronistic. They are, that is to say, universals already – were already understood as such in the eighteenth century – and any audience may still claim them for its own. To take away their intrinsic anachronism and universality, supposedly for the benefit of us in the here and now, by turning them into twenty-first-century icons and anti-icons, or political figures or social types of whom we approve or disapprove, has nothing to do with 'relevance'; it amounts to mean-spirited belittlement.

Not only does Handelian opera have its own inbuilt universalism – its universalist concept, one might say – it has its own inbuilt irony too. At the end of *Alexander's Feast* there is a rather unusual circumstance, when the words beginning 'Let old Timotheus' are sung first in recitative, then as a chorus. But something rather similar happens all the time in a typical *opera seria* scene, where almost everything is looked at from two distinct points of view. A dramatic situation develops; but then, as it threatens to absorb us – to become 'real' – we are withdrawn from it again; it is suspended and distilled in the music, and that procedure says, in effect, we need not pretend that this is real – stand back from it, and reflect on it, whether we do not find our aesthetic sense delighted, or our thoughts disturbed, or our hearts touched. 'From my great griefs I have made my little songs.'

If a Handel opera is faithfully performed – in all its dimensions – if, to borrow another Wagnerian phrase, 'the deeds of music are made visible',[75] the universality and the irony will be there already.

And since we are in Wagnerian vein, let us not forget another of his *obiter dicta*: 'now that I have created the invisible orchestra, I should like to create the invisible stage'.[76] In one sense that sounds like a counsel of despair; but there are occasions when it feels like the best of advice. Either the spectacle is an integral and important part of the opera or it isn't. And if it isn't, the logical thing to do is not arbitrarily to substitute a different spectacle which has nothing to do with the expressive character of the music or the idiom in which it speaks, but to perform the opera in concert. In fact, with first-rate musicians, nicely dressed, in a handsome eighteenth-century room, such a performance can bring us within smiling distance of Elysium.

[75] Richard Wagner, 'Über die Benennung "Musikdrama"', 1872.

[76] Cited in Lucy Beckett, *Richard Wagner, Parsifal* (Cambridge University Press, 1981).

Appendix

An overview of the repertory of the Royal Academy of Music

The nine seasons of the Royal Academy of Music fall conveniently into three 3-year periods.

First season 1720 (April and May only – more a trailer or a taster than a full season)

	Opera	Composer	Librettist	Source librettist	Performances
New operas:	*Numitore*	Porta	Rolli	not known	7
	Radamisto	Handel	Haym?/ Rolli?	Lalli (1710/12)	10
	Narciso	D. Scarlatti/ Roseingrave	Rolli	Capece (1714)	5
				Total performances	**22**

Second season 1720–21

	Opera	Composer	Librettist	Source librettist	Performances
New operas:	*Astarto*	Bononcini	Rolli	Zeno with Pariati (1707)	23
	Arsace	Orlandini/ Amadei	Rolli	Salvi (1715)	9
	Muzio Scevola	Amadei / Bononcini/ Handel	Rolli	Stampiglia (1710)	10
	Ciro	Bononcini	Rolli	Noris	8
Revivals:	*Radamisto*	Handel			7
				Total performances	**57**

Third season 1721–22

	Opera	Composer	Librettist	Source librettist	Performances
New operas:	*Floridante*	Handel	Rolli	Silvani (1696)	15
	Crispo	Bononcini	Rolli	Lemer (1721)	18
	Griselda	Bononcini	Rolli	not known (not Zeno)	16
Revivals:	*Radamisto*	Handel			4
	Astarto	Bononcini			6
	Arsace	Orlandini/ Amadei			3
				Total performances	**62**

Comments 1720–22

During the first brief season only one Italian singer unquestionably of the first rank was engaged, Handel's old colleague from Roman days, Margherita Durastanti. The other principals were Anastasia Robinson, Ann Turner Robinson and the tenor Alexander Gordon. Towards the end of the season Francesca Margherita de L'Épine came out of retirement to take the place of Ann Turner Robinson in the last 1720 performances of *Radamisto*. In September 1720 a new group of Italians arrived, including Senesino, Salvai and Boschi; so for 1720–21 a full season could be planned.

At the same time as these new Italian singers, Bononcini appeared on the scene as Handel's principal composer colleague. His operas proved at least as popular as Handel's, and since he was the more productive, Bononcini evenings outnumbered Handel evenings. The Directors were also happy to look to other sources for their programmes: Thomas Roseingrave, perhaps with the encouragement of Handel, was able to demonstrate his enthusiasm for the music of Domenico Scarlatti by adapting (as *Narciso*) Scarlatti's Roman opera *Amor d'un ombra e gelosia d'un aura*; Filippo Amadei, a cellist in the orchestra, was commissioned to adapt Orlandini's *Amor e maestà*, and even to enter the lists with Handel and Bononcini in the composite *Muzio Scevola*. Amadei was another of the musicians whom Handel will have known since his Italian years, when he worked for much the same patrons as Handel did: Pamphili, Ottoboni, Ruspoli.

All the librettos for these three seasons were provided by the Italian Secretary of the Academy, Paolo Rolli. There is one exception, or presumed exception: the libretto of *Radamisto*, which is generally attributed to Haym. The evidence for this attribution is partly late (Burney) and partly internal: for *Radamisto* is an excellent example of the '*forbice tanta, penna poca*' method ('much work for the scissors, little for the pen') that was Haym's hallmark. Possibly, as Clausen has suggested,[1] Handel began work on the opera before Rolli's central position in the workings of the Academy had been clearly established.

At the end of the third season, in the light of a nervy anti-Catholic mood that had developed at the time of the Atterbury Plot, both Bononcini and Rolli were dismissed. Anastasia Robinson, herself a Catholic, who had found working with Bononcini thoroughly congenial (especially during the 1721–22 season, when she became temporary prima donna during

[1] H. D. Clausen, 'Der Einfluss der Komponisten auf die Librettowahl der Royal Academy of Music (1720–1729)', *VIHAK* 5 (1994), 58–9.

the illness of Durastanti), may have regretted these developments; but she remained with the company.

Handel's operas were all dedicated to members of the Royal Family (as was Scarlatti's); others were dedicated to mere nobility. In financial terms these were the Royal Academy's most successful seasons.

Fourth season 1722–23

	Opera	Composer	Librettist	Source librettist	Performances
New operas:	*Ottone*	Handel	Haym	Pallavicino (1719)	14
	Coriolano	Ariosti	Haym	Pariati (1717)	13
	Erminia	Bononcini	Rolli	not known (1719)	8
	Flavio	Handel	Haym	Noris (1682/1693)	8
Revivals:	*Muzio Scevola*	Amadei/ Bononcini/ Handel			3
	Ciro	Bononcini			5
	Floridante	Handel			7
	Crispo	Bononcini			4
				Total performances	**62**

Fifth season 1723–24

New operas:	*Farnace*	Bononcini	?Haym	Morani	6
	Vespasiano	Ariosti	?Haym	Morselli	9
	Giulio Cesare	Handel	Haym	Bussani (1677/1685)	13
	Calfurnia	Bononcini	Haym	Braccioli	11
	Aquilio Consolo	Ariosti	?Haym	Silvani (1708)	4
Revivals	*Ottone*	Handel			6
	Coriolano	Ariosti			2
				Total performances	**51**

Sixth season 1724–25

New operas:	*Tamerlano*	Handel	Haym	Piovene (1711/1719)	12
	Artaserse	Ariosti	Haym	Zeno with Pariati (1705)	10
	Rodelinda	Handel	Haym	Salvi (1710)	14
	Dario	Ariosti	Haym	Silvani (1691)	6
Pasticcio:	*Elpidia*	Vinci/ Handel	Haym	Zeno (1697)	11
Revivals:	*Giulio Cesare*	Handel			10
				Total performances	**63**

Comments 1722–25

In January 1724 the regular days for opera performances were changed from Wednesday and Saturday to Tuesday and Saturday.[2]

Viewed from a Handelian perspective these three seasons mark the culmination of the Royal Academy of Music enterprise. After Rolli had been dismissed, Handel for some years worked exclusively with Haym as his librettist, a man who, as far as can be judged from only indirect evidence, was happier than Rolli could ever be to serve as the composer's humble assistant. Posterity has judged three of the operas of these years, *Giulio Cesare*, *Tamerlano* and *Rodelinda*, to rank with Handel's supreme operatic achievements; another, *Ottone*, was in its own time one of the most admired for its musical beauties. The principal roles in all these operas were composed for the voices and theatrical gifts of two of the greatest singers of the age: Senesino and Cuzzoni. Handel's previous leading ladies, Durastanti and Anastasia Robinson, stepped aside and at the end of the 1723–24 season retired. Handel's position in London musical life seemed more assured than ever: apart from his salary from the Academy, he was granted a royal pension in 1723, presumably linked with his new position as teacher of music to the princesses.[3]

Although Bononcini left the establishment at the end of 1721–22, his operas continued to be performed and, more readily forgiven than Rolli, he was re-engaged, for one season only, in 1723–24. (*Erminia*, the new Bononcini opera staged in 1722–23, was a revised version of an opera composed in 1719 for Rome.) Meanwhile, Ariosti joined the team.

The Royal Academy's first pasticcio, *Elpidia*, marks Handel's first engagement with Vinci (the composer of the new Neapolitan generation who seems to have meant most to him), and also his first with Zeno, though he will have known something of Zeno's work from his colleagues' contributions to the repertory. Haym draws on some of the same sources as Rolli had used: Zeno and Pariati, Salvi, and of the older Venetians, Noris. One thing that does by now catch the eye is that Handel was more willing – keen, perhaps – to work with old-fashioned, seventeenth-century librettos.[4]

Although these years were financially less stable than the earlier ones there are various indications that the prestige of Italian opera now stood high. The theatre was expensively refurbished for the start of the 1723–24

[2] The *Daily Courant* reported the change, 6 January 1724, without explanation. *Documents I*, p. 668.

[3] D. Hunter, 'Handel among the Jacobites', *ML* 83 (2001), 552.

[4] The often-cited letter from Riva to Muratori, written in September 1725, alludes to this. See Deutsch, pp. 185–6.

season, and the reputation of the company was now so distinguished that in 1722–23 and 1723–24, plans were laid to take it to Paris to stage some of their productions there before the singers dispersed to their various Italian bases for the rest of the summer. Performances – of *Ottone* and *Giulio Cesare* – materialised only in 1724, and then in concert rather than in fully staged form.[5]

Seventh season 1725–26

	Opera	Composer	Librettist	Source librettist	Performances
New operas:	*Scipione*	Handel	Rolli	Salvi (1704)	13
	Alessandro	Handel	Rolli	Mauro (1690/91)	13
Pasticcios:	*Elisa*	(Porpora/?Ariosti)	Haym	not known	6
Revivals:	*Ottone*	Handel			9
	Rodelinda	Handel			8
	Elpidia	Vinci/Handel			5
				Total performances	**54**

Eighth season 1726–27

New operas:	*Lucio Vero*	Ariosti	?Haym	Zeno (1700)	6
	Admeto	Handel	?Haym? Rolli	Aureli/Mauro (1660/1681)	19
	Astianatte	Bononcini	Haym	Salvi (1701)	9
Revivals:	*Floridante*	Handel			2
	Ottone	Handel			2
				Total performances	**38**

Ninth season 1727–28

New operas:	*Teuzzone*	Ariosti	?Haym	Zeno (1706)	3
	Riccardo Primo	Handel	Rolli	Briani (1710)	11
	Siroe	Handel	Haym	Metastasio (1726)	?17
	Tolomeo	Handel	Haym	Capece (1711)	7
Revivals:	*Radamisto*	Handel			?7
	Alessandro	Handel			?7
	Admeto	Handel			?10
				Total performances	**?62**

5 *Documents I*, pp. 713–14.

Comments 1725–28

Expectations raised by the knowledge that Faustina had been engaged to come to London for the 1725–26 season rose to fever pitch when it was announced that she was unavoidably delayed. As a stop-gap *Scipione* was written and composed in haste round the established trio of stars: Senesino, Cuzzoni and Boschi. From the production of *Alessandro* onwards these last seasons of the Royal Academy were dominated by the rivalry between the established prima donna, Cuzzoni, and the newcomer, Faustina; none of the other singers rose beyond the rank of 'lampstands' (Berenstadt's term).

The eighth season, 1726–27, resembles the fifth, 1723–24, in the sense that the three composers officially linked to the Academy all had an equal share in the repertory of new works, though Handel's *Admeto* enjoyed more performances than the Ariosti and Bononcini works together. And when one adds in the seventh and ninth seasons and the revivals during these years, it is clear that Handel is now emphatically the dominant figure in the establishment. The statistics for the last season are not quite certain, but over the three seasons Handel performances outnumber those of other composers by four to one: approximately 120 to 30. His late Academy operas have not enjoyed the same critical esteem as those of the years 1722–25, and the reason for this has commonly been sought in his need to think too much of satisfying the rival parties and their primary loyalty to Cuzzoni and Faustina. But beyond the obvious need to compose effectively for his singers, it is not easy to imagine Handel being brow-beaten in quite this way. In any case the view of contemporary audiences seems to have been different; in terms of the number of performances given in their first season, *Admeto* and, more surprisingly, *Siroe* were more successful than any other Handel opera composed for the Royal Academy.

Haym continued as Italian Secretary of the Academy, but Rolli was now so far readmitted as to share with Haym responsibility for the librettos. Their sources are now chiefly modern and 'reformed' – *Admeto* is the only opera with some slight admixture of seventeenth-century Venetian brio – and with *Siroe* and the engagement with Metastasio Handel comes as close as he was ever to come to the vanguard of continental taste.

During the eighth season, in February 1727, Handel became a British subject. It is of course coincidental that the full titles of all his operas in the last two seasons concern kingship of somewhere or other: *Admeto, Re di Tessaglia; Riccardo primo, Re d'Inghilterra; Siroe, Re di Persia; Tolomeo, Re di Persia.*

Select bibliography

Bauman, Thomas and Marita P. McClymonds (eds.), *Opera and the Enlightenment*, Cambridge University Press, 1995.

Bianconi, Lorenzo (ed.), *I libretti italiani di Georg Friedrich Händel e le loro fonti*, I* and 1**, Florence: Olschki, 1992.

Buelow, George J. and Hans Joachim Marx (eds.), *New Mattheson Studies*, Cambridge University Press, 1983.

Burney, Charles, *A General History of Music from the Earliest Ages to the Present Period* (London: 1776–89), in 2 vols., Frank Mercer (ed.), London: G. T. Foulis & Co, 1935.

Memoirs of the Life and Writings of the Abate Metastasio, 3 vols., London: Robinson, 1796.

Burrows, Donald, *Handel (The Master Musicians)*, Oxford University Press, 1994.

Burrows, Donald and Rosemary Dunhill (eds.), *Music and Theatre in Handel's World. The Family Papers of James Harris 1732–1780*, Oxford University Press, 2002.

Cannon, Beekman C., *Johann Mattheson. Spectator in Music*, New Haven: Yale University Press, 1968 reprint.

Coke, Thomas, *Vice Chamberlain Coke's Theatrical Papers 1706–1715*, Judith Milhous and Robert D. Hume (eds.), Carbondale and Edwardsville: Southern Illinois University Press, 1982 reprint.

Dean, Winton, *Handel's Operas 1726–1741*, Woodbridge: The Boydell Press, 2006.

Dean, Winton and John Merrill Knapp, *Handel's Operas 1704–1726*, Oxford: Clarendon Press, rev. edn, 1995.

Deutsch, Otto Erich, *Handel: A Documentary Biography*, London: A. & C. Black, 1955.

Dorris, George E., *Paolo Rolli and the Italian Circle in London, 1715–1744*, The Hague, Paris: Mouton & Co., 1967.

Eisenschmidt, Joachim, *Die szenische Darstellung der Opern Georg Friedrich Händels auf der Londoner Bühne seiner Zeit* (Inaugural-Dissertation), Halle, 1940.

Gallarati, Paolo, *Musica e Maschera: il libretto italiano del Settecento*, Turin: EDT, 1984.

The New Grove Dictionary of Music and Musicians, Stanley Sadie (ed.), London: Macmillan, 1980.

George Frideric Handel Collected Documents, Volume 1 1609–1725, Donald Burrows, Helen Coffey, John Greenacombe and Anthony Hicks (eds.), Cambridge University Press, 2013.

George Frideric Handel Collected Documents, Volume 2 1725–1734, Donald Burrows, Helen Coffey, John Greenacombe and Anthony Hicks (eds.), Cambridge University Press, 2015.

Harnoncourt, Nikolaus, *Musik als Klangrede: Wege zu einem neuen Musikverständnis*, Munich and Kassel: Deutscher Taschenbuch Verlag/ Bärenreiter Verlag, 1985.

Harris, Ellen T. (ed.), *The Librettos of Handel's Operas* [in facsimile], 13 vols., New York and London: Garland, 1989.

Hortschansky, Klaus and Konstanze Musketa (eds.), *Georg Friedrich Händel – ein Lebensinhalt. Gedenkschrift für Bernd Baselt (1934–1993),* Halle an der Saale: Händel-Haus, 1995.

Larue, C. Steven, *Handel and His Singers: The Creation of the Royal Academy Operas, 1720–1728,* Oxford University Press, 1995.

Leopold, Silke, *Händel. Die Opern,* Kassel, Basel, London: Bärenreiter, 2009.

McCredie, Andrew D., *Instrumentarium and Instrumentation in the North German Baroque Opera,* University of Hamburg *Habilitationsschrift,* Hamburg, 1964.

McGeary, Thomas, *The Politics of Opera in Handel's Britain,* Cambridge University Press, 2013.

Mainwaring, John. *G. F. Händel, nach Johann Matthesons deutscher Ausgabe von 1761 mit anderen Dokumenten herausgegeben,* Bernhard Paumgartner (ed.), Zurich: Atlantis-Verlag, 1947.

Memoirs of the Life of the Late George Frederic Handel, London: R. & J. Dodsley, 1760.

Mattheson, Johann, *Das Beschützte Orchestre*, Hamburg: Schiller, 1717.

Das Neu- Eröffnete Orchestre, Hamburg, 1713.

Der musicalische Patriot, Hamburg, 1728.

Der vollkommene Capellmeister 1739, facsimile edition, Margarete Reimann (ed.), *Documenta Musicologica V,* Kassel and Basel: Bärenreiter, 1954.

Grundlage einer Ehren-Pforte Hamburg, 1740.

Rätzer, Manfred, *Szenische Aufführungen von Werken Georg Friedrich Händels vom 18. bis 20. Jahrhundert: eine Dokumentation*, Halle an der Saale: Händel-Haus, 2000.

Roberts, John H. (ed.), *Handel Sources: Materials for the Study of Handel's Borrowings,* 9 vols., New York: Garland, 1986.

Sadie, Stanley and Anthony Hicks (eds.), *Handel Tercentenary Collection,* Basingstoke: Macmillan Music Division, 1987.

Smith, Ruth, *Handel's Oratorios and Eighteenth-Century Thought,* Cambridge University Press, 1995.

Strohm, Reinhard, *Die italienische Oper im 18. Jahrhundert*, Wilhelmshaven: Heinrichshofen, 1979.

Dramma per musica: Italian Opera Seria of the Eighteenth Century, New Haven and London: Yale University Press, 1997.

Essays on Handel and Italian Opera, Cambridge University Press, 1985.

Tosi, P. F., *Opinioni de' cantori antichi, e moderni*, Bologna, 1723, tr. J. E. Galliard as *Observations on the Florid Song*, London, 1742.

Williams, Peter (ed.), *Bach, Handel, Scarlatti: Tercentenary Essays*, Cambridge University Press, 1985.

Index

Aachen (Aix-la-Chapelle), 43
Abingdon, Unicorn Theatre, 178
Académie de Musique et de Danse, Paris, 99
Accademia degli Infuocati, Florence, 165
Adelung, Johann Christoph, 120
Addison, Joseph, 20, 23, 123, 169, 172
Alden, David, 186, 193, 194
Algarotti, Francesco, 170, 180
Amadei, Filippo, 198, 199, 200
Anne, Princess, 58
Anne, Queen, 16, 18, 19, 21, 73
Annibali, Domenico, 38, 176
Arbuthnot, Dr John, 18, 19, 24
Arcadia (Accademia degli Arcadi), 13–14, 57, 68, 85, 87, 167
Ariosti, Attilio, 30, 200, 201, 203
  Artaserse, 200
  Aquilio Consolo, 200
  Coriolano, 30, 171, 200
  Dario, 200
  Elisa, 202
  Lucio Vero, 202
  Teuzzone, 202
  Vespasiano, 200
Ariosto, Ludovico, 32, 59, 60, 151
  Orlando furioso, 59, 151
Aristotle, 54, 72, 80, 81
Arne, Thomas Augustine, 32, 47, 109, 159, 177
  Comus, 47
Arteaga, Stefano, 79
Atterbury plot, 66, 199
Augusta, Princess of Saxe-Coburg, 40, 41

Babell, William, 123
Bach, Johann Sebastian, 148, 178
Baldi, Antonio, 191
Baretti, Joseph, 79–80
Bayreuth, 197
Beard, John, 37
Beggar's Opera, The, 28, 29, 32, 75, 122
Berenstadt, Gaetano, 171, 203
Bernacchi, Antonio Maria, 32, 191
Bertolli, Francesca, 33
Blathwayt, Colonel John, 25
Boethius, 65
Boiardo, Matteo Maria,
  Orlando innamorato, 58-9
Bononcini, Giovanni, 29, 30, 49, 51, 87, 160, 161, 199, 201, 203
  Astarto, 30, 198
  Astianatte, 30, 202
  Calfurnia, 200
  Ciro, 198, 200
  Crispo, 198, 200
  Griselda, 198
  Erminia, 200, 201
  Farnace, 200
  Xerse, 160
Bordoni, Faustina (see Faustina)
Boschi, Giuseppe Maria, 166, 168, 170, 199, 203
Brandenburg-Prussia, 1
Brockes, Barthold Hinrich, 2
Brown, Lady Margaret, 45
Burlington, 3rd Earl of (Richard Boyle), 19, 24, 33, 73
Burney, Dr Charles, 44, 59, 68, 69, 80–2, 122, 145, 156–7, 176
Burrows, Donald, 18, 42, 136

Caffarelli, Gaetano, 81, 176
Caldara, Antonio, 13
Calzabigi, Raniero de, 81
Campioli, Antonio Gualandi, 163
Cannons, 24
Capece, Carlo Sigismondo, 50, 51, 60, 70, 71, 198, 202
Carestini, Giovanni, 38, 77, 81, 176, 177
Carli, Antonio Francesco, 166, 168
Carmelite order, 12
Caroline, Queen, 17, 44
Carsen, Robert, 186, 194
Cassiodorus, 164
Cavalli, Francesco, 51, 160
Chandos, 1st Duke of (James Brydges), 24
Chimenti, Margherita, 43

Chrissochoidis, Irene, 44
Cicero, 54
Colman, Francis, 57
Colonna, Cardinal Carlo, 12
Conradi, Madame, 164
Conti, Gioacchino, 38, 176, 177
Corago, Il (Pierfrancesco Rinuccini), 180
Corelli, Arcangelo, 12, 13, 15, 109–10, 157, 167
Corneille, Pierre, 56, 72, 79, 85, 170
  Pertharite, 56, 85–6
Covent Garden Theatre, 32, 36–42, 45, 46, 135–6, 175, 176
Croce, Benedetto, 79
Cuzzoni, Francesca, 27–8, 30, 88, 134, 170, 171, 176, 191, 201, 203

Dahlhaus, Carl, 184
Dean, Winton, 9, 85, 88, 144, 150–1, 162, 172, 173, 177, 178, 189, 190
Dent, Edward J., 68
Destouches, André Cardinal, 49, 59
Doni, Giovanni Battista, 56
D'Oyley Carte Opera Company, 183
Dresden, 25, 26, 50, 53
Drury Lane Theatre, 47
Dryden, John, 57
  Albion and Albanius, 57
  Alexander's Feast, 40
Dublin, 46, 47
Durastanti, Margherita, 27, 166, 170, 191, 199, 200, 201
Düsseldorf, 16

Emslie, Barry, 196
English National Opera (ENO), 186, 187, 192, 193, 194
English Touring Opera (ETO), 187–8

Fanshawe, Richard, 23
'Farinelli' (Carlo Broschi), 35, 39, 41, 44, 76, 81, 173
'Faustina' (Faustina Bordoni), 27–8, 30, 88, 134, 170, 171, 176, 203
Feind, Barthold, 2, 8, 63, 163
Ferrara, 58, 60
Feustking, Friedrich Christian, 6, 8, 49, 94, 105
Florence, 11, 12, 14, 15, 50, 51, 53, 70, 71, 117, 126, 132, 165, 166
  Teatro del Cocomero, 102, 165
Fougeroux, Pierre Jacques, 171
'Francesina' (Elisabeth Duparc), 43, 44
Frilli, Stefano, 166
Frederick, Prince of Wales, 36, 40–1, 43

Galliard, John Ernest, 174, 191
Galuppi, Baldassare, 46–7, 82
Gasparini, Francesco, 49, 50
Gay, John, 19, 29, 75 (see also *Beggar's Opera, The*)
George I, King (Georg Ludwig, Elector), 16, 18, 23, 24, 27, 31, 73, 88
George II, King, 17, 23, 36–7, 39, 41, 43, 73
Gibson, Elizabeth, 25
Gluck, Christoph Willibald, 82, 120, 179
Glyndebourne Festival Opera, 186, 187, 188, 192, 193, 194
Goethe, Johann Wolfgang von, 109, 121
Gordon, Alexander, 199
Göttingen, 177–8
Gravina, Gian Vicenzo, 87, 167
Grimani, Cardinal Vincenzo, 14–15, 49
Guarini, Battista,
  Il pastor fido, 23, 49, 57

Hagen, Oskar, 177–8
Halle (Saale), 1–5, 156
  Marktkirche, 3
  Stadtgymnasium, 2–3, 62, 137
  University, 2, 5
Hamburg, 1, 2, 5–10, 14, 57, 62, 92, 100, 109, 123, 159, 162–3, 165
  Opera House (Theater am Gänsemarkt), 5, 92, 99, 137, 162, 168
  Staatsoper, 192
Handel, George Frideric, works
Operas, pasticcios and related works
  Admeto, 31, 50, 52, 56, 70, 71, 133, 134, 171, 177, 202, 203
  Agrippina, 14, 15, 16, 27, 48, 49, 52, 102, 107–20, 126, 130, 131, 132, 166, 167, 168, 178
  Alcina, 32, 38, 39, 41, 51, 52, 58, 60, 61, 66, 136, 143, 145, 147, 149, 151–2, 153, 175
  Alessandro, 28, 46, 52, 70, 71, 72, 88–91, 133, 134, 176, 182, 202
  Alessandro Severo, 44
  Almira, 6, 7, 8, 10, 49, 52, 69, 92–102, 112–3, 123, 125, 130, 134, 144, 146, 159, 163, 164, 166, 167, 175, 177, 191, 192
  Amadigi di Gaula, 17, 19, 21, 28, 49, 52, 59, 73, 130, 131, 168, 169
  Arianna in Creta, 32, 39, 51, 52, 61, 67, 135, 136, 175
  Ariodante, 32, 38, 39, 51, 52, 60, 61, 71, 72, 76–7, 136, 146–50, 154–6, 175, 186, 194–5
  Arminio, 51, 61, 71, 177

Atalanta, 40, 41, 51, 52, 136–7
Berenice, 42, 51, 71
Daphne, Die verwandelte, 6–8, 48, 49, 52, 163
Deidamia, 45, 46, 48, 51, 52, 72, 137, 175
Ezio, 32, 50, 66, 69, 70, 77, 82, 135, 139
Faramondo, 44, 51, 69, 190
Flavio, 50, 52, 54, 56, 88, 128, 129, 130, 133, 134, 200
Floridante, 26, 49, 66, 72, 88, 133, 191, 198, 200, 202
Florindo, Der beglückte, 6–8, 48, 49, 52, 163
Giove in Argo, 45, 46, 47
Giulio Cesare in Egitto, 50, 52, 56, 72, 84, 128–9, 133, 135, 171, 178, 186, 188–9, 192, 193, 200, 201, 202
Giustino, 51, 175, 177
Imeneo, 45, 46, 47, 51, 74, 137, 175
Lotario, 31, 50, 51, 52, 55, 84, 134–5, 175, 191
Muzio Scevola, 26, 30, 49, 54, 56, 72, 133, 170, 190, 198, 199, 200
Nero, 6, 8, 10, 48, 49, 92, 163, 164
Oreste, 39, 175
Orlando, 26, 32, 51, 52, 53, 58, 60, 70, 71, 128, 144–6, 147, 151, 152–4, 176
Ottone, 27, 50, 51, 67, 72, 133, 177, 187, 190, 191, 200, 201, 202
Parnasso in Festa, 32, 58
Partenope, 50, 68, 191
Pastor fido, Il, 22–3, 37, 39, 48, 49, 52, 57, 58, 59, 72, 84, 126, 131, 136, 175
Poro, 38, 50, 52, 61, 66, 69, 82, 135, 173
Radamisto, 30, 49, 56, 62, 73, 74, 132–3, 145, 171, 175, 191, 198, 199, 202
Riccardo primo, 40, 50, 52, 67, 72, 73, 88, 133, 202, 203
Rinaldo, 19, 21–2, 23, 28, 31, 32, 37, 38, 48, 49, 52, 57, 59, 60, 66, 67, 72, 73, 84, 102, 121–6, 127, 128, 130–1, 168, 169, 186, 190, 192, 194
Rodelinda, 36, 50, 52, 55, 56, 71, 72, 84, 85–7, 88, 133, 137–43, 154, 177, 178, 200, 201, 202
Rodrigo (Vincer se stesso è la maggior vittoria), 14, 15, 16, 49, 52, 55, 71, 83, 102–6, 107, 117, 125, 126, 131–2, 166, 167
Rossane, 46
Scipione, 50, 71, 72, 88, 133, 134, 191, 202, 203
Serse, 43, 44, 47, 51, 52, 55, 68, 156–61, 178, 186–7, 192, 193
Silla, 22, 49, 53, 72, 74, 84
Siroe, 50, 56, 66, 69, 72, 82, 133, 171, 202, 203
Sosarme, 50, 51, 55, 70, 71, 135
Tamerlano, 50, 52, 54, 56, 66–7, 72, 84, 88, 129, 133, 144, 191, 200, 201
Terpsicore, 58
Teseo, 19, 21, 28, 49, 52, 59, 72, 84, 131, 168, 169
Tolomeo, 30, 50, 61, 65, 71, 72, 171, 202, 203
Other works
Aci, Galatea e Polifemo, 117–18
Acis and Galatea, 32, 33, 40
Alexander's Feast, 40, 45, 71, 197
L' Allegro ed il Penseroso, 43
Athalia, 31
'Brockes Passion' (Der für die Sünden der Welt gemarterte und sterbende Jesus), 2
Cantata: *Agrippina condotta a morire*, 126
Cantata: *Ah crudel, nel pianto mio*, 126
Cantata: *Apollo e Dafne*, 125
Cantata: *Clori, Tirsi e Fileno*, 116–17
Cantata: *Da quel giorno fatal*, 116–17
Cantata: *Hendel, non può la mia Musa*, 13
Cantata: *Qual ti riveggio*, 126
Cantata: *Un sospir a chi si muore*, 126
Choice of Hercules, The, 71
Concerti Grossi, Op. 6, 43, 45
Deborah, 31, 33
Deutsche Arien, 2
Esther, 33, 39, 40
Funeral Anthem for Queen Caroline, 43, 44
Israel in Egypt, 43, 45
Messiah, 13
Ode for the Birthday of Queen Anne, 18
Organ concertos, 38, 39, 109, 126
Resurrezione, La 13, 71, 113, 115
Saeviat tellus, 125
Saul, 43, 45, 46
Trio sonatas, Op.2, 126
Trionfo del Tempo e del Disinganno, Il, 13, 45, 111, 123–5, 167
'Utrecht' Te Deum and Jubilate, 18
Handel Opera Society, 178
Hanover, 16, 17, 18, 50, 58, 70, 88, 162, 169
Harnoncourt, Nikolaus, 138, 166
Harris, James, 45
Harris, Thomas, 45
Hasse, Johann Adolf, 35, 81, 138, 157, 173
Hawkins, John, 17
Haydn, Joseph, 146
Haym, Nicola Francesco, 30, 31, 49, 50, 65, 71, 72, 84–7, 88, 139, 198, 199, 200, 201, 202, 203
Haymarket, The King's / Queen's Theatre in the, 1, 16, 19, 20, 24, 32, 33, 35, 37, 38, 39, 42, 45, 59, 85, 102, 127, 132, 167–8, 171, 175, 177, 183

Heidegger, John Jacob, 25, 30, 31, 35, 43, 44, 45, 73
Heinichen, Johann David, 164
Hepokoski, James, 184
Herder, Johann Gottfried, 63
Herodotus, 55
Hervey, Lord John, 40
Hill, Aaron, 21–2, 28, 33, 49, 59, 60, 73
Hinsch, Heinrich, 49
Hoffmann, E. T. A., 120
Holdsworth, Edward, 41
Houdar de la Motte, Antoine, 49, 59
Hughes, John, 78
Hume, Robert D., 19, 24, 32, 171
Humphreys, Samuel, 31, 33, 77
Hunold, Christian Friedrich ('Menantes'), 8
Hytner, Nicholas, 186

Jacobites, 30, 66 (see also Atterbury plot)
Jennens, Charles, 12, 41, 45, 47
Johnson, Dr Samuel, 61
Jones, Andrew V., 87, 182, 187
Jonson, Benjamin
  The Alchemist, 16, 132
Journals
  Daily Courant, 201
  London Daily Post, 39, 41
  Old Whig, 39
  The Bee, 35
  The Craftsman, 35
  The London Journal, 27
  The Spectator, 20, 23, 85, 123, 169
  The Universal Journal, 29
  The Universal Spectator, 66

Keiser, Reinhard, 4–5, 6, 8–9, 11, 99, 107, 109–11, 147
  Almira, 6
  Claudius, 93
  Octavia, 8, 62–3, 100, 107, 110–11, 113–15, 118–19
King, Richard G., 182
Kirkendale, Ursula, 7, 13
Kleefeld, Wilhelm, 147
Knapp, John Merrill, 9, 162, 172, 173–4, 189
Kreienberg, Christoph Friedrich, 18
Krieger, Johann Philipp, 4
Kuhnau, Johann, 3
Kupfer, Harry, 193
Kusser, Johann Sigismund, 162, 163, 164

L'Épine, Francesca Margherita de, 199
Lampe, John Frederick, 32, 33
  Dragon of Wantley, The, 47

Larue, C. Steven, 27, 170
Legrenzi, Giovanni, 51
Leipzig, 2, 3, 4
Leo, Leonardo, 81
Leopold, Silke, 156
Lessing, Gotthold Ephraim, 165
Lincoln's Inn Fields Theatre, 32, 35, 37, 42, 45, 46, 175
Lindgren, Lowell, 59, 160
Little Theatre, Haymarket, 32, 42, 46, 175
Littlebury, Isaac, 55
Livy, 55, 62
London (see under separate theatres)
Lotti, Antonio, 50
  Teofane, 26
'Lucchesina' La (Maria Antonia Marchesini), 43
Lully, Jean-Baptiste, 49, 162, 163

McLauchlan, Fiona, 190
McVicar, David, 186, 188–9
Mainwaring, John, 3, 7, 10, 11, 12, 13, 15, 16, 24, 43, 63, 138, 164, 167
Manchester, 1st Duke of (Charles Montagu), 16
Marchesini, Maria Antonia (see 'Lucchesina')
Maria Casimira, Queen, 70, 71
Marx, Hans .Joachim, 13, 162, 163
Mattheson, Johann, 3, 5, 6, 7, 8, 9–10, 11, 92, 107, 109, 137–8, 142, 162, 163, 164–5, 166, 180
  Beschützte Orchestre, Das, 109, 147
  Cleopatra, 8, 10, 164
  Critica Musica, 10
  Ehrenpforte, 4, 5, 6, 8, 9, 10, 92
  Musikalische Patriot, Der, 7, 92
  Vollkommene Capellmeister, Der, 108, 163, 164
Mauro, Ortensio, 17, 50, 70–1, 88, 89–91, 202
Medici, family, 11, 12, 14, 70, 72, 165
Metastasio, Pietro, 28, 34, 50, 61, 65, 66, 69–70, 76, 79, 80, 81, 82, 83, 87, 88, 167, 172–3, 174, 181, 202, 203
  Alessandro nell'Indie (Poro), 50, 66, 69, 173
  Attilio Regolo, 173
  Demofoonte, 172–3
  Didone abbandonata 28, 83
  Ezio, 50, 66, 69, 74–5, 77
  Siroe, 50, 66, 69, 83, 203
Middlesex, Earl of (Charles Sackville), 46, 47
Milhous, Judith, 19, 24, 32, 171
Miller, James, 20
Milton, John,
  Paradise Lost, 87

Minato, Niccolò, 51, 55, 160
Molière (Jean-Baptiste Poquelin), 79
Montagnana, Antonio, 32, 43
Monteverdi, Claudio, 64
L'incoronazione di Poppea, 161
L'Orfeo, 129
Mozart, Wolfgang Amadeus, 1, 159, 184
Cosi fan tutte, 196
Idomeneo, 159
Le nozze di Figaro, 161
Muratori, Ludovico Antonio, 55, 83

Naples, 15, 28, 50, 51, 117, 166, 169, 170
Newcastle, Duke of (Thomas Holles), 24, 25, 26
'Nicolini'/'Nicolino' (Nicola Grimaldi), 16, 169–70, 171, 172
Noris, Matteo, 50, 198, 200, 201

'Opera of the Nobility, The', 32, 35, 36, 37, 39–40, 42, 43, 44, 47
Orlandini, Giuseppe Maria, 198, 199
Ottoboni, Cardinal Pietro, 12, 13, 57, 199

Pamphili, Cardinal Benedetto, 12–13, 57, 199
Pancieri, Giulio, 49
Pariati, Pietro, 51, 167, 198, 200, 201
Paris, 28, 41, 170, 183, 202
Pellegrini, Valeriano, 166
Pendarves, Mrs., 176
Pepusch, Johann Christoph, 32
Pergolesi, Giovanni Battista, 81, 169, 177
Salustia, 169
Perrucci, Andrea, 180
Perti, Giacomo Antonio, 50, 51, 85
Pescetti, Giovanni Battista, 45, 46
Angelica e Medoro, 45
Pilotti-Schiavonetti, Elisabetta, 169
Piovene, Count Agostino, 50
Plato, 65
Plutarch, 49, 55, 62
Pope, Alexander, 19, 41, 63, 108, 192
Poppe, Gerhard, 95, 104
Porpora, Nicola Antonio, 35, 51, 81, 202
Porta, Giovanni
Numitore, 198
Price, Curtis, 132
Provenzale, Francesco, 169
Purcell, Henry, 20, 23, 29, 60, 109, 134, 159
The Fairy-Queen 20, 183
Pythagoras, 65

Quantz, Johann Joachim, 9, 26
Quinault, Philippe, 49

Racine, Jean, 70, 79, 170
Ralph, James, 30
Rameau, Jean-Philippe, 41
Les Indes Galantes, 61
Reinhold, Thomas, 37
Reynolds, Sir Joshua, 64, 120
Rich, John, 36–7, 38, 45, 175
Richter, Karl, 189
Riemschneider, Johann Gottfried, 32
Riva, Giuseppe, 29–30, 83, 85, 201
Roberts, John L., 7, 8, 108
Robinson, Anastasia, 27, 199, 201
Robinson, Ann Turner, 199
Rolli, Paolo Antonio, 25, 30, 31, 34, 49, 50, 51, 54, 60, 71, 72, 73, 78, 84, 85, 87–91, 198, 199, 200, 201, 202, 203
Rome, 7, 12, 13, 14, 15, 27, 50, 51, 53, 70, 108, 109, 116, 160, 166, 167
Roseingrave, Thomas, 198, 199
Rossi, Giacomo, 22, 31, 49, 50, 72, 73, 84
Rossini, Gioacchino, 1, 170
Rotth, August Christian, 3
Roubiliac, Louis-François, 45
Rowe, Nicholas, 67
Royal Academy of Music, 22, 23–31, 32, 34, 45, 53, 54, 56, 67, 68, 84, 85, 87, 132–3, 166, 167, 168, 170–1, 174, 198–203
Ruspoli, Francesco Maria, 12, 13, 57, 166, 199

Sallé, Marie, 38, 39, 41, 58, 135–6, 164, 172, 175
Salvai, Maria Maddalena, 199
Salvi, Antonio, 14, 49, 50, 51, 55–6, 70–2, 82, 85– 6, 138–9, 165, 167, 198, 200, 201, 202
Sartorio, Antonio, 50
Sartorio, Girolamo, 162
Savage, Roger, 173, 185, 186
Sawyer, John, 112, 116
Saxony, 1
Scarlatti, Alessandro, 13, 15, 51, 72, 109, 169
Scarlatti, Domenico, 12, 13, 15, 50, 51, 71, 199
Narciso, 198, 199, 200
Scheibe, Johann Adolf, 8
Scriblerus Club, 19
'Second Academy, The', 30, 31–5, 53, 72, 84, 134, 174–5, 176
Sellars, Peter, 193
'Senesino' (Francesco Bernardi), 25, 26, 27, 29, 32, 33, 35, 44, 134, 170, 171, 172, 176, 191, 199, 201, 203
Settle, Elkanah, 23
Shaftesbury, 3rd Earl of, 20, 28, 63, 65
Shaftesbury, 4th Earl of (Anthony Ashley-Cooper), 43, 47, 63, 159

Shakespeare, William, 20, 60, 77, 163
  Macbeth, 60
  A Midsummer Night's Dream, 20, 183
  The Tempest, 60
Smith, John Christopher, junior, 11, 42
Smith, Ruth, 67
Snow, Valentine, 137, 147
Sophie, Dowager Electress of Hanover, 17, 169
Spanish Succession, War of, 11–12, 14, 66
Spectator, The (see Journals)
Spenser, Edmund
  The Faerie Queene, 60
Stampiglia, Silvio, 49, 50, 51, 68, 69, 72, 82, 160, 167, 198
Steele, Sir Richard, 20, 171, 172
Steffani, Agostino, 16–17, 29, 50, 70, 189, 191
Strada del Pò, Anna Maria, 32, 33, 38, 43, 151, 176
Strauss, Richard, 196
Strohm, Reinhard, 69, 72, 143, 180–1, 185
Suetonius, 49
Swift, Jonathan, 19, 192
Swiney, Owen, 68

Tacitus, 49, 62
Tasso, Torquato, 49
Telemann, Georg Philipp, 4, 9, 10, 109, 138
Theobald, Lewis
  The Rape of Proserpina, 36, 37, 171
Thomasius, Christian, 2
Tiepolo, Giambattista, 171
Timms, Colin, 17
Tosi, Pier Francesco, 173–4, 191

Utrecht, Treaty of, 18

Vanbrugh, Sir John, 24, 28, 167
Vauxhall Gardens, 45
Venice, 14, 15, 27, 49, 50, 51, 84, 165, 166
  Teatro dei SS Giovanni e Paolo, 162
  Teatro San Giovanni Grisostomo, 14–15, 102, 165, 168
Veracini, Francesco Maria
  Adriano in Siria, 40
Verdi, Giuseppe, 1, 128, 140, 146, 184
Vienna, 5, 28, 49, 51, 53, 79, 85
Vickers, David, 68
Vinci, Leonardo, 34, 50, 81, 157, 201
  Didone abbandonata, 42
  Elpidia (pasticcio), 34, 200, 201, 202
Visconti, Lucchino, 185
Vivaldi, Antonio, 51
Voltaire (François-Marie Arouet), 54, 60, 86

Wagner, Richard, 184, 185, 197
  Der fliegende Holländer, 184
  Parsifal, 183
Wagner, Wieland, 197
Walpole, Horace, 120
Walsh, John (father / son), 45, 132
Waltz, Gustavus, 37
Weber, Carl Maria von, 163
Weissenfels, 2, 4, 6, 8
Westminster Abbey, 1
Westphalia, Peace of, 1
Wilde, David, 196
William, Prince of Orange, 58
Wyche, John, 10

Young, Cecilia, 37

Zachow, Friedrich Wilhelm, 3
Zeno, Apostolo, 34, 69, 70, 72, 79, 80, 81, 82, 83, 85, 167, 198, 200, 201, 202

Lightning Source UK Ltd.
Milton Keynes UK
UKHW030401020219
336619UK00012B/411/P

9 780521 521604